The Essential
Mary Handbook

D1016553

The Essential Mary Handbook

A SUMMARY OF BELIEFS, PRACTICES, AND PRAYERS

With a Glossary of Key Terms and
Cross-Referenced to the
Catechism of the Catholic Church

A REDEMPTORIST PASTORAL PUBLICATION

Liguori
LIGUORI, MISSOURI

Edited and Compiled by Judith A. Bauer
Published by Liguori Publications
Liguori, Missouri
http://www.liguori.org

Library of Congress Cataloging-in-Publication Data

Bauer, Judith A.
    The essential Mary handbook : a summary of beliefs, practices, and prayers
/ compiled by Judith A. Bauer.
        p. cm.
    ISBN 0-7648-0383-2
    1. Mary, Blessed Virgin, Saint—Prayer-books and devotions—English. 2.
Mary, Blessed Virgin, Saint—Theology. I. Bauer, Judith A., 1941– .
BX2160.2.88   1999
232.91—dc21   98–47844

All scriptural citations, except the Psalms, are taken from the *New Revised
Standard Version of the Bible*, copyright 1989 by the Division of Christian Education of the National Council of the Churches of Christ in the USA. All
rights reserved. Used with permission.

Psalms quoted are taken from the *Christian Community Bible*, copyright 1995
Bernardo Hurault and published by Claretian Publications, Quezon City,
Philippines and Liguori Publications, Liguori, Missouri, USA. All rights reserved.

Excerpts from the English translation of the *Catechism of the Catholic Church* for the
United States of America, © 1994, United States Catholic Conference, Inc.—Libreria
Editrice Vaticana. Used with permission.

Excerpts from *Vatican II: The Conciliar and Post Conciliar Documents*, edited by
Austin Flannery, O.P., © 1975, Costello Puiblishing Company, Northport, N.Y.,
are used by permission.

The English translation of the Litany of the Blessed Virgin Mary from *Order of
Crowning an Image of the Blessed Virgin Mary* © 1986, International Commit-
tee on English in the Liturgy, Inc. All rights reserved.

Contents

Contents

Contents

Contents

Section Ten: Shrines of Our Blessed Virgin Mary Around the World 241

Contents

An Outline of Major Texts About Mary in the *Catechism of the Catholic Church*

The Essential
Mary Handbook

SECTION ONE

Mary Today

The glories of Mary have been enshrined in the heart of the Church for two thousand years. She is part of the Scriptures and the liturgy, and a focus of the prayers of her earthly children. She has been honored in art, in poetry, and in song. She has been the subject of the writings of the ancient Fathers of the Church, and the teachings of the popes and the councils.

Mary also holds a secure place in the hearts of the faithful. She is the greatest of all the saints, the closest to Christ, the sinless and virginal Mother born without original sin and, indeed, free from sin her entire life. Mary serves as an outstanding example of virtue—of faith, hope, and love for God and for others.

Having conceived Jesus by the power of the Holy Spirit, she nurtured the son of God to adulthood and stood beside him throughout his ministry and his fulfillment of the plan of salvation. She sorrowed at the foot of the cross as her son died, she joyfully received the fact of his Resurrection, and she awaited with the rest of the disciples the inspiring flame of the Holy Spirit on Pentecost.

At the end of her life, Mary was taken up into heaven, body and soul, where she continues to intercede for her children on earth as our spiritual mother and as a model for us the highest level of human sanctity.

The Church, at the Second Vatican Council, reminds us that we ought to revere the memory of Mary because it was through her that the Son of God came into our history, and it urged that all devotion to Mary lead to Christ: "Let them rightly illustrate the duties and privileges of the Blessed Virgin which always refer to Christ, the source of all truth, sanctity, and devotion" (*Dogmatic Constitution on the Church*, §67).

Because Mary should first and always lead us to Christ, the following sections discuss the Blessed Virgin Mary in her relationship to the Trinity—the Father, Son, and Holy Spirit.

1. Mary and the Trinity

All human beings are made in the image and likeness of God (*CCC* §355–361). Mary is also a being of God's creation (*DCC* §§53, 55, 56), but by virtue of her destiny as the Mother of the Son of God, she is the daughter of the Father, and the temple of the Holy Spirit.

The chapter on the Blessed Virgin contained in the *Dogmatic Constitution on the Church* begins by recalling that the mystery of salvation was planned and realized by the Father, the Son, and the Holy Spirit (*DCC* §52). In *Redemptoris Mater*, Pope John Paul II says: "In the salvific design of the Most Holy Trinity, the mystery of the Incarnation constitutes the superabundant *fulfillment of the promise* made by God to man *after original sin*, after that first sin whose effects oppress the whole history of man (*Redemptoris Mater* §11.1).

This same *Dogmatic Constitution on the Church* chapter on the Blessed Virgin already mentioned concludes with the hope that the faithful will pray to Our Blessed Mother so "she, who aided the beginnings of the Church by her prayers, may…intercede before her Son in the fellowship of all the saints, until all families of people…may be happily gathered together in peace and harmony into one People of God, for the glory of the Most Holy and Undivided Trinity" (*DCC* §69).

Because of Mary's essential involvement with the plan of salvation, any understanding of the Virgin Mary should be clearly linked to the activity of the Trinity. Our salvation unfolds within the framework of the Blessed Trinity because it was brought about by the God who created the covenant with the people of Israel, who sent his Son as savior in the fullness of time, and who through this Messiah redeemed us and distributed to us the adoptive fire of the Holy Spirit.

Despite Mary's essential role as the mother of God, she herself is not a divine person. She is the mother of the divine person of the Son alone; she is not the mother of the whole Trinity. That very same divine being is at once the Son of God as to his divinity and the son of Mary as to his humanity.

Nevertheless, Mary is intimately involved in union with God in the Trinity. She achieved this union and involvement with God in the Trinity because of her steadfast faith, her resolute hope, and her deepest love. All human beings, as well, long for this same goal— union with the Trinity; this is what we call "heaven" where we experience communion with the Trinity and the Virgin Mary, the angels, and all the saints (*CCC* §1024).

2. Mary and God, the Creator-Father

In the New Testament, the Father is the architect of the plan of salvation. Christ referred every one of his works and actions back to him. God the Creator-Father is also the architect of Mary's role in salvation. She is not outside the salvation plan of God the Father, but rather she owes her role in this great mystery to her Creator, to a free choice on his part, which Mary did not earn by merit or by any other means.

It is the Father who decided on Mary's mission and the events of her life as they relate to our salvation. Mary was present in the mind of God from the very beginning. As the first reading for the feast of the Presentation of Mary says: "The LORD created me at the beginning of his work, the first of his acts of long ago. Ages ago I was set up, at the first, before the beginning of the earth" (Prov 8:22–23). The *Dogmatic Constitution on the Church* puts it this way: "The Father of mercies *willed* that the Incarnation should be preceded by assent on the part of the predestined mother…" (*DCC* §56).

As well, Mary's motherhood of Christ and of us can be seen as an expression of the motherly care of God, who in Isaiah is seen as both Father and Mother (Isa 49:15, 66:13). This maternal relationship with God resulted for Mary in an incomparable grant of sanctifying grace, which she received at the time of her Immaculate Conception in the womb of her own mother. And because of the grace of her divine motherhood, she is the also the divinely adopted daughter of God. The Church in her Liturgy of the Hours for August 15 calls her the "Mother of her Creator" and Dante, in his *Divine Comedy*, appropriately has Saint Bernard call her "Daughter of your Son."

Mary's role as the Father's Daughter who responsibly serves as a lynchpin in God's plan is seen as "full of grace" (Lk 1:28) and as one who has "found favor with God" (Lk 1:30). These words of the messenger, tinged with revelation and promise, enable us to understand that among all the blessings in Christ, this is a special blessing that has been conferred on Mary. She is full of the grace that she has received from God as his most excellent daughter who has humbly agreed to be the Mother of God. She is the one whom the Father has chosen as the Mother of his Incarnated Son, and, as Pope John Paul II points out:

> Together with the Father, the Son has chosen her, entrusting her eternally to the Spirit of holiness. In an entirely special and exceptional way Mary is united to Christ, and similarly she is eternally loved in this "beloved Son," this Son who is of one being with the father, in whom is concentrated all the "glory of grace" (*Redemptoris Mater* §8).

In this role as holy daughter and holy mother, Mary is an emblem of all who await salvation. She is the Daughter of Israel who represents those poor and humble of the Lord who "confidently hope for and receive salvation from him" (*DCC* §55). Mary's role is not just an individual one, but she also assumes a broader role as a minister of salvation for the whole human race. She echoes the words of the Father on Mount Tabor ("Listen to him!": Mt 17:5) when she says at the wedding feast of Cana: "Do whatever he tells you" (Jn 2:5). Thus she even tells us how to behave toward her son Jesus—we must listen to him carefully and follow the instructions that he gives.

Lastly, our devotion to Mary brings us forward to the love of the Father, to the search for the will of God in all things (*DCC* §65). It is her perfect faith that provides the clearest model for us of that significant virtue. As the *Dogmatic Constitution on Divine Revelation* teaches, "'The obedience of faith' (Rom 16:26) must be given to God who reveals himself. By faith man freely commits his entire self to God" (§5). This faith Mary achieved most perfectly at the moment of the Annunciation where she entrusted herself to God completely with the full obedience of mind and will.

Through Mary, as she reminds us in her *Magnificat* (Lk 1:45–55), we can see Our Father as the "Mighty One" who is just and merciful, and who is forever faithful to his promises, who through her has made possible our salvation.

3. Mary, Mother of Jesus Christ, Mother of God

The Scriptures do not specifically apply the expression "Mother of God" to Mary. However, they do say that Jesus is the Son of God (Lk 1:35; Gal 4:4) and that Mary is the mother of Jesus (Jn 2:1; Matt 1:18; Lk 1:43). Even given this lack of directness, the fact of Mary's divine motherhood cannot be separated out from the faith of believing Christians: Mary is the mother of the true Son of God; Mary is truly the mother of Jesus Christ. As Saint Ignatius of Antioch (d. 107) says so plainly: "Our God, Jesus Christ, was carried in Mary's womb."

As the Church pondered the mysteries of Christ and his mother, its understanding deepened. By the third century, the title *Theotokos*, meaning "mother of God" or "the one who gave birth to God," was granted to Mary. Its application spread and it was adopted by the Council of Ephesus in 431. Cyril of Alexandria, for example, declared in his *First Anathema Against Nestorius:*

> If anyone does not confess that the Emmanuel is truly
> God and that for this reason the Holy Virgin is mother of

7

God (since she bore in the flesh the Word of God made flesh), let him be anathema.

Several councils recognized Cyril's words as the genuine presentation of Christian faith and from that time on, the title *Theotokos* expressed a dogma recognized by all members of the Church.

By acknowledging Mary as the Mother of God, we confess that she gave birth to a divine being with a true human nature. This is the center of our understanding of Jesus Christ, for a belief in Mary's divine motherhood is also linked to the doctrine of the Incarnation.

Another outcome of the affirmation of Mary as the Mother of God is the necessity of affirming that there are two real natures in Jesus Christ, one divine and one human (*CCC* §464–469). This union of two natures in the single person of Jesus Christ is called by theologians the "hypostatic union" (*CCC* §252).

Pope John Paul II states it this way in his encyclical *Redemptoris Mater*: "The dogma of the divine motherhood of Mary was for the Council of Ephesus and is for the Church like a seal upon the dogma of the Incarnation, in which the Word truly assumes human nature into the unity of his person, without canceling out that nature" (§4).

Mary received the distinction of divine motherhood at the Annunciation when the angel Gabriel came to her and said, "Greetings, favored one! The Lord is with you" (Lk 1:28). The word "favored" in Greek is *kecharitomene*; in the Old Testament, however, the word is associated with the word "grace." Thus Mary is favored with God's grace as he singled her out to be the Mother of his Son, the Mother of God.

This election, this favor, is one of grace—a grace that is defined as an affiliation or union with God. The closer a human being is to God, the greater his or her store of grace, and the greater his or her worth. Thus, through Mary's divine motherhood, she received the highest grace ever given to a living being. Jesus Christ, as a divine person incarnate, was perfectly united to God in the grace of the hypostatic union. But after that perfect union destined for Christ alone comes the grace of Mary's divine motherhood, the first order of grace for human persons.

It is worth noting that Mary is united with Christ in two ways: (1) because she truly gave birth to the human life of the Son of God; and (2) because of her union with God through the spiritual affiliation of grace. All these graces and all of Mary's privileges arise out of the fact of Mary's divine motherhood.

What role does Mary's divine motherhood play in our salvation? Mary physically gave birth to Christ, who as Pope John Paul II asserts, is the central factor in our redemption and sanctification. Since Christ is God and man united, he serves as the mediator between God and humankind. The grace of this union makes him the perfect representative of humanity, of which he is the head and highest priest. And it is Mary, through her divine motherhood, who gave Christ his human nature which allows him to be our representative in the redemption story and our mediator with God. Because of Mary, Jesus is truly God with us. We owe to Mary, through her physical motherhood, the accomplishment of our salvation.

Because of Mary's physical motherhood, we can also see how she partakes of the mediation of Christ. As the mother of the mediator between the Father and us, Mary also takes on the role of intercessor on our behalf. This role as mediator is separate from the mediation of Jesus with his Father. It does not make Mary an independent operator nor does it put her on the same level as her Son, for she is a human being who is also redeemed by Jesus Christ. Her place is a relative one and flows from "the superabundance of the merits of Christ, rests on his mediation, depends entirely on it and draws all its power from it" (*DCC* §60).

4. Mary, Mother of the Messiah, Mother of the Redeemer

Christ is always seen at the center of God's plan of redemption. Both the Apostles' Creed and the Nicene Creed declare our redemption as the mission of Jesus Christ. As the *Catechism of the Catholic Church* declares, Jesus Christ is also at the living center of catechesis:

> "At the heart of catechesis we find, in essence, a Person, the Person of Jesus of Nazareth, the only Son from the Father...who suffered and died for us and who now, after rising, is living with us forever (*Catechisi tradendi* §5). To catechize is "to reveal in the Person of Christ the whole of God's eternal design reaching fulfillment in that Person. It is to seek to understand the meaning of Christ's actions and words and of the signs worked by him" *(Catechisi tradendi §5)*. Catechesis aims at putting "people...in communion...with Jesus Christ: only he can lead us to the love of the Father in the Spirit and make us share in the life of the Holy Trinity" (*Catechisi tradendi* §5) (*CCC* §426).

Mary is the Mother of the Redeemer and the mother of the Redeemer's mission as well. It was she who cooperated fully in the mystery of our salvation which hinged on the "on the welcome Mary gave that mission on behalf of all men" (*CCC* §502).

Mary's cooperation with God's redemptive plan continued throughout her life and did not cease even when she reached heaven. As the *Catechism of the Catholic Church* states:

> This motherhood of Mary in the order of grace continues uninterruptedly from the consent which she loyally

gave at the Annunciation and which she sustained without wavering beneath the cross, until the eternal fulfillment of all the elect. Taken up to heaven she did not lay aside this saving office but by her manifold intercession continues to bring us the gifts of eternal salvation (*CCC* §969).

From the point of view of Mary's relationship with Christ, the *Dogmatic Constitution on the Church* points out that her role consists of being the "gracious mother of the divine Redeemer here on earth, and above all others and in a singular way the generous associate and humble handmaid of the Lord" (*DCC* §61).

Mary is also introduced as the mother of Jesus Christ, the Messiah. The title "Messiah" is equivalent to the word *Christ* which means "the anointed one," the promised one who became incarnate of the Virgin Mary by the power of the Holy Spirit and who saved Israel by fulfilling the promises of a Messiah.

Mary is the Jewish woman, wholly human, who is Jesus' mother. She is the God-bearer, the mother of a divine and human person. This is the mystery of the Incarnation, that true and singular event which the *Catechism of the Catholic Church* summarizes in sections 465 through 468.

Through the Incarnation, Mary gifts us with our Redeemer who, though existing before all time, assumes human flesh in order to be the mediator, the Redeemer, and the highest expression of all humankind. It was Mary's free-will choice to accept the Son of God. It was the Son of God's free choice to come as our savior.

From the time of the Incarnation, Mary's life was linked with that of her son. Since Jesus was both a private person and a public Messiah, Mary is associated with Jesus as both a mother and as a colleague in the plan of redemption. With her whole heart, Mary gives herself to God's saving plan, and as Vatican II points out, she devoted herself totally, as a handmaid of the Lord, to the person and work of her Son, under and with him, serving the mystery of redemption, by the grace of Almighty God. Rightly, therefore, the Fathers see Mary not merely as passively engaged by God, but as freely cooperating in the work of man's salvation through faith and obedience (*DCC* §56).

Mary is the mother of Jesus who redeems us through his vanguishment of Satan. As the *Catechism of the Catholic Church* summarizes:

Victory over the "prince of this world" (Jn 14:30) was won once for all at the Hour when Jesus freely gave himself up to death to give us his life. This is the judgment of this world, and the prince of this world is "cast out" (Jn 12:31). "He pursued the woman" (Rev 12:13–16), but had no hold on her: the new Eve, "full of grace" of the Holy Spirit, is preserved from sin and the corruption of death…."Then the dragon was angry with the woman, and went off to make war on the rest of her offspring" (Rev 12:17). Therefore the Spirit and the Church pray: "Come, Lord Jesus" (Rev 22:17, 20), since his coming will deliver us from the Evil One (*CCC* §2853).

The *Catechism* uses the liturgy of Saint John Chrysostom to sum up, in another form, this mystery:

"O holy-begotten Son and word of God, immortal being, you who deigned for our salvation to become incarnate of the holy Mother of God and ever-virgin Mary, you who without change became man and were crucified, O Christ our God, you who by your death have crushed death, you who are one of the Holy Trinity, glorified with the Father and the Holy spirit, save us!" (*CCC* §469).

Because of Mary's close union with Christ and his work of redemption, any honor and devotion to Mary should be expressed in the liturgy, the great retelling of our salvation story, by keeping the feasts of Mary or by taking her as our spiritual example of how to live out the promises of our holy Baptism.

5. Mary's Mission Under the Holy Spirit

The Holy Spirit is the divine Person who brings us the plan of redemption accomplished in Christ. By his outpouring he makes Christ known to us and unites us with him, making us children of the Father (*CCC* §§686, 689, 690). Believers must walk in the Spirit in order to live the truth of their faith as Christians. Mary, the first believer, also must be transformed by the Spirit.

The *Catechism of the Catholic Church* gives many references to Mary's cooperation with the Holy Spirit. Mary is prepared by the Holy Spirit so that the Father can find a dwelling place for his Son and his Spirit among human beings. In this sense, Mary is called the "Seat of Wisdom" (*CCC* §721). Prepared by the grace of the Holy Spirit, Mary, the most humble of creatures, was conceived without sin in the womb of her mother Anne and made suitable to receive the gift of the eternal Son (*CCC* §722). In the tradition of the Eastern Church, Mary is proclaimed as the All-Holy One and is praised as free from "every stain of sin, as though fashioned by the Holy Spirit and formed as a new creature" (*DCC* §56).

In Mary, the Holy Spirit fulfills the loving plan of the Father by making her virginity fruitful. Through the Spirit, she conceives and gives birth to the Son of God (*CCC* §723). The Annunciation is the Pentecost anticipated in Mary, for the Holy Spirit has brought about in her a new state of being that makes possible a response of total faith.

Through the power of the Holy Spirit, Mary makes the Son of God manifest. She makes him visible in the flesh to the poor, the humble, and the Gentiles at the time of his birth, for these are the first to accept him (*CCC* §724). Finally, Mary, through the Holy Spirit, begins to bring all people, who are the target of God's redeeming love, to Christ (*CCC* §525). Mary stands in for us at the foot of the cross, at the joy of the Resurrection, and in the Cenacle where the newly born Church waits for the coming of the Holy Spirit, who is the transmitter of our rebirth as children of God.

Mary should never be seen as a competitor or a substitute for the Holy Spirit; rather she is a way to make the effects of the Spirit apparent to us and therefore she is a facilitator of our understanding of the Holy Spirit's great work. She is a signal expression of perfect cooperation with the inspirations of the Holy Spirit. Mary leads souls to Jesus in total dependence on the Holy Spirit. This picture of Mary's role in salvation leaves no doubt as to why the mystery and the outcome of Pentecost are primary over any devotion to Our Blessed Virgin.

6. Mary and the Church

Mary's relationship to the Church involves three particulars—all affirmed by Vatican II: (1) Mary is the Mother of the Church; (2) Mary is part of the Church as the preeminent member of the Mystical Body; and, (3) Mary is the prototype of the Church.

MARY AS MOTHER OF THE CHURCH

The *Catechism of the Catholic Church* clearly outlines Mary's motherhood in relation to the Church (*CCC* §963)—a motherhood that flows from her motherhood to Christ and her inseparable union with him. This union, says the *Dogmatic Constitution on the Church*, "is made manifest from the time of Christ's virginal conception up to his death" (*DCC* §57).

At the same time, however, Mary is also a member of the human race begot through Adam and thus is united to all those who are to be saved. Mary is the Mother of the Church, that is, mother of the faithful as first in the order of grace. Saint Augustine says that Mary is clearly "the mother of the members of Christ...since she has by her charity joined in bringing about the birth of believers in the Church, who are members of its head."

The *Catechism* quotes Vatican II in explanation of this fact:

> In a wholly singular way she cooperated by her obedience, faith, hope and burning charity in the work of the Savior in restoring supernatural life to souls. For this reason she is a mother to us in the order of grace.
>
> This motherhood of Mary in the order of grace continues uninterruptedly from the consent which she loyally gave at the Annunciation and which she sustained without wavering beneath the cross, until the eternal fulfillment of all the elect (*DCC* §§61,62).

Mary has been recognized as the mother of all human beings since the Middle Ages, but she only recently was officially proclaimed, by Pope Paul VI at the close of Vatican II's third session, as "Mother of the Church." This title expresses the core of Mary's motherly care. Mary is the universal mother of the whole people of God, and in the Church she occupies the place of mother—the whole Church invoking the mother of its Lord as its own mother as well.

MARY AS A MEMBER OF THE CHURCH

Even though she is the Mother of the Church, Mary nevertheless remains a member of the Church—though "a preeminent and as a wholly unique" one (*DCC* §53). She is our sister by reason of her human nature. She is the model for all believers whose responses should echo her generous *Yes*: "Let it be with me according to your word" (Lk 1:38).

Mary is a member of the Church because she belongs to the people whom Jesus restored to his Father and because she also benefited from the grace of redemption, which came to her in an anticipatory way at the time of her Immaculate Conception. If graces come to us through her mediatorship, it is only through her dependence on and intercession with the divine Son that these gifts accrue to us.

A masterpiece of God, Mary is still very much a part of the community of God's creatures. It is through her love and perfection that we are able to see the destiny that God has in store for us. Her Assumption into heaven serves for us as a precursive sign of that which all believers are called to experience in their own resurrection.

MARY AS A TYPE OF THE CHURCH

Mary is a type of the Church in its mission of being a pilgrim people of faith. The *Catechism* speaks of the relationship between Mary and the Church in this way:

> After speaking of the Church, her origin, mission, and destiny, we can find no better way to conclude than by looking to Mary. In her we contemplate what the Church already is in her mystery on her own "pilgrimage of faith," and what she will be in the homeland at the end of her journey. There, "in the glory of the Most Holy and Undivided Trinity," "in the communion of all the saints" (*DCC* §69), the Church is awaited by the one she venerates as Mother of her Lord and as her own mother (*CCC* §972).

The *Catechism* continues by pointing out the Mary images in the Church in other ways as well. She is the icon of the Church in her heavenly glory which represents the Church as it will be perfected in the world to come. She also models for the people of God who are still on their earthly journey of faith the certain hope and comfort that await them on the day of their own resurrection.

Mary is the symbol and most perfect realization of the Church (*CCC* §507), the model of the Church as Mother and teacher (*CCC* §2030), and the emblem of the Church at prayer (*CCC* §2679).

We can understand the similarity between the Church and Mary by looking at another comparison—that of Mary as the new Eve, who by her obedience unties the knot of the old Eve's disobedience. Mary is not directly called the "new Eve" in the Scriptures, but this idea is seen by some scholars as arising from scriptural references in which Christ is called a second or new Adam (Rom 5:19–20). Mary is the new Eve in fulfillment of the promise made to Adam and Eve to "put enmity between you and the woman, and between your offspring and hers (Gen 3:15).

7. Mary's Life of Faith

Mary is the woman of faith without any equal. Her cousin Elizabeth says of her: "Blessed is she who believed that there would be a fulfillment of what was spoken to her by the Lord" (Lk 1:45). Mary responded at the Annunciation with an entrustment of her whole being to God. This action represents a perfect definition of faith.

In his encyclical *Redemptoris Mater*, Pope John Paul II compares Mary's faith to that of Abraham, whom Saint Paul calls "our father in faith" (see Rom 4:12). The pope goes on to point out:

> Abraham's faith constitutes the beginning of the Old Covenant; Mary's faith at the Annunciation inaugurates the New Covenant. Just as Abraham *"in hope believed against hope*, that he should become the father of many nations" (see Rom 4:18), so Mary at the Annunciation,

having professed her virginity ("How shall this be, since I have no husband?") *believed* that through the power of the Most High, by the power of the Holy Spirit, she would become the Mother of God's Son in accordance with the angel's revelation (*Redemptoris Mater* §14.1).

Mary's answer of "yes" was filled with faith and was the starting point of her whole journey, her own pilgrimage of faith. Her faith continued to grow throughout her life until it reached its supreme test when Mary witnessed the death of her Son on the cross. Mary's faith never diminished, and through this faith she accepted the sword that "will pierce your soul too" (Lk 2:35) and, with this final agreement, she became perfectly united with Christ in his suffering (*CCC* §165).

8. Mary's Life of Prayer

Mary is a model of prayer for all the children of God. Her prayer is characterized by a pure intention and a giving heart with which she offered her whole being in a trustful promise to do the will of God.

Mary's prayer is shown to us in the fullness of time when "God sent his Son, born of a woman, born under the law, in order to redeem those who were under the law, so that we might receive adoption" (Gal 4:4–5). Mary's prayer meshed perfectly with God's plan of action. At the Annunciation Mary's prayer was summed up in her wholehearted "yes." Her generous prayer continues in her *Magnificat*, which can be seen as a prayer of the whole Church. Her prayer endures throughout the hopeful waiting, the events of the Incarnation, and the birth of the Son of God.

Mary models the prayer life of the Church. At every significant turn of events, she points to Christ. Her "let it be" is the essence of Christian prayer, entirely directed toward the Person of God. She has prayed and pondered in her heart over the events of her life (Lk 2:19, 51). She is at the center of those gathered in prayer in the upper room awaiting the coming of the Holy Spirit at Pentecost: "All these were constantly devoting themselves to prayer, together with certain women, including Mary the mother of Jesus..." (Acts 1:14).

The *Catechism* expresses the essence of Mary's prayer thusly:

> That is why the Canticle of Mary, the *Magnificat* (Latin) or *Megalynei* (Byzantine) is the song both of the Mother of God and of the Church; the song of the Daughter of Zion and of the new People of God; the song of thanksgiving for the fullness of graces poured out in the economy of salvation and the song of the "poor" whose hope is met by the fulfillment of the promises made to our ancestors, "to Abraham and to his posterity for ever." (*CCC* §2619)

Mary is the perfect pray-er in her role as a symbol of the Church. When we pray with her or to her we gather in the spirit of the beloved disciples and follow with her and them the Father's plan of salvation, the sending his Son to save us. We announce her as Jesus' mother, for she has become the mother of all of us who are yet on earth and bound on the journey of faith.

Summing up the prayer of Mary, the *Catechism* makes this point:

> Because of Mary's singular cooperation with the action of the Holy Spirit, the Church loves to pray in communion with the Virgin Mary, to magnify with her the great things the Lord has done for her, and to entrust supplications and praises to her (*CCC* §2682).

SECTION TWO

Mary in the Scriptures and the Early Writings of the Church

1. Mary Prefigured in the Old Testament

Mary is not mentioned directly by name in the Old Testament; however, she can be recognized in some Old Testament passages as being prophetically prefigured as the Mother of the Messiah. Many Scripture scholars dispute whether any Old Testament passages can be classified as Marian in character. Here, however, we are speaking about the larger sense of these passages as supported by Tradition and the faith of the people of God, and read in the light of Jesus' life, death, Resurrection, and ascension in the New Testament. The *Dogmatic Constitution of the Church* points out the important of Hebrew Scriptures for understanding the person of Mary. It gives a perspective from which to view Mary's relationship to the words of the Old Testament:

> The sacred writings of the Old and the New Testaments, as well as venerable tradition, show the role of the Mother of the Saviour in the plan of salvation in an ever clearer light and call our attention to it. The books of the Old Testament describe the history of salvation, by which the coming of Christ into the world was slowly prepared. The earliest documents, as they are read in the Church are understood in the light of a further and full revelation, bring the figure of a woman, Mother of the Redeemer, into a gradually clearer light. Considered in this light, she is already prophetically foreshadowed in the promise of victory over the serpent which was given to our first parents after their fall into sin (see Gn 3:15). Likewise she is the virgin who shall conceive and bear a son, whose name shall be called Emmanuel (see Isa 7:14; Mi 5:2–3; Mt 1:22–23). She stands out among the poor and humble of the Lord, who confidently hope for and re-

ceive salvation from him. After a long period of waiting, the times are fulfilled in her, the exalted Daughter of Sion and the new plan of salvation is established, when the Son of God has taken human nature from her, that he might in the mysteries of his flesh free man from sin (*DCC* §55).

Using the previous paragraph as a guide, this section will examine the three Old Testament passages given above as they are traditionally seen in relation to the Blessed Virgin Mary.

GENESIS 3:15

After the fall of Adam and Eve in the Garden of Eden, God saw fit to punish both the tempted, Eve and Adam, as well as the tempter, Satan, who was disguised as a serpent. After exiling Eve and Adam, God addressed these pivotal words to Satan—words that have come to be known as the *Protoevangelium*, the sacred promise made by God to restore his fallen people or, in other words, the first pledge of the Good News.

> "I will put enmity between you and the woman,
>   and between your offspring and hers;
> he will strike your head,
>   and you will strike his heel."

Mary is the fulfillment of these words because of the fact that the complete and never-ending enmity put between the Woman and Satan was confirmed in Mary alone, and because of the fact that it was Jesus Christ who crushed Satan's head and Christ was the offspring of Mary.

The early Fathers and the Doctors of the Church also saw this passage as a reference to Mary, and this Old Testament passage is used by Pope Pius XII to point out in his message *Fulgens Corona* the role of this scriptural passage as a foundation to the doctrine of the Immaculate Conception:

> We are taught that God, Creator of all things, after the sad fall of Adam, addressed the serpent, the tempter and corrupter, in these words, which not a few Fathers, Doctors of the Church and many approved interpreters applied to the Virgin Mother of God: "I will put enmities between thee and the woman, and thy seed and her seed" (Gn III, 15). Now, if at any time the Blessed Mary were destitute of Divine grace even for the briefest moment, because of contamination in her conception by the hereditary stain of sin, there would not have come between her and the serpent that perpetual enmity spoken of from earliest tradition down to [this] time.

In *Redemptoris Mater*, Pope John Paul II cites Genesis 3:15 to show that Mary is already prophetically foreshadowed in that promise made to Adam and Eve after their fall into sin (§7.2). Later he unites Genesis 3:15 with the events of Cana and Calvary and also attaches it to the woman in Revelation 12:1, presenting Mary as the person who holds a singular place in the plan of salvation.

This passage of Genesis also is interpreted as linking Mary with Eve. Eve and Mary are connected as two women and two virgins instrumental in the events that befell humankind through their relationships to Christ and Adam. Eve, however, was responsible for the death of sin, and Mary was responsible for life through Christ. The birth of Jesus from Mary is seen as a new beginning since the story of humankind starts on a new path begun by Christ, God and man together.

ISAIAH 7:14–16

In 724 B.C. the northern Jewish kingdom of Israel, and Damascus, were seeking to force the southern Jewish kingdom of Judah into an alliance against Assyria. To have a more pliable instrument at the helm of Judah, they plotted to replace King Ahaz with their own choice. In the face of this pressure Ahaz was assured by the prophet Isaiah that all would go well, provided that the King of Judah spurned the human assistance of Assyria against Israel and Damascus and placed his entire trust in God. Then Isaiah foretold the collapse of the Israel-Damascus alliance. King Ahaz was not to be afraid of their threats; their plan would fail. To help the King's faith Isaiah offered him a sign, a miracle, as proof that he spoke in God's name. When, on a spurious pretext, King Ahaz refused to ask for a sign, Isaiah gave him the prophetic sign of the Virgin Birth.

> Therefore the Lord himself will give you a sign. Look, the young woman is with child and shall bear a son, and shall name him Immanuel. He shall eat curds and honey by the time he knows how to refuse the evil and choose the good. For before the child knows how to refuse the evil and choose the good, the land before whose two kings you are in dread will be deserted (Isa 7:14–16).

This text is often seen as the famous Emmanuel prophecy, referring to Jesus and Mary his mother. However, in a literal sense, the young woman referred to here is the wife of Ahaz the King. The son to be born to them is the holy king Hezekiah who is probably the "Emmanuel" promised to the people of southern Israel, Judah. Because of Hezekiah, the House of David would not vanish. His birth occurred while the country was ravaged by wars, but, within a short time, the kings at Damascus would be defeated. Hezekiah would eat bread and honey, that is, products of the land and the food of the poor at about the time he reached the age of reason and was able to know good from evil.

Matthew, in 1:23, cites this verse of Isaiah in the dream of Joseph explaining the Annunciation. Just prior to this reference, Matthew tells the genealogy of Jesus, through Joseph, who belongs to the royal line of David. The use of the word *Immanuel*, which, as Matthew says, means "God is with us," is also significant since it identifies Jesus with the title Immanuel. Jesus was born in poverty of the woman Mary, just as had been foretold.

In the *Dogmatic Constitution on the Church*, Vatican II puts forward the Scripture passage from Isaiah 7:14 with Genesis 3:15. In both, Yahweh envisions a plan of salvation in which a woman plays a significant role. Isaiah 7:14 is described as an "oracle" pointing to Mary in Matthew 1:23. In using the Scripture text of Isaiah 7:14, the Fathers of Vatican II gave a Marian interpretation not pertaining directly to the event described in the passage but attached to the text by the tradition of believers.

In the *Catechism of the Catholic Church*, the text of Isaiah 7:14 is included in the explanation of the sentence from the Creed: "I Believe in Jesus Christ, the Only Son of God." The *Catechism* reads:

> The gospel accounts understand the virginal conception of Jesus as a divine work that surpasses all human understanding and possibility. "That which is conceived in her is of the Holy Spirit," said the angel to Joseph about Mary his fiancée. The Church sees here the fulfillment of the divine promise given through the prophet Isaiah: "Behold, a virgin shall conceive and bear a son" (*CCC* §497).

MICAH 5:2–3

The prophet Micah, a contemporary of Isaiah, warned that Israel was to be downsized to a mere shadow of herself before she could again be worthy of God's promised mercy. Not only would the Northern Kingdom of the Jews be exiled, Jerusalem itself was earmarked for destruction. But the final unification of the people would be ahieved by a mighty ruler from a humble town—a ruler whose origins are eternal, and who is born of a woman.

> But you, O Bethlehem of Ephrathah,
>> who are one of the little clans of Judah,
> from you shall come forth for me
>> one who is to rule in Israel,
> whose origin is from of old, from ancient days.
> Therefore he shall give them up until the time
>> when she who is in labor has brought forth;
> then the rest of his kindred shall return
>> to the people of Israel.
>
> (Mic 5:2–3)

A surface reading of this text can be made in the light of God's promise that Jerusalem, the Daughter of Zion, will be saved from the Babylonian captivity. Later, Mary is seen symbolically as the "Daughter of Zion." Zion is the place where David, a messianic king in the line of the promised Messiah, had his ancient throne; and the text speaks of a ruler to be born in Bethlehem-Ephrathah and from the ancient House of David.

Traditionally, this passage, along with the one from Isaiah, is seen as foreshadowing the Nativity, the arrival of the Messiah. Micah prophesies that a new King would come forth from the humble city of Bethlehem. This ruler would exist from days of old, yet will be brought forth by the birth pains of a woman. God would leave Israel at the mercy of its enemies until this woman bears a child. This child will unite the scattered Jews and form a holy people finally secure from their enemies.

This passage is in tune with the two previous ones: it is God's plan to leave Israel at the mercy of its enemies.

2. Old Testament Women As Types of Mary

Many other Old Testament texts have been applied to Mary throughout the centuries, both in the liturgy and by individual commentators. These passages, though, refer to Mary in the sense that they have been adapted to her in an indirect way. This adjustment of Hebrew Scripture to Mary provides important insight to her as shown by the place these texts take in the thought of the Church Fathers and other theologians. Here are some of the types of Mary in the Old Testament.

SARAH

Sarah was the wife of Abraham to whom God had promised posterity without number despite the fact that she was childless and far beyond childbearing age. By bearing a child, Sarah brings God's promise to Abraham to pass and helps her husband live out his faith in God. Through the power of God she brought forth a son, Isaac, who ensured the continuation of God's saving plan (Gn 17:1—21:7).

Sarah was a precursor of Mary in the manner of the birth of her son. Sarah's infertility is ended when the Lord says to Abraham: "Is anything too wonderful for the LORD? At the set time I will return to you, in due season, and Sarah shall have a son" (Gn 18:14). This announcement mimics the one given to Mary by Gabriel, the angel messenger from God: "The Holy Spirit will come upon you, and the power of the Most High will overshadow you; therefore the child to be born will be holy; he will be called the Son of God....For nothing will be impossible with God" (Lk 1:35, 37).

Sarah was also a type of Mary through the birth of her son. Just as Sarah gave birth to Isaac, head of the chosen people, so Mary gave birth to Christ the Redeemer, the foundation of the Church. Sarah and Mary are both seen as our mothers in faith.

Abraham, who was tested by God who asked him to sacrifice his son Isaac, is also a model of how to react to the divine request. Abraham was chosen by God and he freely responded in a positive way. Abraham's faith can be seen as similar to Mary's, as Pope John Paul II points out in his encyclical *Redemptoris Mater*:

> Mary's faith can also be *compared to that of Abraham*, whom Saint Paul calls "our father in faith" (cf. Rom 4:12). In the salvific economy of God's revelation, Abraham's faith constitutes the beginning of the Old Covenant; Mary's faith at the Annunciation inaugurates the New Covenant. Just as Abraham *"in hope believed against hope, that he should become the father of many nations"* (cf. Rom 4:18), so Mary, at the Annunciation, having professed her virginity ("How shall this be, since I have no husband?" *believed* that through the power of the Most High, by the power of the Holy Spirit, she would become the Mother of God's Son in accordance with the angel's revelation: "The child to be born will be called holy, the Son of God" (Lk 1:35).

REBEKAH

Rebekah is the second mother figure of Israel. She is the mother of Jacob who is later called Israel. She is described in Genesis 24:16: "The girl was very fair to look upon, a virgin, whom no man had known." As her story continued and she is married to Isaac, we discover she is barren up to the moment when she prays to God to deliver her from this situation. She gives birth to Esau and Jacob, but has a special spot in her heart for Jacob. It is through her clever influence that she wins for Jacob the blessing of the aging and blind Isaac. Jacob has to flee from Esau, thus creating an exile of the mother from her preferred child.

In Paul's letter to the Romans, he explains Rebekah's role in the history of God's people, Israel:

> [S]omething similar happened to Rebecca when she had conceived children by one husband, our ancestor Isaac. Even before they had been born or had done anything good or bad (so that God's purpose of election might continue, not by works but by his call) she was told, "The elder shall serve the younger" (9:10–12).

Paul's commentary points out the dramatic way that God freely elects persons of faith to carry out the plan of salvation. Both Rebecca and Mary have been given this vocation by God. Rebecca's action in helping Jacob to steal his father's blessing from Isaac is also in God's plan, for he had revealed to her the future of her two children before they were born. Mary forms a parallel to Rebekah's cooperation in the final stages of salvation history.

RACHEL

It is from Rachel that the most authentic of the Israelite tribes arises, since she is the mother of Joseph and Benjamin by Jacob. Her story is one of utmost and unswerving love and devotion.

Rachel possessed a beauty that drew Jacob as a magnet to her and caused him to serve her father Laban for fourteen years so that he might win her as his wife (Gen 29:1–30). Hence, Rachel is a figure of the unsurpassed beauty of Mary's soul, which is praised in the age-old prayer of the Church: "You are all-beautiful, O Mary, and there is no stain of sin in you." Just as Rachel's beauty entranced Jacob, so Mary's beauty of soul attracted God who chose her to be the earthly mother of his son, Jesus.

Rachel overcomes her infertility through the help of God, just as Mary's virginity is blessed through the overshadowing of the Holy Spirit and she gives birth to Jesus. Rachel steals the household goods of her father, Laban, so that the patrimony of Israel may be preserved just as Mary protects the heritage of the New Covenant. In a similar fashion to Mary's giving birth to Jesus in Bethlehem, Rachel gives birth to Benjamin on the way to Bethlehem as she and Jacob are returning to the house of his father Isaac.

LEAH

Leah is the sister of Rebecca and also the wife of Jacob. She is the mother of eight of the twelve tribes of Israel through her sons Reuben, Simeon, Levi, Judah, Issachar, Zebulun, and the sons of her slave—Gad and Asher (also fathered by Jacob). Through God's plan, Leah is the ancestor of two of the great figures of Israel, namely, Moses and David. Judah, one of Leah's sons, is the originator of the line of David.

Leah is faithful to her husband, Jacob, even though he very obviously preferred Rachel. Mary is also faithful to the life of her family throughout the hidden years and in the public life of Jesus. Mary and Leah are connected through Judah, for Jesus is a descendant of Judah.

DEBORAH AND JAEL

Deborah, a prophetess and the wife of Lappidoth, is one of the greatest of the judges of Israel (Judg 4:4). She was the inspirer of the Israelite actions against the twenty-year oppression of Jabin, the

Canaanite King of Hazor. The tribes of Israel had not prevailed in a war for one hundred seventy-five years when she collected an army of ten thousand men and gave it to Barac, who put the enemy to flight (Judg 4:4ff.). Deborah responded to this victory with her canticle of praise (Judg 5:1–31).

This canticle is one of the oldest texts of the Hebrew Scriptures, perhaps going back to 1200 B.C. It is written or sung not by Deborah but about her—her leadership, courage, and divine inspiration. The song is about one hundred lines long and is about water and glory— the mediation of Yaweh through a storm brings about victory and God's glory. Jael, another woman, caps off the victory by killing the commander of the Canaanites. Water is a sign of victory, just as Jesus changed the water into wine, thereby manifesting his victory over sin.

Deborah calls on her children to follow the ways of the God. Mary, at Cana, pleads with the servants to do whatever Jesus tells them. Deborah is called the mother of Israel, just as Mary is the mother of the divine Son through whom she became the mother of all the faithful. Mary's son conquers Satan, implacable adversary of her people, just as Deborah and Jael conquer the Canaanite King. Jael is acclaimed as blessed among woman (Judg 5:7, 24), just as Mary is saluted at the Visitation. Mary is connected to Deborah and Jael through the words of her *Magnificat* where she says, "He has thrown down the rulers from their thrones but lifted up the lowly." They are thus types of Mary who through her divine Son conquered Satan, the enemy of her people, became the mother of the faithful, and is also called blessed among women.

JOCHEBED

Jochebed, the mother of Moses, Miriam, and Aaron, is also considered as a mother of Israel. Jewish tradition has Jochebed miraculously giving birth to Moses without pain. She also managed to protect him from the Pharaoh's order to kill all newborn Jewish males for three months. Mary is the mother of Jesus, who is the Messiah and savior of all Christians. She gives birth to Jesus miraculously and together with her husband, Joseph, protects him from the murderous intent of Herod.

MIRIAM

Miriam, the sister of Moses, saved him from the death that the Pharaoh had ordered for all male Hebrew babies (Ex 2:1–8). Miriam watches after Moses as he is floated in the Nile in a basket of reeds and sees the Pharaoh's daughter discover him. Cleverly, Miriam suggests Moses' own mother as a nursemaid to the child.

Miriam also possessed the gift of prophecy (Ex 15:20–21) and was at the head of the women as one of the leaders of the crossing of the Red Sea (Mic 6:4), afterward singing the refrain to their hymn of thanksgiving (Ex 15:20–21). The fact that there are seven texts that speak of Miriam indicate her place as a woman leader in Israel. The prophet Micah says of her: "For I brought you up from the land of Egypt, and redeemed you from the house of slavery; and I sent before you Moses, Aaron, and Miriam" (Mic 6:4).

Just as Miriam is intimately involved in the history of salvation through her protection of Moses, so Mary is a human implement of salvation through her protection of Jesus. As Miriam was seen as a prophetess, so Mary was also granted the gift of prophecy. Miriam whose name signifies "lady princess" is most probably the person after whom all the Marys of the New Testament have been named. As Miriam was instrumental in saving her people from the slavery to Pharaoh, Mary, in association with her son, helped her people overthrow Satan and the shackles of sin. Both Miriam and Mary were singers of great songs of thanksgiving.

JUDITH

Judith was a widow of Israel, who combined great beauty with uncommon goodness (Jdt 8:7–8). When her city of Bethulia was an object of siege by Holofernes and was on the brink of giving in, she inspired her people and overcame the monarch with clever strategy, thus preserving God's chosen. They blessed her with the words, "You are the glory of Jerusalem, you are the great boast of Israel; you are the great pride of our nation!" (Jdt 15:9).

The words of praise directed at Judith by her people are also directed to Mary by the Church, for she is the true glory of Judah and the joy of Israel. She crushed the head of Satan, the enemy of the human race, and freed humanity from the shackles of sin forever. She also sang a song of praise to God, one whose words can be applied to Mary:

> I will sing to my God a new song;
> O Lord, you are great and glorious,
>> wonderful in strength, invincible.
> Let all your creatures serve you,
>> for you spoke, and they were made.
> You sent forth your spirit, and it formed them;
>> there is none that can resist your voice.
>
> (Jdt 16:13–14)

ESTHER

Esther was queen of King Ahasuerus (Est 2:17). By her courage and cleverness she prevented the extermination of the Jews that had been planned by the evil Haman. Armed with faith in God, Esther went before the king at the risk of her very life and begged for her people's safety. Her beauty and goodness saved her and the Hebrew people. Thus, Esther is a type of Mary who won God's love by her splendid goodness, saving her people from Satan by the Redeemer whom she bore, all the while becoming Queen of the World in the process.

RUTH

Ruth was the Moabite daughter-in-law of Naomi who returned with her to Bethlehem after her husband had died. Ruth went to the barley fields to glean grain where Boaz, a wealthy kinsman of Naomi, noticed her and made sure that she was protected from the young men in the field and had adequate water to drink. Boaz and Ruth married and has a son of whom was said:

> "He shall be to you a restorer of life and a nourisher of your old age; for your daughter-in-law who loves you, who is more to you than seven sons, has borne him."...They named him Obed; he became the father of Jesse, the father of David (Ruth 4:15, 17).

Ruth is among the mothers of Israel just as Mary is the mother of God's new people. Ruth is the servant of the Lord, as is Mary in Luke 1:38. Ruth is listed in Matthew's genealogy of Jesus; Mary is the last of the five mothers of Israel mentioned (Mt 1:1–16). Ruth did as her mother-in-law Naomi advised: "All that you tell me I will do" (Ruth 3:5) just as Mary accepts God's request by saying: "Let it be with me according to your word" (Lk 1:38).

BATHSHEBA: QUEEN MOTHER

Bathsheba is the wife of Uriah, one of David's commanders whom David had killed out of lust for Bathsheba. She became David's wife, though the genesis of this union was unlawful. Through David, Bathsheba becomes the mother of Solomon, the next king. It is through Solomon that Bathsheba is connected to Jesus. Later, as Queen

Mother, Bathsheba opens the way for her son Solomon to become the king, an event within the salvation plan of God.

Any comparison of Bathsheba with Mary must center on the notion of "Queen Mother." Bathsheba was an active player and an assertive protector of the House of David and of the power of her son. The Queen Mother had significant influence in the kingdom, a power arose out of her son's status. Mary's activity as Queen Mother also arises out of her relation to her son and his status as savior and Redeemer. Mary also preserves the kingdom of our Lord through her role as the leading believer in his Word.

3. Symbols of Mary in the Old Testament

Mary is also seen as foreshadowed by many of the objects in the Old Testament.

JERUSALEM

Jerusalem, as the Holy City, is seen as a type of Mary. All the praises said of this city of Israel can be applied to her. "Great things have been foretold of you, O city of God" (Ps 87:3).

GARDEN OF EDEN

The Garden of Eden as created by God was a land of grace and plenty, a paradise of pleasure, where God placed the first man (Gen 2:8–10). This sacred ground is a type of Mary, watered by God with generous grace. The new Eden (Mary) is holier and more divine than the old Eden, which had Adam dwelling there. In Mary, it is God who has made his dwelling, filling her with his grace.

NOAH'S ARK

Noah's Ark (Gn 6:14—8:19) was the means for preserving the earthly life of the human race. Mary—through her son Jesus—is the instrument for safeguarding the future of the human race. The Ark floated on waters that covered the earth; Mary lived her human life above the waters of sin, escaping entirely safe and sound. The earth was reinhabited by those who took refuge in the Ark. Heaven is peopled by those who found a place of refuge in Mary.

ARK OF THE COVENANT

The Ark of the Covenant (Ex 26:33; 40:20) points to Mary in a variety of ways, as set forth by Saint Ambrose: "The Ark contained the Tablets of the Law; Mary contained in her womb the heir of the Testament. The Ark bore the Law; Mary bore the Gospel. The Ark made the voice of God heard; Mary gave us the very Word of God. The Ark shone forth with the purest of gold; Mary shone forth both inwardly and outwardly with the splendor of virginity. The gold which adorned the Ark came from the interior of the earth; the gold with which Mary shone forth came from the mines of heaven."

JACOB'S LADDER

Jacob's Ladder also foreshadows Mary. On the way to Mesopotamia, the patriarch Jacob had a dream one night. He saw a ladder extending from the earth to heaven, and by it angels ascended and descended (Gen 28:12–15). Mary is the ladder by which the Son of God descended from heaven to earth and assumed human nature. And on this ladder, he led all creatures back to the Father.

STAFF OF AARON

As the Lord commanded, the rod (or staff) of Aaron was brought into the Lord's presence in the Tent and put together with the rods of the eleven other heads of Israel's tribes. It alone sprouted and gave forth fruit (with shoots and blossoms) despite the fact that it had no human help—no roots or nourishment (Num 17:16–24). Mary is God's rod who became the living temple of the Holy Spirit and without human intervention carried to term and brought forth the blessed fruit that gives spiritual life to all—Jesus Christ. She is the one flower of innocence that sprang forth from our corrupt nature.

GIDEON'S FLEECE

Gideon's fleece also points to Mary. God had used the fleece to give Gideon a sign that he was with him. On the first morning, dew was on the fleece alone while all the neighboring ground was dry. The next morning, the fleece was dry and the ground was wet (Judg 6:36–40). Mary is God's fleece, and the dew which wets it in the silence of the night represents the descent of the Word of God into her most pure womb. Mary "conceived the Lord and was entirely imbued with Him as with a sweet dew, without any harm to her virginity" (Saint Ambrose).

Another parallel is that Mary was filled with God's grace from the first moment of her conception, while all others remained deprived of it; and Mary alone was preserved from sin while the whole world was given over to it.

TEMPLE OF SOLOMON

The Temple of Solomon was the glory of the ancient world. The king beautified it with lavish ornament, with gold, silver, and precious stones, for God was to reside there. Solomon placed within the Temple the Ark of the Covenant containing the Tablets of the Law (1 Kgs 16–17). In the New Covenant, God ornamented Mary as his temple—with all the adornments of his grace and virtues. She is the temple of the real Holy of Holies enclosed within herself—she is the Temple of the Lord.

4. Mary in the New Testament

The main purpose of New Testament writings is to tell the story of Jesus Christ. References to Mary in the gospels and epistles are given in relationship to the mystery of Jesus. Thus the figure of Mary that emerges from the New Testament is one that is created of bits and pieces.

PARENTS

By ancient tradition the Church honors Mary's parents as Joachim and Anne. Nothing truly trustworthy is known about these two people since the information about them is based on the apocryphal writings known as the *Protoevangelium of James*, or the *Book of the Nativity of Mary* as it is sometimes called. These works, written to make up for the lack of detail about Mary in the New Testament, were composed in the second century. There is no doubt that the authors included much that was pure speculation. Joachim and Anne are celebrated as saints which they surely must have been in order to have reared a child of such sanctity.

Mary was a descendent of the line of King David through her father Joachim and perhaps through her mother Anne as well. Her birth from David's seed had been predicted by Isaiah 11:1, Jeremiah 23:5 and 33:15, and Zechariah 3:8 and 6:12. Saint Paul declared to the Romans that Jesus was of the seed of David according to the flesh (Rom 1:3). He told his listeners in Antioch that Jesus, the Savior, was brought to Israel from the seed of David (Acts 13:23). Paul also urged Timothy to remember that "Jesus Christ, raised from the dead, a descendant of David—that is my gospel" (2 Tim 2:8).

An often-asked question is this: Were Joachim and Anne parents to other children? In John 19:25 the writer says: "Meanwhile, standing near the cross of Jesus were his mother, and his mother's sister, Mary the wife of Clopas, and Mary Magdalene." Depending on the punctuation of the sentence, four women may be present as witnesses to the crucifixion: the mother of Jesus, her sister, Mary the wife of Clopas, and Mary Magdalene. In this sense there is an anonymous woman who is considered the sister of Mary. She may be her sister-in-law or she may be a sister in the sense of a cousin or relative, or she may be related by blood. From this gospel passage, it is unclear whether or not Mary had a sister in our modern meaning of the word.

ENGAGEMENT

In Matthew 1:18 we read that Mary was betrothed to a man named Joseph. The apocryphal writings represent him as an old man, a widower at the time of the marriage. They add picturesque accounts of the miraculous sign by which he was chosen as Mary's betrothed from among several candidates chosen by the High Priest—by a dove which flew from his staff and alighted on his head or by the sudden flowering of his staff.

We understand from Luke 1:27 and from the genealogies of the gospels that this Joseph was a descendent of David (Mt 1:1–17, Lk 3:23–38). Even though descended from King David, Joseph was a carpenter, a worker in wood (Mt 13:55, Mk 6:3).

At the beginning of Chapter 2 of Luke, Joseph appears again as Mary's companion—her betrothed. It is important to note that Jewish weddings of this period usually consisted of two steps: a betrothal, which was equivalent to our marriage, and the formal marriage proper.

ANNUNCIATION

In the pages of Luke, we entertain a more detailed picture of Mary. Luke, the gospel writer, transmits the spoken words of Mary and enables us to form a more definitive portrait. Luke begins at the beginning, showing Mary in her personal life as a young virgin called upon to be the mother of Jesus, the Savior. He prepares us for the words of the angel Gabriel to Mary by prefacing this event with the story that foretells the birth of John the Baptist. This birth is also foretold though an annunciation to Zechariah. Here is Luke's account:

In the sixth month the angel Gabriel was sent by God to a town in Galilee called Nazareth, to a virgin engaged to a man whose name was Joseph, of the house of David. The virgin's name was Mary. And he came to her and said, "Greetings, favored one! The Lord is with you." But she was much perplexed by his words and pondered what sort of greeting that might be. The angel said to her, "Do not be afraid, Mary, for you have found favor with God. And now, you will conceive in your womb and bear a son, and you will name him Jesus. He will be great, and will be called the Son of the Most High, and the Lord God will give to him the throne of his ancestor, David. He will reign over the house of Jacob forever, and of his kingdom there will be no end." Mary said to the angel, "How can this be, since I am a virgin?" The angel said to her, "The Holy Spirit will come upon you, and the power of the Most High will overshadow you; therefore the child to be born will be holy; he will be called Son of God. And now, your relative Elizabeth in her old age has also conceived a son; and this is the sixth month for her who was said to be barren. For nothing will be impossible with God." Then Mary said, "Here am I, the servant of the Lord; let it be with me according to your word" (Lk 1:26–38).

The narrative begins at the sixth month of Elizabeth's pregnancy with the angel Gabriel's appearance to Mary. This is the same Gabriel who announces himself as standing "in the presence of God" in the story of Zechariah (Lk 1:19). Even though this appearance by Gabriel marks a unique moment in salvation history—the Incarnation of the Son of God—Luke's account centers primarily on the person of Mary who is called a virgin three times in this passage.

At the beginning, God greets Mary through the angel Gabriel with a term that in Greek means that Mary is already filled with grace even before she agrees to be the mother of the Messiah. Next, we see a Mary who is distraught and troubled by the words of Gabriel and the full import of his greeting. Gabriel tells Mary to cease being afraid; she has found favor with God and that she is to give birth to a Son who will rule over the house of Jacob forever. The angel gives the title of Jesus to Mary's son and says that he will be called "great" and the "Son of the Most High."

Then Mary asks how this will be possible since she is a virgin; the angel responds that the Holy Spirit, that is, the power of God, will overshadow her. It is through his conception by the Holy Spirit that Jesus is the Son of God. The angel continues by telling Mary that her cousin Elizabeth has also conceived a son, even though she was said to be barren, for "nothing will be impossible with God."

Finally, Mary completes her response to the divine message by saying: "Let it be with me according to your word." At this point, the freely given consent to the summons of God has been given and the angel takes his leave.

During this world-changing encounter with the angel, Mary shows the highest simplicity, great wisdom, and faithful obedience. She fulfilled the plan of God who had selected Mary as the human vehicle for the salvation and freeing of humankind. Mary was totally cooperative and completely free in her answer to the angel's announcement. At that moment the Incarnation took place, and God's New Covenant with his people began.

THE VISITATION AND THE *MAGNIFICAT*

After the revelation by the angel Gabriel and Mary's answer, she quickly went to visit her cousin Elizabeth who lived in a town in the hills of Judea, a place often identified with Ain Karim, about four miles west of Jerusalem. Mary may have been prompted to this journey by a personal decision to aid her kinswoman and to congratulate her on her good fortune, but she also may have been eager to share her own good news with Elizabeth.

As Mary entered the house of Elizabeth and greeted her, the son growing within Elizabeth's womb reacted with a great leap of joy (Lk 1:41, 44). Through the workings of the Holy Spirit, Elizabeth quickly grasped the supernatural importance of this event, emanating as it did from the supreme holiness of Mary and her Son.

Elizabeth greets Mary with a benediction: "Blessed are you among women, and blessed is the fruit of your womb" (Lk 1:42). Elizabeth then declares herself not worthy to welcome such important guests: "And why has this happened to me, that the mother of my Lord comes to me?" (Lk 1:43). These words recall Old Testament happenings: "How can the ark of the LORD come into my care?" (2 Sam 6:9) and the words of Deborah to Jael, "Most blessed of women be Jael" (Judg 5:24).

Then Elizabeth acknowledges the presence of the Holy Spirit who has made this perception possible: "For as soon as I heard the sound of your greeting, the child in my womb leaped for joy" (Lk 1:44). Elizabeth knew that it was Mary's faith that had supported the Incarnation, so she concludes with the words: "And blessed is she who believed that there would be a fulfillment of what was spoken to her by the Lord" (Lk 1:45).

Mary responds to this greeting from Elizabeth with her own song of praise and thanksgiving, containing passages (Lk 1:46–50) that recall the psalms and other writings of the Old Testament. The echoes of the Old Testament in this song help us to understand the unfolding of the whole plan of salvation. It is sweetened with praise and redolent with prophecy.

In the first section, Mary joyfully lauds the mercy, holiness, and power of the Lord who has done "great things" for her. In the second section (Lk 1:51–53), she explains that God is one who exalts the weak and brings down the rich and the power-ful. In the third section (Lk 1:54–55), Mary remembers the promises made by God to Israel and his faithfulness in fulfilling them.

Mary is mentioned in Luke 1:56 as staying with her cousin Eliza-beth for three months. She possibly could have assisted at the birth of John the Baptist since Elizabeth was six-months' pregnant at the beginning of Mary's visit. At the end of the three months, the gospel says, Mary returned home.

JOSEPH'S RESPONSE

The Gospel of Saint Matthew tells the story of the following quandry in the life of Joseph before he formally secured his marriage to Mary and took her into his house: "When his mother Mary had been en-gaged to Joseph, but before they lived together, she was found to be with child from the Holy Spirit (Mt 1:18). We do not know how this discovery was made nor how Joseph was informed of this miracu-lous event.

Joseph's response to this announcement is described in this fash-ion: "Her husband Joseph, being a righteous man and unwilling to expose her to public disgrace, planned to dismiss her quietly" (Mt 1:19). On the face of it, Mary's pregnancy, which was not by Joseph, appeared to be adultery, and thus Joseph, being a follower of the law, faithful to the Torah, decided to quietly divorce Mary.

It is then that the angel of the Lord appears to Joseph in a dream in order to change his course of action: "But just when he had re-solved to do this, an angel of the Lord appeared to him in a dream and said, 'Joseph, son of David, do not be afraid to take Mary as your wife, for the child conceived in her is from the Holy Spirit. She will bear a son, and you are to name him Jesus, for he will save his people from their sins'" (Mt 1:20–21).

The angel's message contains two parts: (1) Mary's pregnancy originates with the Holy Spirit; and (2) Joseph is to ratify the marriage by taking his wife into his home, and when the child is born he is to call him Jesus. Mary is being used by God to carry out his goal of salvation. Mary is still a virgin who has not breached the marriage pledge, and despite the appearance of unlawful behavior, Joseph may be assured that he can go forward with his marriage by bringing Mary into his house.

Then Joseph is informed of the future plan of salvation and, just as Mary cooperated by faith and obedience, so Joseph "did as the angel of the Lord commanded him" (Mt 1:24).

Matthew's Gospel goes on to say that Joseph had "no marital relations with her until she had borne a son" (1:25). The use of the word "until" does not indicate that Joseph had marital relations with Mary after the birth of Jesus. It merely states what happens up to a certain point in the chain of events.

This gospel chapter is concluded by Matthew's stressing of the fact that the conception and birth of this child was a fulfillment of the prophecy of Isaiah: "Look, the virgin shall conceive and bear a son, and they shall name him Emmanuel, which means 'God is with us'" (Mt 1:23).

It is probable that Mary and Joseph understood in an imperfect way the accomplishment of the prophecy of Isaiah in the events that were whirling around them; yet there is no mention here in this gospel that they fully comprehended the complete scope of the plan God had for his people.

BETHLEHEM AND THE BIRTH OF JESUS

As Mary's pregnancy was coming to an end, an edict of the Roman Emperor Augustus was promulgated, ordering a census of all the residents of Herod's domain (Lk 2:1). Similar census counts had already been made in other parts of the Roman Empire. This process required that each citizen be enumerated in the town of their ancestors. Since Joseph was of the line of David, he had to go to

Bethlehem, the birthplace of David and the center of his tribe (Lk 2:3–4).

Mary made the journey of about ninety miles to Bethlehem with Joseph. Luke does not tell us why she went with him. Was it because women also were required to be registered, or was it because she wanted to have the companionship of Joseph when it came time for her delivery?

Upon their arrival in Bethlehem, they met with an unexpected difficulty: there was no place for them to stay. Possibly someone showed the couple a series of caves outside the city where tradition has designated one of these caves as the birthplace of Christ. How long Mary stayed in these poor surroundings is not known. The birth of Jesus may have occurred on the night of the couple's arrival or after some days. We are not told any of these details.

While they were staying in these poor accommodations, Mary gave birth to her "firstborn son and wrapped him in bands of cloth, and laid him in a manger" (Lk 2:7). It is traditionally thought by many of the faithful that Mary give birth without the bodily effects of physical delivery and while still remaining a virgin. The bands of cloth in which Mary wrapped Jesus are the "swaddling clothes"— another sign of the community of the poor, the remnant, whom God prepared to receive his Son.

THE SHEPHERDS AND THE ANGELS

The poverty and improvised conditions of Jesus' birth were in strong contrast to the splendor of the angels who appeared to nearby shepherds, saying "Do not be afraid; for see—I am bringing you good news of great joy for all the people: to you is born this day in the city of David, a Savior, who is the Messiah, the Lord" (Lk 2:10). Next, choirs of angelic hosts appear with their song of praise and glory (Lk 2:14).

The shepherds are unhesitating believers and go quickly to Bethlehem to find the child along with Mary and Joseph. After seeing the signs that were foretold by the angels, the shepherds returned to tell others about the child and they were overcome with awe and amazement (Lk 2:15–18). Mary's response to all these events was one of interior prayer. She "treasured all these words and pondered them in her heart" (Lk 2:19).

At the end of eight days, the time had come to circumcise the child. This was done and Jesus and Mary called him "Jesus, the name given by the angel before he was conceived in the womb" (Lk 2:21).

THE PRESENTATION AND THE PURIFICATION

Mary and Joseph were both Jews, and thus they followed the law of Moses which said that a woman giving birth to a male child would be unclean for a period of forty days. This action of fulfilling the Jewish law is exemplified in Saint Paul's description of Jesus' being "born under the law" (Gal 4:4).

During this time, the new mother was forbidden to enter the Temple. After the forty days, the mother was required to go to the Temple and purify herself through the prescribed sacrifices: a year-old lamb for a sacrifice and a young pigeon or a turtledove as an atonement offering. A young pigeon could be substituted for the lamb if the woman could not afford it.

If the male child was the woman's firstborn, she was also obliged to redeem him from the Lord, whose property he was, by the payment of money to the priests. In fulfillment of these obligations, Joseph and Mary went up to the Temple and offered the sacrifices that were expected of the poor. This is Jesus' first encounter with the Temple which would have such significance in his life and that of his mother as well as his first coming to Jerusalem where their lives would reach such a sad ending.

As they were nearing the gate of the Court of the Women, where the purification rituals were held, Joseph and Mary met a just and devout man named Simeon. Simeon had been promised by the Holy

Spirit that he would not die before he saw the Messiah (Lk 2:25–27). Guided by the Holy Spirit, Simeon recognized the long-awaited Savior in the Child Jesus. He took Jesus into his arms and sang this song of praise, called in Latin *Nunc dimittis*:

> "Master, now you are dismissing
>> your servant in peace,
>> according to your word;
>> for my eyes have seen your salvation,
>> which you have prepared in the
>>> presence of all peoples,
>> a light for revelation to the Gentiles
>> and for glory to your people Israel."
>
> (Lk 2:29–32)

These words of prophecy possibly brought home to the parents that the mission of Jesus would reach out to all peoples, not just to the Jews. The song may also have reminded them of other predictions of Isaiah concerning the Servant of the Lord (Isa 42:6; 49:6).

Commenting on this scene, Saint Bernard says that the day will come when our Lord will be offered not in the Temple nor in the arms of Simeon, but outside the city on the arms of the Cross.

After Simon's blessing, he turns to Mary and reminds her of the suffering that her life would involve: "This child is destined for the falling and the rising of many in Israel, and to be a sign that will be opposed so that the inner thoughts of many will be revealed—and a sword will pierce your own soul too" (Lk 2:34–35).

Mary was met also by the prophet Anna, daughter of Phanuel. Anna, a widow, spent her days and nights fasting and praying at the Temple. This holy woman recognized Jesus, the Savior, and began to speak about this wonder-child to all who were seeking the redemption of Jerusalem (Lk 2:36–38).

THE MAGI

Sometime after Jesus was born in Bethlehem, in the time of King Herod, a caravan stopped one evening at the home of the Holy Family in Bethlehem. This dwelling place is called a "house" in the Gospel of Matthew (2:11), so perhaps by now a more appropriate lodging has been found for the family. The caravan leaders said that they were Magi who had seen the newly created star of the Messiah in the East and had been told by King Herod that the prophet Micah had predicted the Messiah's birth in Bethlehem (Mic 5:1–3).

The Magi had visited with King Herod and informed them of their quest for the Messiah. Herod, ever on guard about any threat to his throne, told the wise men that they should seek the child and, upon finding him, bring word back to him so that "I may also go and pay him homage" (Mt 2:8).

After they heard the king's request, the Magi set out and soon saw the star going before them, stopping over the place where Jesus lived. Joyfully they entered the house and seeing the child with Mary his mother they knelt in homage and give him gifts of gold, frankincense, and myrrh (Mt 2:1–11).

The gifts given by the Magi hint that the Wise Men saw Jesus as more than just an earthly ruler. These gifts are traditionally interpreted as gold for Jesus' kingship, frankincense for his divinity, and myrrh for his humanity.

The Magi were seen as the fulfillment of the prophecies: Simeon's prophecy that Jesus would be a light of revelation to the Gentiles; the Psalmist who said: "All kings bow down to him, and all nations serve him" (Ps 72:11); and Isaiah who says that "all those from Sheba shall come. They shall bring gold and frankincense, and shall proclaim the praise of the LORD" (Isa 60:6). The Magi were warned by a dream not to return to Herod, and they left to return to their own country by another way (Mt 2:12).

FLIGHT INTO EGYPT

After the Magi departed, Joseph was cautioned by an angel about the ominous plans of Kind Herod on the life of Jesus. The angel ordered Joseph: "Get up, take the child and his mother, and flee to Egypt, and remain there until I tell you; for Herod is about to search for the child, to destroy him" (Mt 2:13).

Joseph's journey could have taken several different paths, but any route would take about two weeks of debilitating and difficult travel.

Once there, the Holy Family stayed in Egypt until Herod had died. Matthew reminds us that this trek to another land fulfilled the prophecy: "Out of Egypt I have called my son" (Mt 2:15).

Herod soon realized that he had been deceived by the Magi, and he ordered that all the children in and around Bethlehem who were two years old or under should be killed (Mt 2:16). Matthew also perceives that this slaughter was fulfillment of the words of Jeremiah that there would be wailing and loud lamentation. The gospel does not mention if the news of the slaughter of the Innocents reached the Holy Family in Egypt.

RETURN TO NAZARETH FROM EGYPT

When King Herod had died (about 4 B.C.), the angel appeared again to Joseph in Egypt. He said: "Get up, take the child and his mother, and go to the land of Israel, for those who were seeking the child's life are dead" (Mt 2:20). These directives were followed by Joseph but during his journey, he hears that Archelaus, Herod's older son, has been appointed ruler of Judea. Joseph became afraid of going back to Bethlehem, fearing that Archelaus may persecute the Child Jesus as terribly as did his father (Mt 2:21–22).

Another dream vision calmed Joseph's fears, for he was instructed to go to Nazareth of Galilee. Matthew notes that Jesus took up residence in Nazareth in order to fulfill the prophecy that he would be called a Nazarene (Mt 2:23).

HIDDEN LIFE IN NAZARETH

Jesus stayed in Nazareth until he was approximately thirty years of age (Lk 3:23). Two sentences summarize the hidden life of Jesus: He went down to Nazareth and was obedient to his parents (Lk 2:51), and he increased in wisdom and in years, in divine and human favor (Lk 2:52). Even though he was the Son of God, Jesus made himself submissive to Mary and Joseph, not out of duty as their son but because of the will of his Father in heaven. Jesus also grew in wisdom, and this must have given Mary a great deal of motherly joy.

JESUS IN THE TEMPLE

Devout Jews were obligated to appear in the sanctuary at Jerusalem on the festivals of Passover, Pentecost, and Tabernacles. This obligation began at the completion of every male person's thirteenth year, but some parents began the custom sooner in order to acclimate their sons to the observance of this law. Thus, Mary and Joseph took Jesus to observe Passover in his twelfth year (Lk 2:41–42).

When the observance was ended, Mary and Joseph joined a caravan to return to Galilee. After one day's journey, they came to realize that Jesus was not with the caravan. Fearing that some evil had befallen him, they retraced their steps, asking their friends and relatives if they had seen him.

After three days of searching, during which they had returned to Jerusalem, they found Jesus in the Temple, sitting among the scholars. All those who heard him were amazed at his answers and astonished at the depth of his questions.

When Mary and Joseph saw Jesus they, too, were astonished, not really by his intellectual attainments, but by his offhanded concern of his parents and their sorrow at losing him.

Mary thus asked him: "Child, why have you treated us like this? Look, your father and I have been searching for you in great anxiety" (Lk 2:48). Jesus than asked why they were searching for him. Did they not know that he must be in his Father's house? (Lk 2:49).

The parents of Jesus did know that he was appointed to carry on his Father's business, but they did not understand what he said to them (Lk 2:50). They, with the limits of their human intellect, could not know that this mission might mean the abandonment of family bonds, without even so much as a warning, and the adversity of much sorrow. Mary did not comprehend the mysteries of her Son all at once; rather she kept these events "treasured…in her heart" (Lk 2:51).

WEDDING FEAST AT CANA

The wedding at Cana is the first time we encounter Mary after the incident with Jesus at the Temple. This event, as narrated by Saint John the Evangelist, takes place at the beginning of Christ's public life, in Cana, a city in lower Galilee, about three miles from Nazareth, after the first disciples have joined Jesus (Jn 1:35–51) and before he goes to Jerusalem where he cleanses the Temple. This even occurs on the third day—foreshadowing of the Resurrection.

Mary's presence at these wedding festivities along with Jesus and his disciples colors the whole story of this event. The newlyweds have run out of wine, and Mary then said to her son: "They have no wine" (Jn 2:3). Jesus answered her: "Woman, what concern is that to you and to me? My hour has not yet come" (Jn 2:4).

Mary seems to have asked Jesus to perform a miracle, or at the very least expected Jesus to do something about the situation in some way. In response, Jesus addressed his mother as "woman," a word that seems surprisingly abrupt, but most scholars now think that this form of address does not hint at any rebuke, but rather indicates a high level of regard. It is thought that Jesus chose this less affectionate form of address to show that Mary's motherly control had been superceded once he was about "his Father's business."

The meaning of the question "what concern is that to you and to me?" has often been discussed. The wording is sometimes used when one person is bothering another as in the sense of "What have I done to you that you should treat me like this?" In another context, the sentence has the meaning "That is your business, and I am not involved." Though some people see this statement by Jesus as disrespectful, many others read the sentence as meaning a reluctance on the part of Jesus to be involved. At any rate, the question shows that Mary does not share Jesus' understanding of the work his Father has asked him to do.

Jesus continues with another statement that also has been the subject of dispute. Many see this statement as meaning that Jesus is disassociating himself from the claims being made on his earthly family; and in a sense, this statement parallels the abrupt question Jesus poses to his parents at the Temple: "Why is it that you are looking for me?"

Mary responds to Jesus' off-putting remarks by saying to the waiters: "Do whatever he tells you"—a sentence that echoes the word of the Pharaoh: "Go to Joseph; what he says to you, do" (Gen 41:55). Why would Mary do this after Jesus seems to reject her request? One explanation seems to be that Mary is an example of persistence, ignoring any setbacks until eventually she gains the requested favor. Thus Mary's intercession results in a wonderful miracle, the transformation of water into wine, and a sensitive act of kindness by which a young couple is able to avoid embarrassment. Certainly Mary's actions here can serve as our own guide to a similar persistence in our prayer to Jesus and as an example of the effectiveness of Mary's maternal care.

MARY IN THE PUBLIC LIFE OF JESUS

Mary played only an indirect role in the public life of Jesus. Saint John relates that Mary and the brethren of Jesus accompanied him and his disciples to Capernaum (Jn 2:12) after the wedding at Cana. Capernaum, for a time, was the center of Jesus' public ministry, and the starting point for visits to other parts of Galilee. Mary may have stayed here, but she played no obvious part in Jesus' public life, nor is Mary mentioned among the women who ministered to Jesus and his apostles in Galilee (Mk 15:41).

Only two incidents are recounted in which Mary is referred to, not by name but as the Mother of Jesus. On the first occasion, Jesus was so besieged by a crowd of visitors in a house presumably located in Capernaum that he could not even eat. At that point, his brethren and his mother came to take him away, for some people had even accused him of losing his mind (Mk 3:20).

A crowd had gathered outside, and they went to him, and said: "Your mother and your brothers and sisters are outside, asking for you" (Mk 3:32). When Jesus was informed that his mother and brethren were outside, looking around him at those who sat with him, he said: "Who are my mother and my brothers?...Whoever does the will of God is my brother and sister and mother" (Mk 3:33, 34).

This response is not thought to imply depreciation of his mother, but rather an effort to expand the definition of family to spiritual brothers and sisters. He sets family relationship on a new level in which the bonds of obedience to God are above the blood ties of a natural family.

The same effort to exalt the concept of spiritual family is seen on another occasion when a woman exclaimed: "Blessed is the womb that bore you and the breasts that nursed you!" (Lk 11:27). In response, Jesus amended her statement by saying: "Blessed rather are those who hear the word of God and obey it!" (Lk 11:28).

MARY BENEATH THE CROSS

Mary is not encountered again in the gospels until we find her standing beneath the cross together with John, the beloved disciple, and the holy women. John's account of the crucifixion (Jn 19:16–42) is a series of short episodes. At the middle of this account, there occurs a scene picturing Mary at the foot of the cross of Jesus (Jn 19:25). Preceding this appearance of Mary is the story of the soldiers who divided up the clothing of Jesus and cast lots for his seamless tunic (Jn 19:23–24).

John's Gospel continues: "When Jesus saw his mother and the disciple whom he loved…he said to his mother, 'Woman, here is your son.' Then he said to the disciple, 'Here is your mother.' And from that hour the disciple took her into his own home" (Jn 19:26–27).

In this passage Mary is called "woman," exactly as she had been at the marriage feast at Cana. This title is not Mary's personal name, so we can guess here that she is considered not as an individual person but as the woman to whom a special role has been allocated.

Now that the final events in our salvation story have come to pass, she and the Beloved Disciple are the receivers of Jesus' love. They represent all of Jesus' brothers and sisters who are there and who will come into the community of believers. Mary is symbolic of this community as its mother. Her deeper spiritual motherhood begins at the foot of the cross as Jesus accomplishes all that he has been asked to do. The victory is achieved.

Mary and the Beloved Disciple stand in for all Christians as they look upon Jesus and believe. From the flowing blood and water from the side of Jesus, they receive his blessing. The Church is paid for by the cross and the water which flows from the side of Christ (Baptism) and his blood (Eucharist). Mary and John are symbols of the call to discipleship which reaches its highest level in a believing community and in the love and care they have for one another.

MARY AND THE RESURRECTION

Scripture does not tell us about Mary's role in the burial of Jesus. How she spent the days between her son's burial and his Resurrection is also not recorded. Some writers, including Saint John Chrysostom, consider it self-evident that the Risen Christ first appeared to his Mother, though we have no mention of this in the New Testament.

The forty days before the Ascension was no doubt a time of great joy; Acts 1:13–14 does tell us that Mary was present in the upper room united in prayer with the apostles, the holy women, and the disciples of our Lord. Since she was united in prayer with the apostles, she must have witnessed the outpouring of the Holy Spirit on the day of Pentecost and the other events marking the beginning of Christ's Church on earth (Acts 2:1).

Nothing further is told about Mary in Acts, and the rest of the epistles, too, are silent about her. Scriptures do not even refer in direct words to her Assumption, which was the high point of her life on earth and the beginning of her joy with her Son in heaven.

WOMAN OF THE APOCALYPSE

In Revelation, John describes a woman whom he saw in a vision: she was clothed with the sun, the moon was beneath her feet, and on her head was a crown of stars. "She was pregnant and was crying out in birth pangs, in the agony of giving birth" (Rev 12:2). She gives birth on earth to a male child, who is the Son of God, and who is caught up to his throne (Rev 12:5). Then the dragon, or Satan, who was lying in wait to kill the child pursues the woman into the desert and tries to destroy her, but she escapes with divine help and lives securely there for three and a half years (Rev 12:6–9).

This mysterious figure has often been identified with Mary, especially in modern times. But, at Bethlehem Mary did not give birth to

Jesus in pain, nor did she flee to the desert after the Ascension. The early tradition of the Church regards this woman, before the birth of the child, as a symbol of the Israel of the Old Testament; after the birth of the child and his ascension into heaven, the woman is seen to represent the Israel of the New Testament, the Church.

Does this woman in the vision, then, have anything to do with Mary? Many modern readers of John hold the opinion that the mysterious image has two meanings. In the first meaning, the woman clothed with the sun is indeed the Church—but this does not exclude Mary, who herself is a representative of the Church. A meaning combined from the two interpretations is certainly a possibility since Mary is not merely the individual mother of Jesus but the representative of the whole people of God.

SUMMARY

One commentator on Mary summarizes Mary's place in the Scriptures in this way:

> Thus Scripture presents Mary "through a glass in a dark manner" (1 Cor 13:12). Almost every passage referring to her can be—and has been—interpreted in quite different ways. Foretold by the Prophets, but in rather equivocal terms, praised by the angel, yet seemingly sometimes reproached by her Son, aware of her destiny, yet not quite comprehending it, becoming a mother for the second time under the Cross but mysteriously, finally appearing as a "sign" in the heavens—yet not she but the Church."

In spite of all this ambiguity, she remains a significant part of the mystery of our salvation and a figure close by the side of her son, on earth as in heaven.

5. Mary in the Apocrypha

The label "apocrypha" is given to a number of works written in imitation of the Scriptures or connected to the Scriptures in some way. Apocrypha, which means "hidden" or "secret," are not accepted as part of sacred Scripture but some of these writings from the early days of the Church have exercised a tremendous influence on the popular imagination. Some of these apocryphal works contain information about Mary, and many attempt to fill in the gaps of the story told in the gospels.

PROTOEVANGELIUM OF JAMES

This book probably originated in the second century as an expansion of the birth story of Jesus. It seems to be the first Christian writing to show an independent interest in the person of Mary. It was originally titled *The Nativity of Mary*.

The author recounts, in the fashion of a legend, the background and life of Mary. He gives elaborate and creative details to flesh out the bare-bones gospel picture of Mary: her miraculous birth after the angel's announcement to her aged parents Joachim and Anne; Mary's presentation in the Temple at the age of three; Mary's engagement to Joseph, an old man vying with a group of youths for Mary's hand, and who is chosen by God through the sign of a dove; the Annunciation wherein Gabriel appears to Mary twice: once while she is drawing water at the well, and the second time when she is spinning at home; the birth of Jesus in a cave outside Bethlehem; the midwife's testimony to Mary's virginity, and Mary's vindication before the High Priest.

The *Protoevangelium* is an important work because it seems to have given rise to three Marian feasts: the Conception of Mary, the Nativity of Mary, and the Presentation of Mary in the Temple.

SIBYLLINE ORACLES

The *Sibylline Oracles* are a Jewish-Hellenist work written about the second century. One part of this work contains a long, poetic section that refers to the "holy virgin" or the "virgin Mary," and seems to paraphrase Luke's annunciation and birth stories, adding such features as the virgin's laughter, which is echoed after the birth of Jesus by the laughter of the heaven. This book also states that God allotted seven periods of penance for sinful humans "thanks to the Holy Virgin."

TRANSITUS MARIAE

These are legendlike writings which describe the passage of Mary from this life to the life hereafter. According to many of these fictional accounts, Mary died a natural death in Jerusalem surrounded by the apostles and the evangelists—Peter, Andrew, Philip, Simon, and Thaddaeus. After they had carried Mary's body to a new tomb in Gethsemane, a sweet odor was emitted from the sepulcher. After three days, invisible angels were heard glorifying God, and on the third day, the apostles saw her spotless body was taken into paradise.

OTHER APOCRYPHA

In the *Ascension of Isaiah*, a second-century revision of an earlier Jewish work, tells of the miraculous appearance (rather than birth) of the Christ Child. In the *History of Joseph the Carpenter*, a narrative dating from the fourth or fifth century, Mary is seen as comforting Joseph in his old age and in his dying illness and urges that Joseph be invoked by the poor. In the *Arabic Gospel of the Infancy*, two miracles of the Infant Jesus are recorded. These miracles were worked for women who appealed to Mary, his mother. Finally, the *Book of the Resurrection of Christ*, a third- or fourth-century work, contains a story of the apostles asking Mary to pray to the Lord to reveal to them the things that are in heaven.

SECTION THREE

Mary in the
Liturgy of the Church

The Blessed Virgin Mary occupies a place in the Church which is highest after Christ. While Mary's role is subordinate to Christ, she is also, by virtue of her sinless humanhood, closest to us. Mary is an important figure to the faithful, because she is linked to the mystery of Christ's sacrifice on the cross from which our salvation flows.

The chief expression of our Catholic faith always lies in the worship of God through the liturgy—a liturgy that unites the Church, as Christ's body, with his eternal worship of the Father, and so allows us to share, through the Holy Spirit, in the hope of our own resurrection. Because we believe that those who have gained their eternal reward as members of the communion of saints can intercede for us with God, and because of Mary's status as the preeminent member of this company of saints, we honor her through liturgical celebrations and feast days.

As Pope Paul VI says in his apostolic exhortation on devotion to Mary, "We must first turn our attention to the sacred liturgy. In addition to its rich doctrinal content, the liturgy has an incomparable pastoral effectiveness and a recognized exemplary value for the other forms of worship" (*Marialis Cultus*, §1).

In the public liturgy of the Mass, Mary is honored in several ways: in the eucharistic prayers, in the prefaces, and in solemnities, feasts, memorials, and votive masses.

1. Eucharistic Prayers, Prefaces, and Solemn Blessings

The Mass, as the perfect sacrifice, gains its efficacy from the sacrifice of the cross, which the Mass continues (*CCC* §1362). Mary's association with the Mass is a frequent one.

First, she is named in the confession in the Preparatory Prayers of the Mass: "I ask blessed Mary ever virgin, all the angels and saints, and you, my brothers and sisters, to pray for me...." Mary is also named in the Profession of Faith in the Nicene Creed (when it is said): "Came down from heaven: by the power of the Holy Spirit he was born of the Virgin Mary...."

Next Mary is recalled in the Eucharistic Prayer of the Mass. She is commemorated in the ancient Roman Canon, in descriptive words of doctrinal significance: "In union with the whole Church we honor Mary, the ever-Virgin Mother of Jesus Christ our Lord and God." In Eucharistic Prayer No. 2, Mary is included in the words: "By the power of the Holy Spirit he took flesh and was born of the Virgin Mary." Further, we say in the Communion prayer, "[M]ake us worthy to share eternal life with Mary, the virgin Mother of God..." The community says in Eucharistic Prayer No. 4: "He was conceived through the power of the Holy Spirit and born of the Virgin Mary...." and also "[G]rant also to us, your children, to enter into our heavenly inheritance in the company of the Virgin Mary, the Mother of God...." As Pope Paul VI reminds us,

> This daily commemoration, by reason of its place at the heart of the divine Sacrifice, should be considered a particularly expressive form of the veneration that the Church pays to the "Blessed of the Most High" (cf. Lk 1:28) (*Marialis Cultus* §10).

Mary is further remembered in some of the Prefaces of the Eucharistic Prayer: the second preface for Advent and the second preface for Ordinary Time.

2. Solemnities, Feasts, Memorials, and Votive Masses

To appreciate the full extent of the veneration offered to Mary in the public liturgy of the Church, it is necessary to study the propers of the Masses for her feasts, both general and local. At once, the person examining these elements will see the use made of the Old Testament—especially the words of the Psalms, and of such books as

Ecclesiasticus and Proverbs. Scriptural readings from the New Testament are also set forth in order to remind us of the whole part that Mary plays in the story of salvation.

The general Roman calendar lists fifteen feasts of the Blessed Virgin Mary throughout the liturgical year. In the United States, the feast of Our Lady of Guadalupe, the Mother of the Americas, is added, bringing the total to sixteen. These feasts celebrate either Mary's remarkable involvement in the birth and life of Jesus, the working of grace in her life, or the importance she has in the lives of the faithful because she is the model of perfect discipleship.

To understand the meaning of the Church's celebration of Mary, it may be helpful to think of Mary's feasts as being divided into three groups: the celebration of the Mother of God, the feasts of the Blessed Virgin, and the feasts of our Lady.

Christmas: The greatest Marian feast has been that of Christmas, which, since the fourth century, has celebrated the Virgin Mary as mother of the Savior, for as the Lord said through the prophet, "Look, the virgin shall conceive and bear a son, and they shall name him Emmanuel" (Mt 1:23). This honoring of Mary is not confined to Christmas; it really begins with Advent and runs through the feast of the Baptism of Our Lord, which begins Christ's public life.

Feasts of the Blessed Virgin: The second group of Marian observances comprise those feasts which commemorate real or apocryphal observances of Mary's life: the Conception, the Birth, the Presentation, the Annunciation, the Visitation, and the Assumption. These celebrations have as their reference Mary's personal sanctity rather that her place in the our salvation story.

Feasts of Our Lady: This third group is made up of those feasts that honor Mary as a model, advocate, and protectress of humankind.

They venerate our Lady as a patron, under a special title, or as she is represented in a particular place or community. Local or secondary Marian celebrations, of which over nine hundred have been counted, are a way of giving all human beings an opportunity to honor Mary according to particular needs, in their own time and place, but still in the light of our Lady as the giver of Jesus Christ to humankind.

IMMACULATE CONCEPTION OF MARY: DECEMBER 8

This solemnity celebrates Mary's miraculous conception without sin from the very first instant of her human existence and God's provident plan, from the beginning of time, to arrange for the sinlessness of the woman he chose as the Mother of God. It also prepares for the arrival of our Savior and the happy beginning of our plan of salvation.

This feast, originally called the "Conception of Saint Anne," came to the Western Church by way of the Eastern Church, where is was introduced during the eighth century. It spread from Constantinople to Naples and Sicily, and then spread to Normandy and other parts of Europe. The feast spread slowly because of the disputes among theologians over Mary's absolute sinlessness, but finally it was declared an annual feast for the whole Church and given its present rank in 1854 and raised to a holy day of obligation.

The Immaculate Conception is celebrated with great verve in Spain where December 8 is the traditional day of school celebrations, where houses are decorated with flowers and flags, with candles burning in the windows throughout the night on the eve of the feast, and an annual Mother's Day is observed with joyful family celebrations scheduled throughout the country.

The readings for this feast are as follows:

Gn 3:9–20 which recounts our history of sin; Eph 1:3–12 which proclaims God's eternal plan of salvation;

Lk 1:26–38 in which Mary, full of grace, freely agrees to her role as mother of Jesus Christ.

OUR LADY OF GUADALUPE: DECEMBER 12 (IN THE UNITED STATES)

This feast commemorates Mary as the patroness of the Americas and the apparition of our Blessed Virgin to a Mexican native named Juan Diego on the hill of Tepeyac near Mexico City in 1531. The picture of Mary, represented with Aztec features, is now venerated at the Basilica of Our Lady of Guadalupe, and is said to have appeared on the inside of Juan Diego's cloak when he went to the bishop to report his sighting. This feast celebrates Mary's promise to stand as a mother to all peoples, especially the poor.

The readings of the Mass are as follows:

Zech 2:14–17 in which the daughter of Zion is exhorted to rejoice in honor of the coming of the Lord; Rev 11:19, 12:1–6, 10 in which the Ark of the Covenant appears as well as a woman clothed with the sun and crowned with twelve stars—both symbols of Mary; and Lk 11:27–28 in which those who hear and keep the word of God are blessed.

MARY, MOTHER OF GOD: JANUARY 1

This solemnity celebrates the part Mary played in the mystery of salvation, praises the dignity which this mystery brings to the holy Mother, renews adoration of the newborn Prince of Peace, and asks God, through the intercession of Mary, for the gift of peace.

The readings of the Mass are as follows:

Num 6:22–27 which is the Lord's blessing of his people; Gal 4:4–7 which reflects on the new blessings of freedom and maturity brought to humanity in the fullness of time by God's Son who was born of a woman; and Lk 2:16–21 which tells the story of the circumcision and naming of Jesus eight days after his birth, but also shows Mary as keeping in her heart all the astounding events surrounding her Son's birth as a way of inviting us, at the beginning of a new year, to engage in grateful contemplation of the mystery that awaits us.

OUR LADY OF LOURDES: FEBRUARY 11

This optional memorial commemorates the first of Mary's eighteen appearances to Bernadette Soubirous at Lourdes, on February 11, 1858. This is the only celebration of an apparition of Mary in the general Roman calendar, and it remains there because of the significance of Lourdes as a place of pilgrimage and holiness.

Readings for the Mass may be selected from the Common for Feasts of Mary. The suggested first reading is Isa 66:10–14 which speaks of a transformed Jerusalem—a place often linked with Mary—and which promises peace and prosperity to Israel "like an overflowing stream," an image that suggests the healing waters at Lourdes.

ANNUNCIATION OF THE LORD: MARCH 25

This solemnity celebrates the Incarnation of the Word in Mary's womb, nine months before the celebration of the birth of Jesus. This is, as described by Pope Paul VI, a joint feast of Christ—the Word made flesh, who becomes the Son of Mary—and the Blessed Virgin—who becomes the mother of God.

In the early Christian centuries, March 25 was observed as the Day of the Incarnation. Soon, through the working of tradition, other events associated with the history of salvation were considered to have occurred on this day also, among them the crucifixion of Christ, creation of the world, the Fall of Adam and Eve, and the sacrifice of Isaac. Even in ancient times, the papal Curia, on all of its documents, started the year on March 25. In fact, in England, the Feast of the Annunciation, called "Lady Day," marked the beginning of the legal year, even after the Reformation. In central Europe, this feast was sometimes called the "Feast of Swallows" because of the general belief that swallows return from their migration on this day.

In all of medieval Europe, pageants and processions marked the celebration of the Annunciation. In some places the "Golden Mass" was sung, while in others a young choirboy representing Mary was dressed as an angel and suspended on a rope in midair. As the approaching "angel" descended, mothers would place candy on the pews, making their children believe that invisible companions of Gabriel had brought these goodies from heaven.

In Russia, large wheaten wafers were blessed by priests and given to the faithful after the Mass. When they arrived home, each member of the family ate a small piece of the wafer, and the remaining crumbs of the Annunciation bread were buried in the fields in order to ward off disease, frost, and drought.

The Mass readings for this great celebration are these:

> Isa 7:10–14 in which the belief that the child born to Mary is not only a sign of God's power, but is named "God-with-us"; Heb 10:4–10 which reminds us that the it is through his body, taken from Mary's flesh, that the Son fulfills his Father's will and offers God the sacrifice that makes us holy; and Lk 1:26–38 which is the narrative of the Annunciation which emphasizes both the overshadowing of God's grace and his power in the coming of Christ but also Mary's freely given consent.

VISITATION OF THE BLESSED VIRGIN MARY: MAY 31

This feast commemorates Mary's visit to Elizabeth, the mother of John the Baptist, which follows immediately after the account of the

Annunciation in the Gospel of Luke. Notable events occurred at this meeting: the sanctification of John the Baptist in Elizabeth's womb, the proclamation of Mary as the Mother of God, and Mary's triumph of humble agreement in her *Magnificat*.

The readings for this feast are these:

> Zeph 3:14–18 in which the daughter of Zion shouts for joy and Israel sings joyfully as well; Rom 12:9–16 (alternate) which urges the faithful to be generous in their hospitality and look upon the needs of the saints as their own; and Lk 1:39–47 which recounts the visit of Mary to Elizabeth.

This feast was celebrated at a very early date by the Cistercians, Franciscans, Carmelites, and Dominicans. In 1389, Pope Urban VI extended this feast to the universal Church, but the Visitation did not become a universal feast for all practical purposes until the Council of Basel in 1441. The feast of the Visitation was celebrated in recent times on July 2, but was moved to its present day of May 31, probably in order to place it between the celebrations of the Annunciation and the birth of John the Baptist.

IMMACULATE HEART OF MARY:
SATURDAY AFTER THE SECOND SUNDAY AFTER PENTECOST

This optional memorial is designed to honor the "admirable heart of Mary," popularized in the seventeenth century by Saint John Eudes. Since that time, the feast had been celebrated in many countries, especially Poland and France. Finally, in 1944, in honor of the consecration of the Church and the entire world to the Immaculate Heart of Mary, Pius XII proclaimed this a feast of the universal Church. This devotion to Mary's heart is really directed symbolically to her maternity, her sanctity, and her role in the redemptive mission of

Christ. This feast follows after the feast of the Sacred Heart of Jesus. The first reading is chosen from the Common of the Blessed Virgin Mary. The Gospel is Luke 2:41–51, reflecting the pain in Mary's heart when she and Joseph had been searching for Jesus.

OUR LADY OF MOUNT CARMEL: JULY 16

This optional memorial was originally celebrated by the Carmelites to mark the end of the Second Council of Lyons (1272), which allowed their order to continue. It was extended to the whole Church in 1726. Readings are selected from the Common of the Blessed Virgin. Some choices might be as follows:

> Sir 24:1–21 which celebrates Mary as the wisdom of God;
> Zech 2:14–17 which is a call to silence at the coming of
> the Lord; and Lk 2:15–19 which recounts the adoration
> by the shepherds.

DEDICATION OF THE BASILICA OF ST. MARY MAJOR: AUGUST 5

This optional memorial celebrates the dedication of the great church on the Esquiline Hill in Rome, which was built by Pope Liberius and refurbished and dedicated to Mary by Pope Sixtus III (432–440). This memorializes what is probably the first church directly associated with Mary in the West, and acknowledges the tradition of devotion to Mary, the mother of God.

Readings may be taken from the Common of the Blessed Virgin; appropriate choices may be as follows:

> Rev 21:1–5 announces this is God's dwelling among men;
> Lk 11:27–28 in which those who hear the word of God
> and keep it are blessed.

ASSUMPTION OF THE BLESSED VIRGIN MARY: AUGUST 15

This solemnity is possibly the oldest exclusively Marian celebration and remains one of Mary's most important days in the liturgical year. Two other events are connected with this feast—Mary's "falling asleep" or dormition and her coronation in heaven—and are included in the celebration but not expressly commemorated.

In the Eastern churches, this celebration is preceded by a period of fasting similar to that of Lent. Hungarians celebrate the Assumption with great solemnity and include pageants and parades in their observances. This custom arose out of a legend in which the first king of Hungary, Saint Stephen, offered the royal crown to Mary, and thereby chose her as the patroness of the whole country.

The custom of processions on the feast of the Assumption seems to have begun with Pope Sergius I (d. 701) who initiated the practice of having liturgical processions on the major feasts of Mary. In some places in Europe, a statue of Mary is carried through the town, symbolically representing her journey to heaven. A special procession called *Candelieri* is conducted in Sardinia where seven huge candlesticks are carried to the church of the Assumption where they are placed beside Mary's shrine. The origin of this custom goes back to the year 1580 when a deadly plague was miraculously stopped on August 15 after Sardinians had vowed to honor Mary every year by offering her these candles.

It was also a medieval practice to conduct a "Blessing of the Herbs" on the Assumption, and thus this feast was sometimes called "Our Lady's Herb Day" in honor of the custom of blessing the medicinal powers of herbs to make them effective against disease.

Other customs associated with the Assumption include these: Armenians bring the first grapes from their vineyards to church on Assumption day; Sicilians observe an abstinence from fruit during the first two weeks of August in honor of the Blessed Virgin, and on the feast day itself present one another with baskets of fruit; in Latin countries, especially Portugal, the boats of fishermen are blessed on the afternoon of the Assumption; and in England and Ireland it is an ancient, Assumption-day custom to bathe in oceans, rivers, or lakes to preserve good health through Mary's intercession.

Despite the varied methods of celebration, this feast is one that honors Mary's resurrection, her destiny, the glorification of her sinless soul and virginal body, and the consoling image for all of humankind of the ultimate and final hope of heaven.

The readings for this feast are as follows:

For the Mass of the Vigil:

1 Chr 15:3–4, 15, 16; 16:1–2 wherein the Ark is transferred; 1 Cor 15:54–57 which asks of death, where is your victory? Where is your sting?; and Lk 11:27–28 in which a woman in a crowd blesses the womb that bore Jesus.

For the Mass of the Day:

Rev 11:19; 12:1–6, 10 which tells of the great portent of the woman and the dragon; 1 Cor 15:20–26 in which Christ, the first fruits, has been raised up from the dead; and Lk 1:39–56 which is Mary's *Magnificat*.

QUEENSHIP OF MARY: AUGUST 22

This memorializes the queenship of the Blessed Virgin Mary, who, says Pope Pius XII, "is to be called Queen not only by reason of her divine Maternity, but also because by the will of God she has had an outstanding part in the work of our eternal salvation." This celebration, which occurs seven days after the feast of the Assumption, is part of the prolonged celebration of that feast.

The readings may be taken from the Common of the Blessed Virgin; choices may be as follows:

Isa 9:1–6 which promises a child-king; Lk 1:28–36 which
talks of Mary's royal child; and Lk 1:39–47 which tells of
Mary's blessedness.

BIRTH OF MARY: SEPTEMBER 8

This feast celebrates the miraculous birth of Mary as told in the apocryphal writing of the *Protoevangelium* and reflects that the life and holiness of Mary are God's gifts to his people.

This feast, which seems to have originated in Syria and Palestine in the sixth century, was adopted by the Roman Church at the end of the eighth or ninth century. It was observed among all nations by the end of the twelfth century and was considered one of the major feasts of Mary.

Traditional customs associated with the nativity of Mary connect it with thanksgiving celebrations, the beginning of Indian summer, and the fall planting season. Thus a harvest blessing is performed in many churches on this day. In France, September 8 is the occasion of a grape harvest festival, and in the Alps, the moving of cattle and sheep from the high summer pastures is begun.

The readings prescribed for this feast are these:

Mic 5:1–14 names Bethlehem as the place of birth of the
future king; Rom 8:28–30 points to God's foreknowledge
of Mary as his choice; and Mt 1:1–16, 18–23 recounts the
ancestors of Jesus.

OUR LADY OF SORROWS: SEPTEMBER 15

This memorial is an outgrowth of medieval devotion to Mary at the foot of the cross, and has been celebrated by the Servite Order since the seventeenth century. In honor of the sufferings he had endured during his captivity in France, Pope Pius VII extended this observance to the whole Church on his return to Rome. This feast follows directly after that of the Triumph of the Cross and invites us to enter in spirit into Mary's compassion, as she faithfully shares the sufferings of her Son. *Marialis Cultus* calls this a "fitting occasion for reliving a decisive moment in the history of salvation and for venerating, together with the Son lifted up on the cross, his suffering Mother" (§7). In her honor, the great medieval sequence *Stabat Mater,* "At the Cross Her Station Keeping," may be said or sung before the gospel.

The readings on this feast day are these:

> Heb 5:7–9 which points to Jesus' share in our sufferings as our source of eternal salvation; Lk 2:33–35 in which Simeon predicts that Mary's soul will be pierced with sorrows is read for the gospel or Jn 19:25–27 in which the dying Jesus names Mary as the mother of his disciples.

OUR LADY OF THE ROSARY: OCTOBER 7

This memorial commemorates the rosary which presents Mary as the highest example of both contemplative and intercessory prayer. The rosary which combines meditations on the mysteries of Christ with the recitation of the Hail Mary has been prayed in the Western Church at least since the twelfth century; however, this feast also commemorates the defeat of the Turkish fleet at the Battle of Lepanto in 1571 which was attributed to Mary's intercession. The feast of Our Lady of the Rosary was extended to the whole Church after another defeat of the Turks in Hungary in 1716.

The Common of the Blessed Virgin Mary is used from which these readings may be chosen:

Acts 1:12–14 in which Mary and the apostles are together in the Cenacle; Lk 1:28–36 which recounts the Annunciation.

PRESENTATION OF MARY: NOVEMBER 21

This memorial was originally connected with the dedication to Mary of the "New Church" of Jerusalem, situated on the ruins of the Temple, by the Emperor Justinian in 543. Gradually it became associated with the apocryphal story, which is told in the *Protoevangelium of James*, of Mary's being brought to live in the Temple at the age of three. Though this feast was only slowly accepted in the Western Church, it has been celebrated by the Greek Church since the eighth century, and is one of the twelve great feasts of the Eastern liturgical calendar. The real significance of this feast centers around Mary's total offering of self, her dedication to God, and her lifelong purity and holiness, rather than the legend of her presentation in the Temple.

The Common of the Blessed Virgin Mary is used from which these readings are recommended:

1 Chr 15–16 in which the Ark of the Covenant is brought to Jerusalem and is placed in the Tabernacle; Zech 2:14–17 in which God chooses Zion; and Lk 11:27–28 wherein Jesus reminds us that blessed are they who hear the word of God and keep it.

3. Mary in Special Optional Celebrations

In 1992, prompted by the call of Vatican II, which renewed the Church's teaching on the place of the Blessed Virgin Mary in Christ's pascal mystery and which also issued guidelines for the liturgical reform, the U.S. National Conference of Catholic Bishops issued a collection of forty-six Masses in honor of the Blessed Virgin Mary.

These Masses have been composed using several bases: a study of ancient liturgical documents, an examination of the writings of the Fathers of the Church, an analysis of the Church's magisterium, and a desire to balance the old with the new. This collection of Masses covers the cycle of the liturgical year, and their texts support teaching and devotion that fosters genuine honor toward the Mother of God.

Here are the titles and readings for these Masses arranged by season:

ADVENT SEASON

The Blessed Virgin Mary, Chosen Daughter of Israel: During Advent the liturgy brings into clearer focus the figure of the Blessed Virgin, whom the Church proclaims as the joy of Israel and the daughter of Zion. For this Mass, Reading A is Genesis 12:1–7 in which God speaks to our ancestors, to Abraham, and to his offspring forever. Reading B is 1 Samuel 7:1–5, 8b–11, 16, which tells of God's promises to David through the prophet Nathan. The gospel gives the genealogy of Jesus, son of David, son of Abraham (Mt 1:1–17).

The Blessed Virgin Mary and the Annunciation of the Lord: Frequently during Advent, the liturgy reminds us of the Annunciation message of the angel Gabriel to Mary. This freely given consent of our Lady is of cornerstone importance to our story of salvation. In the past, this Mass was celebrated on the ember days of Advent, and was known in the Middle Ages as the "Golden Mass." Reading A gives the prophet Isaiah's promise that a virgin shall conceive (Isa 7:10–14, 8:10c). Reading B, also from Isaiah, retells his promise that the root of Jesse shall come in wisdom and understanding (Isa 11:1–5, 10). The gospel is read from Luke and tells the story of the Annunciation (Lk 1:26–38).

The Visitation of the Blessed Virgin Mary: This Mass celebrates the unfolding of the mystery of salvation as the Virgin Mary bears the Word of God to her cousin Elizabeth. This visitation has its own feast but is appropriate during Advent because of its close association to the celebration of Christmas. This going forth is a reflection of God's plan which he has set in motion to set us free from sin. Reading A is a joyful shout of exultation that the Lord is in the midst of his people (Zeph 3:14–18*a*). Reading B is from the Song of Songs and celebrates the arrival of "my lover" who says, "The voice of my beloved! Look, he comes" (Song 2:8–14). The gospel is Luke's retelling of the visit to Elizabeth and Mary's *Magnificat* (Lk 1:39–56).

CHRISTMAS SEASON

Holy Mary, Mother of God: This Mass celebrates the central mystery of the Blessed Virgin as Holy Mary, Mother of God. It praises Mary's faith and obedience and, though God has singled her out above all others, her humility by which she was pleasing to God. The reading tells us that God sent his Son, born of a woman, to ransom us (Gal 4:4–7). The gospel tells of the journey of the shepherds to Bethlehem to honor the infant Jesus (Lk 2:15*b*–19).

The Blessed Virgin Mary, Mother of the Savior: This Mass celebrates Mary's maternal joys and honors her perfect virginity. The reading proclaims the arrival of a son, "Wonder-Counselor, God-Hero, Father-Forever, Prince of Peace" (Isa 9:1–3, 5–6). The gospel (Lk 2:1–14) relates the story of the birth of Jesus.

The Blessed Virgin Mary and the Epiphany of the Lord: This Mass celebrates the light of revelation to the Jews and the Gentiles and honors the role of Christ as Savior, occurring through the ministry of the Blessed Virgin. The Old Testament reading from Isaiah proclaims the radiant light of the Lord (Isa 60:1–6). The gospel recounts the journey of the Magi, led by the light of the star, to the child and Mary, his mother (Mt 2:1–12).

The Blessed Virgin Mary and the Presentation of the Lord: This Mass commemorates Mary's part in the presentation of our Lord in the Temple in accordance with Mosaic Law and her faithful submission to post-childbirth purification even though she was a virgin before, during, and after the birth of Jesus. The reading (Mal 3:1–4) proclaims the arrival of the Lord, the messenger of the covenant, at the Temple. The gospel recounts Mary's meeting with Simeon in the Temple after the birth of Jesus (Lk 2:27–35).

Our Lady of Nazareth (I and II): This Mass, with its two sets of readings, commemorates our Lady in the service of her family during their life in Nazareth and her participation in the work of salvation. Mass I includes a reading from the Letter of Paul which reaffirms that God sent his Son, born of a woman, and also born under the law (Gal 4:4–7). Gospel A tells of the Holy Family returning to their home in Nazareth where Jesus grew in wisdom and maturity (Lk 2:22, 39–40). Gospel B tells of twelve-year-old Jesus being lost on the Passover journey to Jerusalem. His worried parents found him, and he went back to Nazareth with them (Lk 2:41–52).

The reading of Mass II is Paul's wish that the fullness of Christ's message would live within all who heard it (Col 3:12–17). The gospel is the story of Herod's quest to destroy Jesus, and the return of the family to Nazareth after Herod had died (Mt 2:13–15, 19–23).

Our Lady of Cana: This Mass celebrates Jesus Christ who manifested himself as the Messiah through the sign of Cana, the disciples who believed in him, and his mother who was instrumental in this miracle and in our salvation. The reading tells of the promise of the Israelites to do whatever the Lord has said (Ex 19:3–8*a*). The gospel recounts the wedding feast at Cana where our Lady instructed the servants to do whatever Jesus told them (Jn 2:1–11).

LENTEN SEASON

Holy Mary, Disciple of the Lord: This Mass celebrates Mary as Christ's first and most perfect disciple. It is suitable for Lent which is a journey of the faithful who should listen to the Word of God and follow in Christ's footsteps as Mary does with utmost diligence. The reading points out the delights of wisdom who is portrayed as a woman (Sir 51:13–18, 20–22). Gospel A, in which Jesus is lost in the Temple, tells of Mary who kept all these things in her heart (Lk 2:41–52). Gospel B contains Jesus' promise that his disciples who do the will of the heavenly Father would be as his mother and his brothers (Mt 12:46–50).

The Blessed Virgin Mary at the Foot of the Cross I: This Mass honors the cosharing of our Lady in the Passion and suffering of her son. She does this as the handmaid of the Redeemer, the new Eve, the mother of Zion, and the image of the Church. The reading asks that if the God who did not spare his own Son is in favor of us, who indeed can be opposed (Rom 8:31*b*–39). The gospel tells of Mary's standing at the foot of Jesus' cross (Jn 19:25–27).

The Blessed Virgin Mary at the Foot of the Cross II: This Mass honors Mary as the partner in Christ's Passion and her living martyrdom at the foot of the cross of her son. The reading tells of Judith who averted her people's ruin before God (Jdt 13:17–20). The gospel tells of Jesus' mother who stood, with faithful love, at the foot of the cross (Jn 19:25–27).

The Commending of the Blessed Virgin Mary: This Mass honors the entrustment of our Lord's disciples to his Virgin Mother as her children, and the commending of our Lady by Christ to John, his beloved disciple. In the reading, the mother of the seven Mac- cabean brothers honorably bore witness to their deaths, urging them to remain true to the God who made them (2 Macc 7:1, 20–29). The gospel celebrates Mary's entrustment to John by Jesus (Jn 19:25–27).

The Blessed Virgin Mary, Mother of Reconciliation: This Mass acknowledges Mary's role in reconciling sinners with God, a deepening and extending of her maternal role. It is then especially appropriate where the faithful gather for the sacrament of penance. The reading asks us, on behalf of Christ, to be reconciled to God (2 Cor 5:17–21). The gospel again tells of Mary's entrustment to John as his mother (Jn 19:25–27).

EASTER SEASON

The Blessed Virgin Mary and the Resurrection of the Lord: This Mass celebrates the Lord's Resurrection and the joy that flows to the whole world, to the new Church, and to the Virgin Mother. The world is filled with the radiance of Christ. The reading speaks of the new Jerusalem, arriving as a beautiful bride dressed for her husband (Rev 21:1–5*a*). In the gospel, Mary Magdalene and the other Mary discover that Christ has risen, and he instructs them to go and tell the disciples (Mt 28:1–10).

Holy Mary, Fountain of Light and Life: This Mass celebrates Mary as the mother of our enlightenment by the waters of baptism. Because her womb was the treasury of Christ in whom was contained all salvation and grace, Mary is seen as the sanctuary of the mysteries of God. In the first reading Peter proclaims that everyone must repent and be baptized (Acts 2:14*a*; 36–40*a*, 41–42). Gospel A avows Christ

81

to be the light of the world (Jn 12:44–50). Gospel B reminds the faithful that no one can enter the kingdom of God without a birth in the water and spirit (Jn 3:1–6).

Our Lady of the Cenacle: This Mass honors Mary who was present at the first gathering of the Christ's disciples and who gives us a wonderful model of prayer as she steadfastly waits with the disciples in oneness of mind and heart. The reading tells of the gathering in the upper room where the apostles waited for the power of the Holy Spirit to descend (Acts 1:6–14). In the gospel, Jesus announces that his mother and brothers are those who hear the Word of God and put it into practice (Lk 8:19–21).

The Blessed Virgin Mary, Queen of the Apostles: This Mass celebrates the eminent place of Mary as Queen of the Apostles and urges the faithful to pray as Mary did to spread the glory of God. The reading shows the apostles in prayer with Mary and the sudden arrival of the spirit as tongues of fire (Acts 1:12–14; 2:1–4). The gospel repeats Jesus' commitment of his Mother to John, his beloved disciple (Jn 19:25–27).

ORDINARY TIME: MASSES THAT CELEBRATE MARY'S BOND WITH SCRIPTURE

This series of Masses celebrate memorials of the Mother of God under titles derived from sacred Scripture or those that express Mary's close bond with the Church:

1. *Holy Mary, Mother of the Lord* (Reading: 1 Chr 15:3–4, 15–16; 16:1–2; Gospel: Lk 1:39–47)
2. *Holy Mary, the New Eve* (Reading: Rev 21:1–5a; Gospel A: Lk 1:26–38; Gospel B: Jn 2:1–11)
3. *The Holy Name of the Blessed Virgin Mary* (Reading: Sir 24:17–21; Gospel: Lk 1:26–38)

4. *Holy Mary, Handmaid of the Lord*: (Reading: 1 Sam 1:24–28; 2:1–2, 4–8; Gospel: Lk 1:26–38)

5. *The Blessed Virgin Mary, Temple of the Lord*: (Reading A: 1 Kings 8:1, 3–7, 9–11; Reading B: Rev 21:1–5*a*; Gospel: Lk 1:26–38)

6. *The Blessed Virgin Mary, Seat of Wisdom*: Reading A: Prov 8:22–31; Reading B: 24:1–4, 18–21; Gospel A: Mt 2:1–12; Gospel B: Lk 2:15*b*–19)

7. *The Blessed Virgin Mary, Image and Mother of the Church I*: (Reading: Gen 3:9–15, 20; Gospel: Jn 19:25–27)

8. *The Blessed Virgin Mary, Image and Mother of the Church II*: (Reading: Acts 1:12–14; Gospel: Jn 2:1–11)

9. *The Blessed Virgin Mary, Image and Mother of the Church III*: (Reading: Rev 2:1–5*a*; Gospel: Lk 1:26–38)

10. *The Immaculate Heart of the Blessed Virgin Mary*: (Reading: Jdt 13:17–20, 15:9; Gospel A: Lk 11:27–28; Gospel B: Lk 2:46–51)

11. *The Blessed Virgin Mary, Queen of All Creation* (Reading: Isa 9:1–3, 5–6; Gospel: Lk 1:26–38)

ORDINARY TIME: MASSES THAT CELEBRATE MARY'S FOSTERING OF THE FAITHFUL'S SPIRITUAL LIFE

This series of Masses celebrate the Mother of the Lord under titles referring to her cooperation in fostering the spiritual life of the faithful:

1. *The Blessed Virgin Mary, Mother and Mediatrix of Grace*: (Reading: Esth 8:3–8, 16–17*a*; Gospel: Jn 2:1–11)

2. *The Blessed Virgin Mary, Fountain of Salvation*: (First series reading: Ezek 47:1–2, 8–9, 12; First series gospel: Jn 19:25–27; Second series reading: Song 4:6–7, 9, 12–15; Second series gospel: Jn 7:37–39*a*)

3. *The Blessed Virgin Mary, Mother and Teacher in the Spirit*: (Reading A: Prov 8:17–21, 34–35; Reading B: Isa 56:1, 6–7; Gospel A: Mt 12:46–50; Gospel B: Jn 19:25–27)

4. *The Blessed Virgin Mary, Mother of Good Counsel*: (Reading A: Isa 9:1–3, 5–6; Reading B: Acts 1:12–14, 2:1–4; Gospel: Jn 2:1–11)

5. *The Blessed Virgin Mary, Cause of Our Joy*: (Reading A: Zech 2:14–17, Isa 61:9–11; Gospel A: Lk 1:39–47; Gospel B: Jn 15:9–12)

6. *The Blessed Virgin Mary, Pillar of Faith*: (Reading: Jdt 13:14, 17–20; Gospel: Lk 11:27–28)

7. *The Blessed Virgin Mary, Mother of Fairest Love*: (Reading: Sir 24:17–21; Gospel: Lk 1:26–38)

8. *The Blessed Virgin Mary, Mother of Divine Hope*: (Reading: Sir 24:9–12, 18–21; Gospel: Jn 2:1–11)

9. *Holy Mary, Mother of Unity:* (Reading A: Zeph 3:14–20; Reading B: 1 Tim 2:5–8; Gospel: Jn 11:45–52)

ORDINARY TIME: MASSES THAT CELEBRATE MARY'S MERCY

This series of Mass forms celebrate Mary under titles referring to her mercy and intercession on behalf of the faithful:

1. *Holy Mary, Queen and Mother of Mercy I*: (Reading: Esth 9:12, 14–15, 25, 30; Gospel: Jn 2:1–11)

2. *Holy Mary, Queen and Mother of Mercy II*: (Reading: Eph 2:4–10; Gospel: Lk 1:39–55)

3. *The Blessed Virgin Mary, Mother of Divine Providence*: (Reading: Isa 66:10–14; Gospel Jn 2:1–11)

4. *The Blessed Virgin Mary, Mother of Consolation*: (Reading A: Isa 61:1–3, 10–11; Reading B: 2 Cor 1:3–7; Gospel A: Mt 5:1–12; Gospel B: Jn 14:15–21, 25–27)

5. *The Blessed Virgin Mary, Help of Christians:* (Reading A: Rev 12:1–3a, 7–12ab, 17; Reading B: Gen 3:1–6, 13–15)

6. *Our Lady of Ransom*: (Reading: Jdt 15:8–10, 16:13–14; Gospel: Jn 19:25–27)

7. *The Blessed Virgin Mary, Health of the Sick*: (Reading: Isa 53:1–5, 7–10; Gospel: Lk 1:39–56)

8. *The Blessed Virgin Mary, Queen of Peace*: (Reading: Isa 9:1–3, 5–6; Gospel: Lk 1:26–38)

9. *The Blessed Virgin Mary, Gate of Heaven*: (Reading A: Rev 21:1–5*a*, Reading B: Ps 122: 1–2, 3–4, 8–9)

4. Liturgy of the Hours

The revised book of the Divine Office, now called the Liturgy of the Hours, one of the central pivot points of the daily liturgical prayer of the Roman Rite, contains exceptional illustrations of devotion to our Blessed Lady. Pope Paul VI summarizes in the following words the Marian themes of the Liturgy of the Hours.

> These are to be found in the hymns—which include several masterpieces of universal literature, such as Dante's sublime prayer to the Blessed Virgin—and in the antiphons that complete the daily Office. To these lyrical invocations there has been added the well-known prayer *Sub tuum praisidium*, venerable for its antiquity and admirable for its content. Other examples occur in the prayers of intercession at Lauds and Vespers, prayers which frequently express trusting recourse to the Mother of Mercy. Finally there are selections from the vast treasury of writings on our Lady composed by authors of the first Christian centuries, of the Middle Ages and of modern times (*Marialis Cultus* §13).

The Liturgy of the Hours also contains the very beautiful Common of the Blessed Virgin Mary, filled with psalms and hymns, antiphons and intercessions, prayers and Scripture, as well as readings from such sources as the Second Vatican Council's *Dogmatic Constitution on the Church* and sermons from Saint Sophronius and Saint Aelred.

5. Other Liturgical Celebrations

In other liturgical ceremonies, the Church invokes words of veneration and love addressed to our Lady. The Church prays passionately to Mary on behalf of her children who are facing death and those who have already breathed their last. She asks for comfort from Mary for those who are left behind in sorrow and in grief.

In Baptism, the Church asks for Mary's blessing before immersing candidates in the saving waters of this sacrament of initiation. The Church asks Mary's intercession for mothers who come to church to express their joy and gratitude for the gift of motherhood; and she asks for Mary's assistance for those who follow Christ by embracing the religious life or who receive the Consecration of Virgins.

It is easy and comforting to observe that these liturgical celebrations recognize the unique place that belongs to Mary in the act of Christian worship as befits her role as the holy Mother of God and the associate of the Redeemer.

The Image of Mary Through the Ages

E very age adapts its devotion and prayers to our Blessed Virgin in a way that meets its own particular needs. As each time and place shapes an image of Mary that expresses the beliefs and concerns important to the faithful of that age, Mary's image is altered and seen through a different filter.

As witness to this ever-changing image, Mary has become known throughout history by hundreds of names, including: Mother, Virgin, Queen, Immaculate Conception, Our Lady of Mercy, of Sorrows, of Peace, of Perpetual Help, of Charity, of the Highway, of the Rosary, of Chartres, Lourdes, Fátima, and Guadalupe. Each of these manifestations reveals a lot more about the Church in any particular historical situation than they do about Mary. And because times and cultures vary, the challenge of discipleship and the demands of living the gospel vary and can never be strictly set down. Every age, thus, consciously or unconsciously forms its own ideal of Mary, and her titles can be seen as an expression of this ideal.

1. Mary in the Early Church

The apostolic preaching of the early Church (some of which is written down in the Acts of the Apostles) says practically nothing about Mary. Several reasons have been given for this omission: (1) Mary, though a silent witness to Christ's earthly ministry, was already known to most of the faithful of Palestine, and thus there was little need to record information; (2) Mary was in the forefront in Jesus' life during his early years when there were no disciples present to witness the events surrounding her role, and thus the event of Mary's life were not written down; and, (3) the role of women in the East of that era was downplayed, and writers assumed that Mary, like most women of that age, was just there in the background.

Saint Paul gives the first reference to Mary in his apostolic writing—in a Letter to the Galatians (the earliest book of the New Testament to be written) where he said:

> But when the fullness of time had come, God sent his
> Son, born of a woman, born under the law, in order to
> redeem those who were under the law, so that we might
> receive adoption as children (Gal 4:4–5).

These words of Saint Paul are useful as a reflection of the minds of the first Christians that Mary is the mother of Christ, Son of God, and that she conceived Christ and gave him birth just as all human infants are born of a human mother.

Other evidence of devotion to Mary is found in the art of the catacombs which contain the first paintings of Mary, giving witness to the early honor of the Mother of Jesus; archaeologists have discovered an inscription under Saint Peter's Basilica portraying Mary as a Protectress for departed souls and as their Mediatrix; and leaden seals from the fifth or sixth century have come down to us inscribed with the words *servus Mariae*, or servant of Mary.

Evidence of widening devotion to our Lady is found in second-century baptismal creeds which mention "born of the Holy Spirit and the Virgin Mary." The writings of Saint Ignatius of Antioch (d. after 107) give five references to Mary as a Virgin and Mother. Sometime in the second century, Mary's holiness is further confirmed by Saint Justin (the first person to write fully about Mary) and Saint Irenaeus whose writings propose the Eve-Mary parallel in which Eve's disobedience was undone by Mary's obedience.

In the fourth century, a manuscript fragment in Greek asks the "Mother of God" for protection, this being an early version of the *Sub tuum* prayer which is a forerunner of the *Memorare*.

Later in the same century, Bishop Severian of Gabala (d. after 408) calls the praise of Mary a daily custom, Saint Ephraem (d. 373) refers to Mary's powers of mediation, Saint Ambrose (d. 397) holds up Mary as a model of women and a type of the Church, and Saint Augustine proclaims Mary free from original sin and praises her status as virgin and mother. In fact Saint Augustine (d. 430) spoke of Mary as taking a vow of virginity, and he was the first of the Latin Fathers to also take this formal vow.

In the fifth century, devotion to Mary took on a wider scope when the Council at Ephesus (431), led by Saint Cyril of Alexandria, declared Mary as *Theotokos* (meaning "Godbearer"), or the Mother of God. The church of St. Mary Major in Rome was rebuilt by Pope Sixtus III to commemorate this event. After the Council of Ephesus, feasts celebrating Mary multiplied. Early feasts included the Commemoration of the Virgin observed in parts of Europe, the Annunciation, and the Hypante, that is, the Encounter Between Christ and Simeon.

In 451, the Council of Chalcedon reaffirmed Mary as the Mother of God. By the middle of the fifth century, Mary is introduced into the texts of the Mass. In the *Leonine Sacramentary*, for example, Saint Leo the Great adds to the Canon (Eucharistic Prayer) the reference to Mary: "In communion with and venerating in the first place the glorious ever-Virgin Mary, Mother of God...."

In the sixth century, additional churches are dedicated to Mary, for example the church of Saint Mary in Jerusalem and the church of Saint Mary Antiqua in Rome. By midpoint in this century as well, the Second Council of Constantinople reaffirms the dogma of the divine motherhood, and also in Constantinople, Saint Romanos the Singer composes some of the first hymns in honor of Mary.

The seventh century also saw marks of Marian devotion, especially honoring Mary's holiness and her relationship to Christ. The Third Council of Constantinople (680–681) reiterates Mary's divine motherhood. The Marian antiphon *Ave Maris Stella* is composed; Byzantine Emperor Heraclitus has the image of Mary placed on the masts of his ships.

2. Mary in the Early Middle Ages

By the eighth century, the outlines of Marian liturgy and devotion were much more developed in the East than in the West. Epiphanius (d. around 800), a monk of Constantinople, was the first author of a life of Mary. Much of the contents of his book are fanciful: he said, for example, that when Mary was laid in the tomb, all present looked on as her body became invisible before their eyes. Saint John Damascene (d. after 749), the last of the Fathers in the East, devoted some of his studies to Mary, especially writing on the Incarnation. He expressed his devotion to Mary with exuberance: "What is sweeter than the Mother of God? She holds my mind captive; she has seized my tongue; on her I meditate day and night." Germanus of Constantinople (d. 733), defender of icons, and Andrew of Crete (d. 740) praised Mary's power of intercession, and the later invoked her as "Mary, Help of Christians."

In the West, the Benedictine monk Alcuin (d. 804), one of Charlemagne's ministers, made important contributions to Marian theology and devotion. He composed two votive Masses of our Lady for celebration on Saturday, and he is noted for his poetic inscriptions composed for chapels of our Lady, for example, "May devotion and honor remember you here, Queen of heaven, greatest hope of our life. May you regard with pity the children of God we implore you, Virgin most meek."

Also in the West, Paschasius Radbert (d. 865), a scholar and theologian of the time of Charlemagne, wrote the story of the birth of Mary and discussed the preservation of Mary's physical body during the moment of childbirth.

3. Mary in the High Middle Ages

As European culture revived after the Dark Ages, devotion to Mary grew accordingly. Crowds gathered to celebrate the monastery festivals associated with Mary's feasts. Magnificent cathedrals were built, many of them dedicated to Mary. A rich tradition of Marian sermons, prayers (such as the *Salve Regina*), liturgical offices and Masses, and public declarations of being "slaves of Mary," as that made by Odilo of Cluny (d. 1049), developed.

Saint Peter Damian (d. 1072) sets forth the connection between Mary and the holy Eucharist. He urged devotion to our Lady—recitation of the Little Office (he himself composed an Office of our Lady for daily use), daily recitation of an early form of the Hail Mary, and the Saturday Mass in honor of Mary. Saint Anselm of Canterbury (d. 1099) composed inspiring works about our Lady, whom he called the "reconciler of the World." His prayers and writings, diffused throughout the monastic world, were widely influential and were communicated to the faithful who, through Anselm, began to recognize the power of Mary's intercession.

By the eleventh century, the *Hail Holy Queen* was composed and perfectly suits the attitude of medieval Christians toward Mary who was seen as the merciful intercessor with her Son. Thus enormous devotion poured out toward Mary, expressing itself in hymns (*Alma Redemptoris Mater*), relics (Charles the Bold obtained what he believed to be the dress of Mary), art (one of the great Marian mosaics is placed in the Cathedral at Torcello, Italy), and architecture (the Cathedral of Notre Dame at Chartres is begun).

Two theological topics influenced Marian devotion in the twelfth century: (1) focus on Mary's compassion on Calvary and the interpretation of our Lord's words, "Woman, here is your son" (Jn 19:26), as applicable to Mary's spiritual motherhood; and, (2) Mary's assistance to all Christians as influenced by the doctrine of the Assumption. One of the active theologians was Saint Bernard of Clairvaux (d. 1153), a Cistercian, who developed a Mary-based spirituality and who is often thought of as the medieval doctor of our Lady. Many books expounding the miracles of Mary were also written, among them, the influential book by William of Malmesburg (d. around 1143) called the *Miracles of the Blessed Virgin Mary*.

Doctrine and devotion reinforce each other in the thirteenth century. Along with the great cathedrals dedicated to Mary, Marian spirituality was evident in the lives of Saint Francis (d. 1226), Saint Dominic (d. 1221), Albert the Great (d. 1280) who called on Mary under the title "Mother of the Church," Saint Bonaventure (d. 1274) who said "I have never read of any saint who did not have a special devotion to the glorious Virgin," Saint Thomas Aquinas who evolved a harmonious theology of Mary, and Duns Scotus (d. 1308) who was the first to set forth good reasons for the doctrine of Mary's Immaculate Conception.

The fourteenth century saw the rise of the universities; Oriel College, for example, was founded at Oxford and dedicated to Mary. In this century also, Dante sketches a portrait of Mary in *The Divine Comedy*, showing that he is the "supreme poet of Mary."

Saint Bridget of Sweden (d. 1375) revealed her visions of the Blessed Virgin and wrote twenty-one meditations covering the life of Mary.

4. Mary in the Fifteenth Century

The invention of the printing press in the fifteenth century gives widespread impetus to the dissemination of books about Mary: John Lydgate (d. 1450), commissioned by the English King Henry V, composed the life of Mary in verse; Saint Bernardine of Siena (d. 1444) wrote about the seven words of Mary; Thomas à Kempis (d. 1471), in *The Imitation of Christ*, emphasized recourse to Mary in achieving the ideal of a deeper, richer spiritual life; the *Little Office of the Blessed Virgin Mary* was printed in 1457; and the Dominican Alan de la Roche (d. 1475) wrote *The Utility of Mary's Psalter*, upholding the power of the rosary to prevail with Mary.

The rosary increased in importance as a devotion to Mary. The first Confraternity of the rosary was established in 1475; and the rosary was approved by Pope Alexander VI in 1495.

5. Mary in the Reformation

The Reformation mounted an attack on Marian devotion, not directly but via opposition to calling upon the saints or Mary for assistance. Neither Luther nor Calvin completely banished devotion to Mary, but limited it to the emulation of the humble and submissive Virgin rather than the Queen of Heaven or the Spiritual Mother of the Church.

The Council of Trent (1563) defended the invocation of Mary, as well as imitation of the saints, from the attacks of the reformers. Both Catholic and Protestant positions tended to harden throughout the struggles that followed, and so devotion to Mary along with the doctrine of the Real Presence in the Eucharist became subjects for argument. Saint Peter Canisius (d. 1597) wrote the *Incomparable Virgin Mary*, the first major defense of Catholic doctrine and devotion to Mary.

6. Mary in the Seventeenth Century

The Church's internal development of devotion to Our Lady continued: the Litany of the Blessed Virgin was prescribed for the universal Church in 1601; the feast of the Holy Name of Mary was extended to the whole Church in 1683, as was the feast of the Rosary in 1716; and the feast of Our Lady of Mount Carmel was instituted in 1726.

A hundred years after the Reformation, devotion to Mary reached a second peak, especially in France, which took its place as a spiritual leader of Western Catholicism. In the French School of Spirituality, Cardinal Pierre de Bérulle (d. 1629) linked devotion to Mary to the mystery of the Word-made-flesh. It was due to Bérulle that the blossoming of French culture in the seventeenth century included a devotion to the Blessed Virgin Mary.

Also in France, Jean Jacques Olier (d. 1657), founder of the Sulpician Order, applied mystical language to Marian devotion and encouraged the role of Mary in the development of the spiritual life, especially for seminarians. Saint John Eudes (d. 1680) composed the first full-length book on the Heart of Mary, *The Admirable Heart of Mary*, which was published after his death. John Eudes saw Mary as the spouse of the priest, and proposed meditation on Christ in the womb of his mother as a devotion that was also taken up by Bérulle and other members of the French school.

With Louis-Marie Grignion de Montfort (d. 1716), author of *The True Devotion to the Blessed Virgin*, a pinnacle of devotion to Mary was reached. He has been called the master of devotion to Mary and believed that it was better to approach God indirectly, through the mediation of his mother, than address him directly. Small signs of love to the Blessed Virgin were insufficient for salvation, said de Montfort. Instead, a complete interior surrender to her was necessary so that Mary could form her "slave" exactly as she saw fit.

Devotional practices to Mary often became bizarre, with confraternities of the "slaves of Mary" wearing chains around their necks or wrists as signs of bondage. Some even vowed martyrdom in defense of belief in the Immaculate Conception, which, at that point, was not yet official Catholic doctrine.

7. Mary in the Eighteenth Century

The philosophical movement of the Enlightenment which rejected the Church's authority to determine what was true or not true in favor of reliance on human reason was a feature of the eighteenth century. Few Enlightenment scholars had much use for what they considered to be the excesses of Marian devotion. Increasingly, the Church lost secular power and influenced by the cult of reason, struck Marian feasts from local church calendars, let shrines fall into disuse, and discouraged excessive forms of devotion to Mary.

In the midst of this decline in devotion to Mary, Saint Alphonsus Liguori published his classic book *The Glories of Mary*, a work intended to reactivate devotion to our Lady and defend it from attack.

For Alphonsus Liguori, Mary's role was to revive souls that had fallen from divine grace and to reconcile them to God. Shortly after publication of *The Glories of Mary,* in 1754, Our Lady of Guadalupe was declared the patroness of Mexico, despite the fact that apparitions were considered by Enlightenment observers as just one more out-of-hand religious superstition.

8. The Nineteenth Century and Mary

After the Enlightenment and the French Revolution, an authentic note of Marian devotion came back into favor, especially among newly founded religious orders such as the Marists, Oblates of Mary Immaculate, and the Claretians. Efforts to recruit the laity were also put forth, such as that of G. J. Chaminade (d. 1850) who worked with lay sodalities, and who later founded the Marianists. This was the beginning of what was called "the age of Mary."

Demand was growing for recognition of the doctrine of Mary's Immaculate Conception. In this climate of renewed devotion, Pope Pius IX wrote the first encyclical concerning Mary in 1849 and, in 1854, solemnly declared the dogma of the Immaculate Conception in the bull *Ineffabilis Deus.* Devotion to Mary was further influenced by the encyclicals of Leo XIII, "The Pope of the Rosary," who, between 1883 and 1902, issued eleven encyclicals on the rosary and on Mary, calling her Mediatrix of All Graces, Mother of the Redeemed, and Guardian of the Faith, and advocating devotion to her as the salvation of society.

By the middle of the century, apparitions of Mary were chronicled all over Europe, especially in France. In 1830, our Lady appeared to Saint Catherine Laboure and asked for the Miraculous Medal to be issued. In 1846, our Lady appeared at La Salette. Our Lady appeared to Saint Bernadette at Lourdes in 1858, and appeared at Pontmain in 1871. Toward the end of the century, in 1879, our Lady appeared on the wall of a church in Knock, Ireland. Under the influence of these events, Mary herself became an object of devotion, losing much of her connection to the Trinity and to Christ, with whom she was linked by the early Church.

9. Twentieth Century and Beyond

The zealous apostolate of Mary continued into the twentieth century. The Legion of Mary was established by Frank Duff in 1921, while sodalities reblossomed and strong Marian devotion was fostered by new secular institutes.

Apparitions of Mary also continued. At Fátima, in 1917, our Lady appeared to three small children. Our Lady appeared at Beauraing, Belgium, in 1932–1933, and in Banneaux, Belgium, in 1937.

The popes also extended the role of Mary in the Church through a series of encyclicals, apostolic letters, addresses, and observance of a Marian Year in 1954. In 1904, in his encyclical *Ad Diem Illud*, Pope Pius X developed the idea of Mary's spiritual motherhood, saying "Mary is our sure way to Christ." Pope Benedict XV made never-ending appeals to the Queen of Peace during World War I. Pope Pius XI commemorated the Council of Ephesus and spoke of Mary's contributions to Christ's work of redemption. He portrayed her as associated with this work not only in Bethlehem as Mother of God but also at Calvary.

Pope Pius XII showed great interest in Mary in the following: In 1942, he dedicated the world to the Immaculate Heart of Mary in keeping with her wishes expressed at Fátima. In the encyclical *Mystici Corporis*, he outlined the role played by Mary in human salvation and explained how she is spiritually the Mother of Christ's members; he proclaimed the spiritual power of Mary's rosary in the encyclical *Ingruentium Malorum*; and in *Ad Caeli Reginam,* he declared the Queenship of Mary and establishes it as a feast.

Particularly important among his works was the definition of the dogma of the Assumption of Mary in the bull *Munificentissimus Deus* in 1950, and the directives of the encyclical *Mediator Dei*, issued in 1947, in which Pope Pius XII dealt with Mary in the sacred liturgy: the liturgy was declared to be the norm of devotion to Mary, though other forms of piety were also approved.

Other features of twentieth-century devotion of Mary have been Marian congresses on the local, national, and international levels, and the growth of pilgrimages to many of the shrines to Mary. Many traditional devotional practices in regard to Mary were in the process of being reassessed in the light of renewed scriptural studies after World War II. This focus was obvious from the orientation of the Second Vatican Council when it published *Lumen Gentium* (*Dogmatic Constitution on the Church*) which, in Chapter 8, sets forth for the first time a synthesis of teaching concerning the position that Mary holds in the mystery of Christ and the Church.

Pope Paul VI led the way to renewed devotion to Mary by declaring her the "Mother of the Church" in 1964, and urging prayer to her during the months of May and October. He advised sound, biblically and pastorally oriented devotion to Mary that is faithful to tradition, and reminded us that it is in the history of salvation that we will find the most perfect expression of Mary.

During the time of Pope Paul VI much rethinking was apparent as a result of Vatican II. A *Roman Missal* was published in 1969 with an approach to Mary based on her role in the mystery of Christ and the Church. Some minor feasts were eliminated, but many more prayers and readings are added for the feasts and memorials that remain. A revised *Roman Missal* was published in 1975 which included votive Masses of "Mary Mother of the Church" and the "Holy Name of Mary." The new *Liturgy of the Hours* was published in 1970 with much use made of the *Magnificat*, Marian antiphons, hymns, and readings.

Paul VI further added to the treatment of the liturgical expression of Marian piety through his Apostolic Constitution *Marialis Cultus*. This document indicated which Marian practices are completely valid and concluded with the theological and pastoral value of devotion to Mary.

In 1978, Archbishop Karol Wojtyla of Krakow was elected Pope John Paul II and dedicated his pontificate to Mary, taking the motto *Totus Tuus*, or "All Yours, O Mary." In 1982, he visited Fátima and reconsecrated the world to the Immaculate Heart of Mary. In his encyclical, *Redemptoris Mater*, issued in 1987, Pope John Paul reflected on the role of Mary in the mystery of Christ and on her active presence in the life of the Church. Central to consideration of Mary, said John Paul, was the fact that she is the Mother of God, since by the power of the Holy Spirit she conceived in her virginal womb and brought into the world Jesus Christ, the Son of God, who is one being with the Father and the Holy Spirit.

John Paul II, throughout his reign, celebrated Mary's role in the Church. He devoted more than sixty of his Wednesday afternoon catechetical talks to the topic of Mary. In general-audience topics in May of 1997 he reflected on these ideas: (1) The words, "Behold your Mother," express the intention of Jesus to inspire in his followers an attitude of love for and trust in Mary; (2) while the gospels do not mention Jesus appearing to Mary after the Resurrection, it was fitting that she should have been the first to experience his glory; (3) Mary's powerful intercession obtains for the Church an ever-fresh outpouring of the enlightening and strengthening gifts of the Holy Spirit.

As the twentieth century draws to a close, devotion of Mary is still being reassessed in scriptural, pastoral, and ecumenical perspectives. Devotion to Mary within the liturgy is being seen as the accepted norm, and practices of piety that favor the Scriptures, Mary in salvation history, in association with the mysteries of Christ, and as mother and type of the Church are being encouraged. Long-standing devotional practices, such as the rosary, the scapular, and the Angelus, are undergoing examination and restatement in terms of current trends in Christian life—emphasizing Mary's true role in the Church.

SECTION FIVE

Marian Prayers

1. Traditional Prayers in Honor of Our Lady

WE FLY TO YOUR PROTECTION OR *SUB TUUM*

This is probably the most ancient formal prayer to our Lady, written sometime in the third century; it has been found on an Egyptian papyrus that was discovered in 1917. This prayer is often used, as it was when it was first written, in times of trials and persecution. In many places it is said or sung after the rosary or at the end of night prayers.

> We fly to your protection,
> O holy Mother of God;
> despise not our petitions
> in our necessities,
> but deliver us always from all danger,
> O glorious and blessed Virgin.
> Amen.

A variation is as follows:

> We take refuge beneath thy protection,
> holy Mother of God:
> do not turn thy eyes from our prayers
> in our need,
> but forever set us free from all evil,
> thou glorious and blessed Virgin.

Here is a longer version from the Byzantine Rite:

> Oppressed by sin and sadness,
> we have recourse to the Mother of God.

Filled with sorrow for our sins,
we kneel and cry from the depths of our hearts:
O our Queen, come to our aid.
Have compassion on us.

We are overwhelmed to the point of succumbing
under the weight of our sins.
Do not disillusion your servants,
for you are our only hope.

Mother of God,
even though we are unworthy to receive your aid,
we will never cease making your power known.
If you should not be here to intercede for us,
who would free us from such dangers?
Who could have preserved us unharmed until now?
Our Queen,
we will never go far from you,
for you always save your servants
from all their misfortunes.
Amen.

HAIL MARY OR *AVE MARIA*

This prayer is formally known as the "Angelic Salutation" since it is based on a passage from the Gospel of Luke which contains the first line of the prayer. By the beginning of the twelfth century, the first part of the prayer was in common use in the liturgy of the West. The second part of the prayer beginning "Holy Mary" was added about the fifteenth century. As early as the eleventh century, devout persons were reciting the Hail Mary in sets of fifty, much like a litany, and genuflecting or bowing during the repetition of this prayer.

Hail Mary, full of grace.
The Lord is with thee.
Blessed are thou among women,
and blessed is the fruit of thy womb, Jesus.
Holy Mary, Mother of God,
pray for us sinners,
now and at the hour of our death.
Amen.

Here is a version of the Hail Mary from the Byzantine Rite:

Hail, Mother of God, Virgin Mary, full of grace,
the Lord is with you;
Blessed are you among women,
and blessed is the fruit of your womb.
For you have borne Christ,
the Savior and Deliverer of our souls.
Amen.

MEMORARE

This prayer to the Blessed Virgin Mary is named after the Latin word for *remember,* which is the first word of the prayer. Since the monks of the Monastery of Citeaux were devout followers of our Lady, when the prayer appeared in the fifteenth century, it was quickly attributed to Saint Bernard, the founder of this monastery. In reality, the prayer was popularized by a priest named Claude Bernard (d. 1461) and may have been based on a much longer prayer that was used in the Eastern Church.

Remember, O most gracious Virgin Mary,
that never was it known
that anyone who fled to your protection,

implored your help, or sought your intercession
was left unaided.
Inspired with this confidence,
I fly to you, O virgin of virgins, my Mother.
To you I come,
before you I stand, sinful and sorrowful.
O Mother of the Word Incarnate,
despise not my petitions,
but in your mercy, hear and answer me.
Amen.

MAGNIFICAT

This song of praise by Mary is found in Luke 1:46–55.

"My spirit proclaims the greatness of the Lord,
my spirit finds joy in God my savior
For he has looked upon his servant in her lowliness;
all ages to come shall call me blessed.
God who is mighty has done great things for me,
holy is his name;
His mercy is from age to age
on those who fear him.
He has shown might with his arm;
he has confused the proud in their inmost thoughts.

He has deposed the mighty from their thrones
and raised the lowly to high places.
The hungry he has given every good thing;
while the rich he has sent away empty.
He has upheld Israel his servant,
ever mindful of her mercy;

Even as he promised our fathers,
promised Abraham and his descendants forever."

MORNING OFFERING

O Jesus, through the Immaculate heart of your mother, Mary, I offer You today my prayers, my sufferings, my disappointments, my joys, and all my works. I give You these together with all that is offered to You in the Sacrifice of the Mass everywhere in the world. I give this gift of today in reparation for my sins, for the needs of people throughout the world, for the intentions and needs of my loved ones, and for our Holy Father. Amen.

POPE PIUS XII'S CONSECRATION TO THE BLESSED VIRGIN

Most Holy Virgin Mary, tender Mother of all, to fulfill the desires of the Sacred Heart and the request of the Vicar of your Son on earth, we consecrate ourselves and our families to your Sorrowful and Immaculate Heart, O Queen of the Most Holy Rosary, and we recommend to you, all the people of our country and all the world.

Please accept our consecration, dearest Mother, and use us as you wish to accomplish your designs upon the world.

O Sorrowful and Immaculate Heart of Mary, Queen of the Most Holy Rosary, and Queen of the World, rule over us, together with the Sacred Heart of Jesus Christ, Our King. Save us from the spreading flood of modern paganism; kindle in our hearts and homes the love of purity, the practice of a virtuous life, an ardent zeal for souls, and a desire to pray the rosary more faithfully.

We come with confidence to you, O Throne of Grace and Mother of Fair Love. Inflame us with the same Divine Fire which has inflamed your own Sorrowful and Immaculate Heart. Make our hearts and homes your shrine, and through us, make the Heart of Jesus, together with your rule, triumph in every heart and home.

SAINT FRANCIS OF ASSISI'S SALUTATION
TO THE BLESSED VIRGIN MARY

Hail, holy Lady,
most holy Queen,
Mary, Mother of God,
ever-virgin;
Chosen by the most holy Father in heaven,
    consecrated by him
with his most holy and beloved Son
    and the Holy Spirit, the Comforter.
On you descended and in you still remains
    all the fullness of grace
and every good.
Hail, his palace.
Hail, his tabernacle.
Hail, his robe.
Hail, his handmaid.
Hail, his mother.
And hail, all holy virtues,
who by the grace and inspiration of the Holy Spirit,
are poured into the hearts of the faithful
so that, faithless no longer, they may be faithful
    servants of God through you.
Amen.

PRAYER OF PRAISE TO THE IMMACULATE VIRGIN

O pure and immaculate blessed Virgin, sinless Mother of your Son, the mighty Lord of the universe, you who are all pure and all holy, the hope of the hopeless and sinful, we sing your praises. We bless you, as full of every grace, you who bore the God-Man: we all bow low before you; we invoke you and implore your aid. Rescue us, O holy and pure Virgin, from every necessity that presses upon us and from all the temptations of the devil. Be our intercessor and advocate at the hour of death and judgment; deliver us from the fire that is not extinguished and from the outer darkness; make us worthy of the glory of your Son, O dearest and most clement Virgin Mother. You indeed are our only hope, most sure and sacred in God's sight, to whom we honor and glory, majesty and dominion for ever and ever, world without end. Amen.

HAIL, HOLY QUEEN OR *SALVE REGINA*

Hail, holy Queen, Mother of Mercy; hail our life, our sweetness and our hope. To you do we cry, poor banished children of Eve. To you do we send up our sighs, mourning and weeping in this valley of tears. Turn, then, most gracious advocate, your eyes of mercy toward us. And after this our exile show unto us the blessed fruit of your womb, Jesus, O clement, O loving, O sweet Virgin Mary.

REGINA COELI

Queen of heaven, rejoice, alleluia.
For he whom you merited to bear, alleluia.
Has risen as he said, alleluia.
Pray for us to God, alleluia.
Rejoice and be glad, O Virgin Mary, alleluia.
Because the Lord is truly risen, alleluia.

Let us pray: O God, who by the Resurrection of your Son, our Lord Jesus Christ, granted joy to the whole world, grant, we beg of you, that through the intercession of the Virgin Mary, his Mother, we may lay hold of the joys of eternal life, through the same Christ Our Lord. Amen.

AKATHIST HYMN: TWENTY-THIRD CHANT

By singing praise to your maternity, we all exalt you as the spiritual temple, O Mother of God! For the One who dwelt within your womb, the Lord who holds all things in his hands, sanctified you, glorified you, and taught all people to sing to you:

Hail, O Tabernacle of God the Word;
   hail, Holy One, more holy than the saints.
Hail, O Ark that the spirit has gilded;
   hail, sacred Glory of reverent priests.
Hail, unshakable Tower of the Church;
   hail, unbreakable Wall of the Kingdom.
Hail, O you through whom the trophies are raised.
   hail, O you through whom the enemies are routed.
Hail, O Healing of my body;
   hail, O Salvation of my soul.
Hail, O Bride and Maiden everpure.

REJOICE, MOTHER OF GOD

A celebration of the joys of the Blessed Virgin Mary taken from an anthem of the Byzantine Rite. Recalling Mary's joys on earth is felt to be a preparation for sharing eternal joy with Jesus Christ in heaven.

Rejoice, Mother of God, Virgin Immaculate.
Rejoice, you who received joy from the Angel.
Rejoice, you who conceived the brightness of eternal Light.
Rejoice, Mother.
Rejoice, Holy Mother of God and Virgin.
All creation extols you.
Mother of Light, pray for us.

2. Prayers of the Saints to Mary

PRAYER OF SAINT ALOYSIUS GONZAGA

O Holy Mary, my mother, into your blessed trust and custody, and into the care of your mercy I this day, every day, and in the hour of my death, commend my soul and my body. To you I commit all my anxieties and miseries, my life and the end of my life, that by your most holy intercession and by your merits all my actions may be directed and disposed according to your will and that of your Son. Amen.

PRAYER OF SAINT AUGUSTINE

Gracious Lady, you are a mother and virgin; you are the mother of the body and soul of our Head and Redeemer; you are also truly mother of all the members of Christ's Mystical Body. For through your love, you have cooperated in the begetting of the faithful in the Church. Unique among women, you are mother and virgin; mother of Christ and Virgin of Christ. You are the beauty and charm of earth, O Virgin. You are forever the image of the holy Church. Through a woman came death; through a woman came life, yes, through you, O Mother of God.

PRAYER OF SAINT EPHRAEM THE SYRIAN

O Virgin, most pure, wholly unspotted, O Mary, Mother of God, Queen of the universe, you are above all the saints, the hope of the elect and the joy of all the blessed. It is you who have reconciled us with God. You are the only refuge of sinners and the safe harbor of those who are shipwrecked. You are the consolation of the world, the ransom of captives, the health of the weak, the joy of the afflicted, and the salvation of all. We have recourse to you, and we beseech you to have pity on us. Amen.

PRAYER OF SAINT BERNARD

Mary, our Mother, the whole world reveres you as the holiest shrine of the living God, for in you the salvation of the world dawned. The Son of God was pleased to take human form from you. You have broken down the wall of hatred, the barrier between heaven and earth which was set up by the disobedience of Adam and Eve. In you heaven met earth when divinity and humanity were joined in one person, the God-Man.

Mother of God, we sing your praises, but we must praise you even more. Our speech is too feeble to honor you as we ought, for no tongue is eloquent enough to express your excellence. Mary, most powerful, most holy, and worthy of all love. Your name brings new life, and the thought of you inspires love in the hearts of those devoted to you.

PRAYER OF SAINT FRANCIS DE SALES

Most Holy Mary Virgin Mother of God, I am unworthy to be your servant. Yet moved by your motherly care for me and longing to serve you, I choose you this day to be my Queen, my Advocate, and my Mother. I firmly resolve ever to be devoted to you and to do what I can to encourage others to be devoted to you.

My loving Mother, through the Precious Blood of your Son shed for me, I beg you to receive me as your servant forever. Aid me in my actions and beg for me the grace never by thought, word, or deed to be displeasing in your sight and that of your most holy Son. Remember me, dearest Mother, and do not abandon me at the hour of death.

PRAYER OF SAINT JOHN DAMASCENE

Hail Mary, hope of Christians, hear the prayer of a sinner who loves you tenderly, honors you in a special manner, and places in you the hope of his salvation. I owe you my life, for you obtain for me the grace of your Son and you are the sure pledge of my eternal happiness.

I entreat you, deliver me from the burden of my sins, take away the darkness of my mind, destroy the earthly affections of my heart, defeat the temptations of my enemies, and rule all the actions of my life. With you as my guide may I arrive at the eternal happiness of heaven.

PRAYER OF SAINT CATHERINE OF SIENA

O Mary, temple of the Trinity.
O Mary, bearer of fire.
O Mary, dispenser of mercy.

O Mary, restorer of human generation, because the world was repurchased by means of the sustenance that your flesh found in the Word, Christ repurchased the world with his Passion and you with your suffering.

O Mary, peaceful ocean.
O Mary, giver of peace.
O Mary, fruitful land.

You, O Mary, are that new plant from which we have the fragrant flower of the Word, only-begotten Son of God, because this Word was sown in you, O fruitful land. You are the land and the plant.

O Mary, vehicle of fire, you bore the fire hidden and veiled beneath the ash of your humanity. O Mary, vase of humility, in which there burns the light of true knowledge with which you lifted yourself above yourself and yet were pleasing to the eternal Father; hence he took and brought you to himself, loving you with a singular love.

With this light and fire of your charity and with the oil of your humility, you drew and inclined his divinity to come into you—although he was first drawn to us by the most ardent fire of his inestimable charity.

Today, O Mary, you have become a book in which our rule is written. In you, today, is written the wisdom of the eternal Father. In you, today, is manifested the strength and freedom of all humankind.

I say that the dignity of humankind is manifested because when I look at you, O Mary, I see that the hand of the Holy Spirit has written the Trinity in you, forming in you the Incarnate Word, the only-begotten Son of God. He has written for us the wisdom of the Father, that is, the Word. He has written for us his power, because he was powerful in effecting this great mystery. And he has written for us the clemency of that Holy Spirit, because only through grace and the divine clemency was so great a mystery ordained and accomplished.

But today I ardently make my request, because it is the day of graces, and I know that nothing is refused to you, O Mary. Today, O Mary, your land has generated the Savior for us. O Mary, blessed are you among women throughout the ages. Amen.

PRAYER OF SAINT GERTRUDE OF HELFTA

Most chaste Virgin Mary, by the spotless purity with which you prepared for the Son of God a dwelling of delight in your virginal womb, I beg of you to intercede for me that I may be cleansed from every stain. Most humble Virgin Mary, by that most profound humility by which you deserved to be raised high above all the choirs of angels and saints, I beg of you to intercede for me that all my sins may be expiated. Most amiable Mary, by that indescribable love that united you so closely and inseparably to God, I beg of you to intercede for me that I may obtain an abundance of all merits. Amen.

PRAYER OF SAINT ANSELM

O Jesus, Son of God, and you, O Mother Mary, you desire that whatever you love should be loved by us. Therefore, O good Son, by the love you bear your Mother, to grant to me that I may truly love her. And you, O Good Mother, I beg you by the love that you bear your Son, to pray for me that I may truly love him. Behold I ask nothing that is not in accordance with your will. Since this is in your power, will my sins prevent this being accomplished? O Jesus, lover of all, you were able to love criminals and even to die for them. Can you, then, refuse me, who asks only the love of You and your Mother? And you, too, Mary, Mother of He who loved us, who did bear Him in your womb, and feed Him at your breast, are you not able to obtain for one who asks it the love of your Son and yourself?

May my mind venerate you both as you deserve. May my heart love you as it should. May my body serve you as it ought. In your service may my life be spent. Blessed be God forever. Amen, amen.

PRAYER OF SAINT FRANCIS OF ASSISI

Holy Virgin Mary, there is none like you among women born in the world. Daughter and handmaid of the heavenly Father, the almighty King, Mother of our most high Lord Jesus Christ, and Spouse of the Holy Spirit, pray for us to your most holy Son, our Lord and Master.

Hail holy Lady, most noble Queen, Mother of God, and Mary ever Virgin. You were chosen by the heavenly Father, who has been pleased to honor you with the presence of his most holy Son and the Divine Paraclete.

You were blessed with the fullness of grace and goodness. Hail, Temple of God, his dwelling place, his masterpiece, his handmaid.

Hail, Mother of God. I venerate you for the holy virtues that—through the grace and light of the Holy Spirit—you bring into the hearts of your devoted ones to change them from unfaithful Christians to faithful children of God. Amen.

PRAYER OF SAINT JOHN VIANNEY

O most holy Virgin Mary, always present before the most holy Trinity, to whom it is granted at all times to pray for us to your most blessed Son, pray for me in all my needs. Help me, defend me, give thanks for me, and obtain for me the pardon of all my sins and failings.

Help me especially in my last hours. Then, when I can no longer give any sign of the use of reason, give me courage and protect me against all evil spirits. Make in my name a profession of faith. Assure me of my eternal salvation.

Never let me despair of the mercy of God. Help me to overcome the evil spirits. When I can no longer say, "Jesus, Mary, and Joseph, I place my soul in your hands," say it for me. When I can no longer hear human words of consolation, bring me comfort. Stay with me when I stand in judgment before your Son.

If I have to do penance for my sins in purgatory, pray for me after my death. Inspire my friends to pray for me, and thus help gain for me very soon the happiness of being in the presence of God. Lead my soul to heaven where, united with all the elect, I may bless and praise God and yourself for all eternity. Amen.

PRAYER OF SAINT PASCHASIUS

Deign, O Immaculate Virgin, Mother most pure, to accept the loving cry of praise which we send up to you from the depths of our hearts. Though they can but add little to your glory, O Queen of Angels, you do not despise, in your love, the praises of the humble and the poor.

Cast down upon us a glance of mercy, O most glorious Queen;

graciously receive our petitions. Through your immaculate purity of body and mind, which rendered you so pleasing to God, inspire us with a love of innocence and purity.

Teach us to guard carefully the gifts of grace, striving ever after sanctity, so that, being made like the image of your beauty, we may be worthy to become the sharers of your eternal happiness. Amen.

PRAYER OF SAINT JOHN OF THE CROSS

Most holy Mary, Virgin of virgins, shrine of the most Holy Trinity, joy of the angels, sure refuge of sinners, take pity on our sorrows, mercifully accept our sighs, and appease the wrath of your most holy Son. Amen.

PRAYER OF SAINT JOHN BOSCO

O Mary, powerful Virgin, mighty and glorious protector of the holy Church, marvelous help of Christians, you who are as awe-inspiring as an army in battle array; you by whom alone all heresies throughout the world are brought to nothing: in our anguish, our struggles, our distress, guard us from the enemy's power, and at the hour of our death bid our souls welcome into paradise. Amen.

PRAYER OF SAINT CYRIL OF ALEXANDRIA

Hail, Mother and Virgin, Eternal Temple of the Godhead, Venerable Treasure of Creation, crown of virginity, support of the true faith, on which the Church is founded throughout the world.

Mother of God, who contained the infinite God under your heart, whom no space can contain: through you the most Holy Trinity is revealed, adored, and glorified, demons are vanquished, Satan cast down from heaven into hell and our fallen nature again assumed into heaven.

Through you the human race, held captive in the bonds of idolatry, arrives at the knowledge of Truth. What more shall I say of you?

Hail, through whom kings rule, through whom the Only-Begotten Son of God has become the Star of Light to those sitting in darkness and in the shadow of death. Amen.

PRAYER OF SAINT AMBROSE

May the life of Blessed Mary be ever present to our awareness.
In her, as in a mirror, the form of virtue and beauty of chastity
    shine forth.
She was virgin, not only in body, but in mind and spirit.
She never sullied the pure affection of her heart
    by unworthy feelings.
She was humble of heart.
She was serious in her conversations.
She was prudent in her counsels.
She preferred to pray rather than to speak.
She united in her heart the prayers of the poor
And avoided the uncertainty of worldly riches.
She was ever faithful to her daily duties,
Reserved in her conversations, and always
    accustomed to recognize God as the Witness of her thoughts.
Blessed be the name of Jesus.
Amen.

PRAYER OF SAINT ILDEFONSUS OF TOLEDO

I beg you, O holy Virgin, that I may have Jesus from the Spirit from whom you conceived Jesus. May my soul receive Jesus through the Spirit, through whom your flesh conceived the same Jesus. Let it be granted to me to know Jesus from the Spirit, from whom it was given to you to know, to have and to bring forth Jesus. May I in my lowliness speak exalted things of Jesus in that Spirit, in whom you confess yourself to be the handmaid of the Lord, choosing that it be done unto you according to the angel's word. May I love Jesus in that Spirit in which you adore him as Lord, contemplate him as your Son. Amen.

3. Prayers to Mary Under Her Special Titles

PRAYER TO OUR LADY OF GOOD COUNSEL

Most glorious Virgin, chosen to be the Mother of the Eternal Word made man, treasure house of divine graces and advocate of sinner: I, the most unworthy of your children, have recourse to you, begging of you to be my guide and counselor. Obtain for me, through the most Precious Blood of your Divine Son, forgiveness of my sins, and the salvation of my soul. Amen.

PRAYER TO OUR LADY, QUEEN OF PEACE

Most holy Virgin, by your divine motherhood you merited a share in your Divine Son's prerogative of universal kingship, and to be called Queen of Peace. May your powerful intercession guard your people from all hatred and discord among themselves and direct their hearts in the way of peace. Your Son came to teach us this way for the good and well-being of all. Enlighten the rulers of our country and of all countries on earth to follow the path to peace. Grant that there may be peace in our hearts, in our families, and in our world. Amen.

PRAYER TO OUR LADY OF GUADALUPE

Our Lady of Guadalupe, mystical rose, intercede for the Church, protect all who invoke you in their necessities. Since you are the ever Virgin Mary and Mother of the true God, obtain for us from your most holy Son the grace of a firm faith and a sure hope amide the bitterness of life, as well as an ardent love and the precious gift of final perseverance. Amen.

PRAYER TO THE VIRGIN OF THE POOR

Blessed Virgin of the Poor, lead us to Jesus, source of all grace. Blessed Virgin of the Poor, save all nations. Blessed Virgin of the Poor, alleviate suffering. Blessed Virgin of the Poor, pray for each one of us.

Blessed Virgin of the Poor, believe in us and bless us. Mother of the Savior, Mother of God, we thank you. Amen.

PRAYER TO OUR LADY OF FÁTIMA

O Most holy Virgin Mary, Queen of the most holy Rosary, you were pleased to appear to the children of Fátima and reveal a glorious message.

We implore you, inspire in our hearts a fervent love for the recitation of the Rosary. By meditating on the mysteries of the redemption that are recalled therein may we obtain the graces and virtues that we ask, through the merits of Jesus Christ, our Lord and Redeemer. Amen.

PRAYER TO OUR LADY, MOTHER OF CONFIDENCE

O Immaculate Mary, when we show devotion to you under the title of Mother of Confidence, our hearts overflow with consolation and we are moved to hope for every good gift from you. Receive, then, with a mother's compassion, these acts of love with which we pray will make you look with favor on us in every necessity. Above all, we ask you to help us live ever united to you and your Divine Son Jesus. Under your escort we will safely walk along the road and it will be our lot to hear on the last day of our lives those consoling words: Come, faithful servant, enter into the joy of the Lord. Amen.

PRAYER TO OUR LADY OF LOURDES

O ever Immaculate Virgin, mother of mercy, health of the sick, refuge of sinners, comfort of the afflicted, you know my wants, my troubles, my sufferings. Deign to cast on me a look of mercy. By appearing in the Grotto of Lourdes, you were pleased to make it a privileged sanctuary, whence you dispense your favors. Already many sufferers have obtained the cure of their infirmities, both spiritual and corporal. I come, therefore, with the most unbounded confidence to implore your maternal intercession. Obtain, O loving Mother, the granting of my requests. Through gratitude for favors, I will endeavor to imitate your virtues that I may one day share your glory. Amen.

PRAYER TO OUR LADY OF LA SALETTE

Remember, Our Lady of La Salette, true Mother of Sorrows, the tears you shed for me on Calvary. Remember also the care you have always taken to keep me faithful to Christ your Son. After having done so much for your child, you will not now abandon me. Inspired by this consoling thought, I come to cast myself at your feet in spite of my infidelities and ingratitude. Do not reject my prayers, O merciful Virgin, but intercede for my conversion, obtain for me the grace to love Jesus above all things, and to console you by a holy life, that I may one day see you in heaven. Amen.

PRAYER TO THE MOTHER OF OUR REDEEMER

Loving Mother of the Redeemer, gate of heaven, star of the sea, assist your people who have fallen yet strive to rise again. To the wonderment of nature you bore your creator, yet remained a virgin as before. You who received Gabriel's joyful greeting, have pity on us poor sinners. Amen.

PRAYER TO THE HEART OF MARY

O heart of Mary, Mother of God and our Mother; heart most worthy of our love, in which the adorable Trinity is ever well-pleased, worthy of the veneration and love of all the angels and of all humanity; heart most like the heart of Jesus, of which you are the perfect image; heart, full of goodness, ever compassionate toward our miseries; deign to melt our icy hearts and grant that they may be changed into the likeness of your Son. Amen.

PRAYER TO MARY, QUEEN OF THE HOME

O Blessed Virgin Mary, you are the Mother and Queen of every Christian family. When you conceived and gave birth to Jesus, human motherhood reached its greatest achievement. From the time of the Annunciation you were the living chalice of the Son of God made Man. You are the Queen of the home. As a woman of faith, you inspire all mothers to transmit faith to their children.

Watch over our families. Let the children learn free and loving obedience inspired by your obedience to God. Let parents learn dedication and selflessness based on your unselfish attitude. Let all families honor you and remain devoted to you. Amen.

PRAYER TO OUR LADY, SPLENDOR OF THE STARS

Mary, you are the extension of heaven and the foundation of the earth, and the depths of the seas and the light of the sun, the beauty of the moon and the splendor of the stars. You are greater than the cherubim, more eminent than the seraphim, and more glorious than the chariot of fire.

Your womb bore God, whose majesty overwhelms us all. Your lap held the glowing coal. Your knees propped up the lion of majesty. Your hands touched the untouchable and the fire of the divinity that lies therein. You are the basket of this bread of burning flame and the chalice of this wine.

O Mary, you produced in your womb the fruit of the offering. We your servants ask you to guard us from the enemy that attacks us, so that as the water and wine are not separated in their mixture, we too will not be separated from you and your Son, the Lamb of Salvation. Amen.

4. Prayers of the Popes to Mary

TO MARY, MOTHER OF DIVINE LOVE

To you, O Mary, are known all the needs of your people and of the whole Church. Mother of Truth and Seat of Wisdom, dissipate the clouds of error which darken our minds. Amend the strayings of our hearts and inspire in us love for truth and the desire to do good.

Obtain for all people a holy fear of God so that society may know happiness. Give us lively faith that we may trust in those things which are imperishable. Give us that love which is sealed forever in God. Obtain for families fidelity, harmony, and peace. Stir up and confirm in the hearts of those who govern nations a clear notion of their responsibility, and of their duty to foster religion, morality, and the common good.

And just as your mercy is showered upon souls, O Mary, may it likewise flow over all those ills which afflict this people, and indeed the whole Christian family. Have pity on the poor, on captives, on all who bear persecution for the sake of justice, or are stricken by misfortune. Hail, O Mary, Mother of those who wander here below; you are our life, our sweetness, and our hope.

O Mother of Divine Love, send down your motherly blessing on all who pray to you; send it abundantly and consolingly. Amen.

Pope Pius XII

TO OUR LADY OF REST

Hear, O Blessed Virgin, the prayers which we address you, Our Lady of Rest, as we are mindful of that maternal love in which you receive your children.

It is by your powerful intercession, O Mary, that our hearts and minds find rest. We know well our own weakness; but we trust in the everlasting promises, and we hope for eternal happiness as we cling to the crucified Jesus, who has made His cross to be ours as well.

O Mary, under your patronage we find peace in the midst of earthly tribulation. You are the quiet certainty of the strong of soul, ever on guard against the enemy. You are the sanctuary of the pure who remain unstained by earth's corruption. And just as, with you, we find peace during the present life, so shall we find with you, when the days of our pilgrimage are over, everlasting peace in the world to come. Amen.

Pope Pius XII

CONSECRATION OF THE SICK TO MARY

O kind and good Mother, whose own soul was pierced by the sword of sorrow, look upon us while, in our sickness, we arraign ourselves beside you on the Calvary where your Jesus hangs.

Dowered with the high grace of suffering, and hopeful of fulfilling in our own flesh what is wanting in our sharing of Christ's passion, on behalf of his Mystical Body, the Church, we consecrate to you ourselves and our pain. We pray that you will place them on that Altar of the Cross to which Jesus is affixed. May they be little victims of propitiation for our salvation, for the salvation of all peoples.

O Mother of Sorrows, accept this consecration. Strengthen our hopeful hearts, that as partakers of Christ's sufferings we may also share in his comfort now and for evermore. Amen.

Pope Pius XII

PRAYER AT THE LOURDES GROTTO IN THE VATICAN GARDENS

O blessed Virgin, Mother of God, Mother of Christ, Mother of the Church, look upon us mercifully at this hour.

Virgin faithful, pray for us. Teach us to believe as you believed. Make our faith in God, in Christ, in the Church, always to be serene, courageous, strong, and generous.

Mother worthy of love. Mother of faithful love, pray for us. Teach us to love God and our brothers and sisters as you loved them: make our love for others to be always patient, kindly, and respectful.

Cause of our joy, pray for us. Teach us to be able to grasp, in faith, the paradox of Christian joy, which springs up and blooms from sorrow, renunciation, and union with your sacrificed Son. Make our joy to be always genuine and full, in order to be able to communicate it to all. Amen.

Pope John Paul II

PRAYER TO OUR LADY OF APARECIDA

Lady Aparecida, a son of yours who belongs to you unreservedly— *totus tuus*—called by the mysterious plan of Providence to be the Vicar of your Son on earth, wishes to address you at this moment. He recalls with emotion, because of the brown color of this image of yours, another image of yours, the Black Virgin of Jasna Gora.

Mother of God and our Mother, protect the Church, the Pope, the bishops, the priests and all the faithful people; welcome under your protecting mantle men and women religious, families, children, young people, and their educations.

Health of the sick and Consoler of the afflicted, comfort those who are suffering in body and soul; be the light of those who are seeking Christ, the Redeemer of all; show all people that you are the Mother of our confidence.

Queen of Peace and Mirror of Justice, obtain peace for the world, ensure that Brazil and all countries may have lasting peace, that we will always live together as brothers and sisters and as children of God.

Our Lady Aparecida, bless all your sons and daughters who pray and sing to you here and elsewhere. Amen.

Pope John Paul II

PRAYER TO OUR LADY OF EVANGELIZATION

O Mary, Mother of Jesus and Mother of his Church, we are mindful of the role you play in the evangelization of souls who do not yet know Him. We are mindful of how missionaries came with the power of Christ's Gospel and committed the success of their work to you. As the Mother of Divine Grace you were with the missionaries in all their efforts.

And as Mother of the Church you presided over all the activities of evangelization and over the implantation of the Gospel in the hearts of the faithful. You sustained the missionaries in hope and you gave joy to every new community that was born of the Church's evangelizing activity.

You were there with your intercession and your prayers, as the first grace of baptism developed, and as those who had new life in Christ your Son came to a full appreciation of their Christian calling.

We ask you, Mary, to help us to fulfill this mission of evangelization which your Son has given to his Church and which falls to us. Mindful of your role as Help of Christians, we entrust ourselves to you in the work of carrying the Gospel ever deeper into the hearts and lives of all the people. We entrust to you our missionary mandate and commit our cause totally to your prayers.

To Jesus Christ your Son, with the Father, in the unity of the Holy Spirit be praise and thanksgiving forever and ever. Amen.

Pope John Paul II

PRAYER TO OUR LADY, MOTHER OF ADVENT

O Mother of our Advent,
be with us and see to it
that he will remain with us
in this difficult Advent
of the struggles for truth and hope,

for justice and peace:
He, alone, Emmanuel.

Pope John Paul II

PRAYER TO OUR LADY FOR CHRISTIAN UNITY

Spouse of the Holy Spirit and Seat of Wisdom, help us in the great endeavor that we are carrying out to meet on a more and more mature way our brothers and sisters in the faith, with whom so many things unite us, although there is still something dividing us. Through all the means of knowledge, of mutual respect, of love, shared collaboration in various fields, may we be able to rediscover gradually the divine plan for the unity in which we should enter. Mother of unity, teach us constantly the ways that lead to unity.

Allow us in the future to go out to meet human beings and all the peoples that are seeking God and wishing to serve him on the way of different religions. Help us all to proclaim Christ.

Mother of Good Counsel, show us always how we are to serve the individual and humanity in every nation, how we are to lead them along the ways of salvation. How we are to protect justice and peace in a world continually threatened on various sides. Let us entrust to you all the difficult problems of the societies, systems, and states—problems that cannot be solved with hatred, war and self-destruction but only by peace, justice, and respect for the rights of people and nations.

Pope John Paul II

PRAYER TO OUR LADY OF THE THIRD MILLENNIUM

Mother of the Redeemer, with great joy we call you blessed. In order to carry out his plan of salvation, God the Father chose you before the creation of the world. You believed in his love and obeyed his word.

The Son of God desired you for his Mother when he became man to save the human race. You received him with ready obedience and undivided heart.

The Holy Spirit loved you as his mystical spouse and he filled you with singular gifts. You allowed yourself to be led by his hidden and powerful action.

In this third Christian century, we entrust to you the Church which acknowledges you and invokes you as Mother.

To you, Mother of the human family and of the nations, we confidently entrust the whole of humanity, with its hopes and fears. Do not let it lack the light of true wisdom. Guide its steps in the ways of peace. Enable all to meet Christ, the Way and the Truth and the Life.

Sustain us, O Virgin Mary, on our journey of faith and obtain for us the grace of eternal salvation. O clement, O loving, O sweet Mother of God and our Mother, Mary. Amen.

Pope John Paul II

PRAYER OF LOVE FOR MARY

Holy Immaculate Mary, help all who are in trouble. Give courage to the faint-hearted, console the sad, heal the infirm, pray for the people, intercede for the clergy, have a special care for nuns; may all feel, all enjoy your kind and powerful assistance, all who now and always render and will render, you honor, and will offer you their petitions. Hear all our prayers, O Mother, and grant them all. We are all your children: Grant the prayers of your children.
Amen forever.

Pope John XXIII

PRAYER TO THE MOTHER OF THE CHURCH, THE MOTHER OF FAMILIES

May the Virgin Mary, who is the Mother of the Church, also be the Mother of the "Church of the home." Thanks to her motherly aid, may each Christian family become a "little Church" in which the mystery of the Church of Christ is mirrored and given new life. May she, the handmaid of the Lord, be an example of humble and generous acceptance of the will of God. May she, the Sorrowful Mother at the foot of the cross, comfort the sufferings and dry the tears of those in distress because of the difficulties of families.

Pope John Paul II

5. Psalms Associated With Our Lady

The following psalms are some of those which are said as part of the Little Office of the Blessed Virgin Mary.

PSALM 85 (84)

You have favored your land, O Lord;
you have brought back the exiles of Jacob.
You have forgiven the sin of your people;
you have pardoned their offenses.

You have withdrawn your wrath
and turned from your burning rage.

But restore us, God our savior;
put away altogether your indignation.
Will your anger be ever with us,
carried over to all generations?

Will you not give us life anew,
that your people may rejoice in you?
Show us, O Lord, your unfailing love
and grant us your saving help.

Would that I hear God's proclamation,
that he promise peace to his people,
his saints—lest they come back to their folly.
Yet his salvation is near to those who fear him,

and his Glory will dwell in our land.
Love and faithfulness have met;
righteousness and peace have embraced.
Faithfulness will reach up from the earth
while justice bends down from heaven.

The Lord will give what is good,
and our land will yield its fruit.
Justice will go before him,
and peace will follow along his path.

PSALM 95 (94)

Come, let us sing to the Lord,
let us make a joyful sound
to the Rock of our salvation.
Let us come before him giving thanks,
with music and songs of praise.

For the Lord is the great God,
the great King above all gods.

In his hand are the depths of the earth
and the mountain heights.
The sea is his, for he made it,
and his hand shaped the dry land.

Come and worship; let us bow down,
kneel before the Lord, our Maker.
He is our God, and we his people;
the flock he leads and pastures.

Would that today you heard his voice!
Do not be stubborn, as a Meribah,
in the desert, on that day at Massah,

when your fathers challenged me,
and they put me to the test.

For forty years they wearied me and I said,
"They are a people of inconstant heart;
they have not known my ways."
So I declared an oath in my anger,
"Never shall they enter my rest."

PSALM 122 (121)

I rejoiced with those who said to me,
"Let us go to the house of the Lord!"
And now we have set foot
within your gates, O Jerusalem!

Jerusalem, just like a city,
where everything falls into place!
There the tribes go up,
the tribes of the Lord, the assembly of Israel,
to give thanks to the Lord's name,
There stand the courts of justice
the offices of the house of David.

Pray for the peace of Jerusalem:
"May those who love you prosper!
May peace be within your walls
and security within your citadels!"

For the sake of my relatives and friends
I will say, "Peace be with you!"
For the sake of the house of our Lord,
I will pray for your good.

PSALM 123 (122)

To you I lift up my eyes,
to you whose throne is in heaven.

As the eyes of servants look
to the hand of their master,
as the eyes of maids look
to the hand of their mistress,
so our eyes look to the Lord our God,
till he shows us his mercy.

Have mercy on us, O Lord,
have mercy on us,
for we have our fill of contempt.
Too long have our souls been filled
with the scorn of the arrogant,
with the ridicule of the insolent.

PSALM 128 (127)

Blessed are you who fear the Lord
and walk in his ways.
You will eat the fruit of your toil;
you will be blessed and favored.

Your wife, like a vine,
will bear fruits in your home;
your children, like olive shoots
will stand around your table.
Such are the blessings bestowed
upon the man who fears the Lord.

May the Lord bless you from Zion.
May you see Jerusalem prosperous

all the days of your life.
May you see your children's children,
and Israel at peace!

PSALM 132 (131)

O Lord, my heart is not proud
nor do I have arrogant eyes.
I am not engrossed in ambitious matters,
nor in things too great for me.

I have quieted and stilled my soul
like a weaned child on its mother's lap;
like a contented child is my soul.
Hope in the Lord, O Israel,
now and forever.

PSALM 150 (149)

Alleluia!
Praise God in his sanctuary;
praise him in the vault of heaven.
Praise him for his mighty deeds;
praise him for his own greatness.
Praise him with dance and tambourines;
praise him with pipe and strings.
Praise him with clashing cymbals;
praise him with clanging cymbals.
Let everything that breathes
sing praise to the Lord.
Alleluia!

SECTION SIX

Marian Litanies
and Aspirations

Litanies

The word *litany* comes from the Greek word for "entreaty" or "supplication" and simply means "to pray." In the prayer of the Church, a litany consists of a series of invocations, symbolic salutations, and supplications in honor of God directly or indirectly through the intercession of the Blessed Virgin Mary or the saints.

LITANY OF THE BLESSED VIRGIN MARY

This litany was given authorization for general use in 1587 at the Shrine of the Holy House of Loreto; thus, one of its alternate names is the "Litany of Loreto." From time to time, additional invocations have been ordered added to the litany.

> Lord, have mercy. Christ, have mercy.
> Lord, have mercy. Christ, hear us.
>   Christ, graciously hear us.
> God the Father of Heaven, have mercy on us.
> God the Son, Redeemer, have mercy on us.
> God the Holy Ghost, have mercy on us.
> Holy Trinity, one God, have mercy on us.
> Holy Mary, pray for us.
> Holy mother of God, *pray for us.*
> Holy virgin of virgins, *pray for us.*
> Mother of Christ, *pray for us.*
> Mother of divine grace, *pray for us.*
> Mother most pure, *pray for us.*
> Mother most chaste, *pray for us.*
> Mother inviolate, *pray for us.*
> Mother undefiled, *pray for us.*
> Mother most amiable, *pray for us.*
> Mother most admirable, *pray for us.*
> Mother of good counsel, *pray for us.*
> Mother of our Creator, *pray for us.*
> Mother of our Savior, *pray for us.*

Virgin most prudent, *pray for us.*
Virgin most venerable, *pray for us.*
Virgin most renowned, *pray for us.*
Virgin most powerful, *pray for us.*
Virgin most merciful, *pray for us.*
Virgin most faithful, *pray for us.*
Mirror of justice, *pray for us.*
Seat of wisdom, *pray for us.*
Cause of our joy, *pray for us.*
Spiritual vessel, *pray for us.*
Vessel of honor, *pray for us.*
Singular vessel of devotion, *pray for us.*
Mystical rose, *pray for us.*
Tower of David, *pray for us.*
Tower of ivory, *pray for us.*
House of gold, *pray for us.*
Ark of the Covenant, *pray for us.*
Gate of Heaven, *pray for us.*
Morning star, *pray for us.*
Health of the sick, *pray for us.*
Refuge of sinners, *pray for us.*
Comforter of the afflicted, *pray for us.*
Help of Christians, *pray for us.*
Queen of angels, *pray for us.*
Queen of patriarchs, *pray for us.*
Queen of prophets, *pray for us.*
Queen of apostles, *pray for us.*
Queen of martyrs, *pray for us.*
Queen of confessors, *pray for us.*
Queen of virgins, *pray for us.*
Queen of all saints, *pray for us.*
Queen conceived without Original Sin, *pray for us.*
Queen assumed into Heaven, *pray for us.*
Queen of the most holy Rosary, *pray for us.*
Queen of peace, *pray for us.*

    Lamb of God, who takest away the sins of the world,
        Spare us, O Lord.
    Lamb of God, who takest away the sins of the world,
        Graciously hear us, O Lord.
    Lamb of God, who takest away the sins of the world,
        Have mercy on us.

Pray for us, O Holy Mother of God that we may be made worthy of the promises of Christ.

Let us pray. Grant, we beseech Thee, O Lord God, that we your servants may enjoy perpetual health of mind and body and by the glorious intercession of the Blessed Mary, ever Virgin, be delivered from present sorrow and enjoy eternal happiness. Through Christ Our Lord. Amen.

LITANY OF THE IMMACULATE HEART OF MARY

While the Litany of Loreto is sometimes used on public occasions in the Church, this litany is reserved for private use entirely.

    Lord, have mercy on us.
    Christ, have mercy on us.
    Lord, have mercy on us.

    Christ, hear us.
    Christ, graciously hear us.
    God, the Father of heaven, have mercy on us.
    God, the Son, Redeemer of the world, have
        mercy on us.
    God, the Holy Spirit, have mercy on us.
    Holy Trinity, one God, have mercy on us.

    Heart of Mary, *pray for us*.
    Heart of Mary, like unto the heart of God, *pray for us*.
    Heart of Mary, united to the heart of Jesus, *pray for us*.
    Heart of Mary, instrument of the Holy Spirit, *pray for us*.

Heart of Mary, sanctuary of the Divine Trinity,
pray for us.
Heart of Mary, full of grace, *pray for us.*
Heart of Mary, blessed among all hearts, *pray for us.*
Heart of Mary, throne of glory, *pray for us.*
Heart of Mary, most humble, *pray for us.*
Heart of Mary, holocaust of divine love, *pray for us.*
Heart of Mary, fastened to the Cross with Jesus
crucified, *pray for us.*
Heart of Mary, comfort of the afflicted, *pray for us.*
Heart of Mary, refuge of sinners, *pray for us.*
Heart of Mary, hope of the agonizing, *pray for us.*
Heart of Mary, seat of mercy, *pray for us.*

Lamb of God, you who take away the sins of the world,
spare us, O Lord.
Lamb of God, you who take away the sins of the world,
have mercy on us.

Christ hear us.
Christ, graciously hear us.
Immaculate Mary, meek and humble of heart,
make our heart like unto the heart of Jesus.

Let us pray. O most merciful God, who, for the salvation of sinners and the refuge of the miserable, was pleased that the most pure heart of Mary should be most like in love and pity to the divine heart of thy Son, Jesus Christ, grant that we who commemorate this sweet and loving heart may, by the merits and intercession of the same Blessed Virgin, merit to be found like to the heart of Jesus. Through the same Christ our Lord. Amen.

LITANY OF THE QUEENSHIP OF MARY

This litany was composed as part of the Rite for Crowning an Image of the Blessed Virgin Mary. It also may be used for private prayer.

Lord, have mercy.
Christ, have mercy.
Lord, have mercy.

God our Father in heaven, *have mercy on us.*
God the Son, Redeemer of the world, *have mercy on us.*
God the Holy Spirit, *have mercy on us.*
Holy Trinity, one God, *have mercy on us.*

Holy Mary, *pray for us.*
Holy Mother of God, *pray for us.*
Most honored of virgins, *pray for us.*

Chosen daughter of the Father, *pray for us.*
Mother of Christ the King, *pray for us.*
Glory of the Holy Spirit, *pray for us.*

Virgin daughter of Zion, *pray for us.*
Virgin poor and humble, *pray for us.*
Virgin gentle and obedient, *pray for us.*

Handmaid of the Lord, *pray for us.*
Mother of the Lord, *pray for us.*
Helper of the Redeemer, *pray for us.*

Full of grace, *pray for us.*
Fountain of beauty, *pray for us.*
Model of virtue, *pray for us.*

Finest fruit of the redemption, *pray for us.*
Perfect disciple of Christ, *pray for us.*
Untarnished image of the Church, *pray for us.*

Woman transformed, *pray for us.*
Woman clothed with the sun, *pray for us.*
Woman crowned with stars, *pray for us.*

Gentle Lady, *pray for us.*
Gracious Lady, *pray for us.*
Our Lady, *pray for us.*

Joy of Israel, *pray for us.*
Splendor of the Church, *pray for us.*
Pride of the human race, *pray for us.*

Advocate of grace, *pray for us.*
Minister of holiness, *pray for us.*
Champion of God's people, *pray for us.*

Queen of love, *pray for us.*
Queen of mercy, *pray for us.*
Queen of peace, *pray for us.*

Queen of angels, *pray for us.*
Queen of patriarchs and prophets, *pray for us.*
Queen of apostles and martyrs, *pray for us.*
Queen of confessors and virgins, *pray for us.*
Queen of all saints, *pray for us.*
Queen conceived without original sin, *pray for us.*
Queen assumed into heaven, *pray for us.*

Queen of all the earth, *pray for us.*
Queen of heaven, *pray for us.*
Queen of the universe, *pray for us.*

Lamb of God, you take away the sins of the world,
    spare us, O Lord.
Lamb of God, you take away the sins of the world,
    hear us, O Lord.
Lamb of God, you take away the sins of the world,
    have mercy on us.

Pray for us, O glorious Mother of the Lord,
that we may become worthy of the promises of Christ.

Let us pray. God of mercy, listen to the prayers of your servants who
have honored your handmaid Mary as mother and queen. Grant
that by your grace we may serve you and our neighbor on earth and

be welcomed into your eternal kingdom. We ask this through Christ our Lord. Amen.

LITANY OF THE SEVEN SORROWS OF THE BLESSED VIRGIN MARY

Lord, have mercy. *Lord, have mercy.*
Christ, have mercy. *Christ, have mercy.*
Lord, have mercy. *Lord, have mercy.*
Christ, hear us. *Christ, graciously hear us.*
God the Father of Heaven, *have mercy on us.*
God the Son, Redeemer of the world, *have mercy on us.*
God the Holy Spirit, *have mercy on us.*
Holy Trinity, one God, *have mercy on us.*

Mother of Sorrows, *pray for us.*
Mother whose soul was pierced by the sword,
    pray for us.
Mother who fled with Jesus into Egypt, *pray for us.*
Mother who sought Him sorrowing for three days,
    pray for us.
Mother who saw Him scourged and crowned
    with thorns, *pray for us.*
Mother who stood by Him while He hung upon
    the Cross, *pray for us.*
Mother who received Him into your arms when He
    was dead, *pray for us.*
Mother who saw Him buried in the tomb, *pray for us.*

O Mary, queen of martyrs, *save us by your prayers.*
O Mary, comfort of the sorrowful, *save us by
    your prayers.*
O Mary, help of the weak, *save us by your prayers.*
O Mary, strength of the fearful, *save us by your prayers.*
O Mary, light of the despondent, *save us by your prayers.*
O Mary, nursing mother of the sick, *save us by
    your prayers.*

O Mary, refuge of sinners, *save us by your prayers.*

Through the bitter Passion of your Son, *save us by your prayers.*

Through the piercing anguish of your heart, *save us by your prayers.*

Through the heavy weight of your woe, *save us by your prayers.*

Through your sadness and desolation, *save us by your prayers.*

Through your maternal pity, *save us by your prayers.*

Through your perfect resignation, *save us by your prayers.*

Through your meritorious prayers, *save us by your prayers.*

From immoderate sadness, *save us by your prayers.*

From a cowardly spirit, *save us by your prayers.*

From an impatient temper, *save us by your prayers.*

From fretfulness and discontent, *save us by your prayers.*

From sullenness and gloom, *save us by your prayers.*

From despair and unbelief, *save us by your prayers.*

From final impenitence, *save us by your prayers.*

We sinners, *beseech you, hear us.*

Preserve us from sudden death, *beseech you, hear us.*

Teach us how to die, *beseech you, hear us.*

Succor us in our last agony, *beseech you, hear us.*

Guard us from the enemy, *beseech you, hear us.*

Bring us to a happy end, *beseech you, hear us.*

Gain for us the gift of perseverance, *beseech you, hear us.*

Aid us before the Judgment Seat, *beseech you, hear us.*

Mother of God, *beseech you, hear us.*

Mother, most sorrowful, *beseech you, hear us.*

Mother, most desolate, *beseech you, hear us.*

Lamb of God, who takes away the sins of the world, *spare us, O Lord.*

Lamb of God, who takes away the sins of the world, *graciously hear us, O Lord.*

Lamb of God, who takes away the sins of the world,
   have mercy on us.

Christ, hear us. *Christ, graciously hear us.*
Lord, have mercy. *Christ, have mercy.*
Lord, have mercy.

Help us, O Blessed Virgin Mary.
In every time, and in every place.

Let us pray. O Lord Jesus Christ, God and Man, grant, we beseech you, that your dear Mother Mary, whose soul the sword pierced in the hour of your Passion, may intercede for us, now, and in the hour of our death, through Your own merits, O Savior of the world, who with the Father and the Holy Spirit lives and reigns, God, world without end. Amen.

LITANY OF SALUTATIONS TO MARY COMPOSED BY SAINT JOHN EUDES (1601–1680)

Hail Mary, daughter of God the Father.
Hail Mary, Mother of God the Son.
Hail Mary, Spouse of God the Holy Ghost.
Hail Mary, Temple of the Most Blessed Trinity.
Hail Mary, Pure Lily of the Trinity, One God.
Hail Mary, Celestial Rose of the love of God.
Hail Mary, Virgin pure and humble, of whom
   the King of Heaven willed to be born.
Hail Mary, Virgin of virgins.
Hail Mary, Queen of Martyrs, whose soul a
   sword transfixed.
Hail Mary, my Queen and my Mother, my life,
   my sweetness and my hope.
Hail Mary, Mother most amiable.
Hail Mary, Mother most admirable.
Hail Mary, Mother of Divine Love.
Hail Mary, Immaculate, Conceived without sin.

Hail Mary, full of grace, the Lord is with thee.
Blessed are you among women and blessed is the
    fruit of your womb, Jesus.

Blessed be your spouse, Saint Joseph.
Blessed be your father, Saint Joachim.
Blessed be your mother, Saint Anne.
Blessed be your guardian, Saint John.
Blessed be your holy Angel, Saint Gabriel.

Glory be to God the Father, who chose you.
Glory be to God the Son, who loved you.
Glory be to God the Holy Spirit, who espoused you.

O Glorious Virgin Mary,
May all people love and praise you.
Holy Mary, Mother of God, pray for us and bless us,
Now and at death, in the name of Jesus, your Divine Son.
Amen.

Aspirations

Here are short prayers that can be said throughout the day. They help turn our minds to Jesus through Our Lady.

Mary, conceived without sin, pray for us who have recourse to you.

Mary, by your pure and Immaculate Conception, make my body pure and my soul holy.

O Mary, who entered the world without stain of sin, obtain for me from God the grace to leave it without sin.
Jesus, Mary and Joseph, I give you my heart and my soul.

Jesus, Mary and Joseph, assist me in my last agony.

Jesus, Mary and Joseph, may I die in peace, and in your blessed company.

Holy Mary, mother of God and Mother of Mercy, pray for us sinners, now and at the hour of our death.

Mother of God, pray for us. Holy Mary, pray for us.

Mary, Virgin Mother of God, pray to Jesus for me.

Queen of the most holy Rosary, pray for us.

Mary, refuge of sinners, bring all sinners back to Christ.

Our Lady of Sorrow, help me to overcome my despair.

Blessed be the name of Mary. Blessed be the name of Jesus forever.

Holy Mary, our hope, seat of wisdom, pray for us. Heart of Jesus, formed by the Holy Spirit in the womb of the Virgin Mother, pray for us.

Queen of Angels, our help in all our necessities, pray for us.

Mary sorrowing, Mother of all Christians, pray for us who have recourse to thee.

SECTION SEVEN

Novenas to Mary

A novena constitutes nine days of prayer, either public or private, for some special intention or some celebration in the liturgical year. The origin of the idea of a novena would seem to be the nine days that elapsed between the Ascension of our Lord and the coming of the Holy Spirit at Pentecost. The oldest novena in honor of our Lady seems to be that one made in preparation for the feast of the Immaculate Conception, which was first brought to popularity by the Franciscans. Prayers used for the nine days of a novena may be selected from any form of prayer that is approved by an ecclesiastical official of the Church.

1. Novena for the Immaculate Conception

PREPARATORY PRAYER (SAID EACH DAY)

Come, O Holy Spirit, fill the hearts of the faithful and kindle in them the fire of your love.

Virgin most pure, conceived without sin, all fair and stainless in your conception; glorious Mary, full of grace, Mother of God, Queen of Angels, I humbly honor you as Mother of my Savior, who, though He was God, taught me by his own veneration, reverence, and obedience to you, the honor and homage that are due to you. I pray to you, then, to accept this novena which I dedicate to you. You are the safe refuge of the penitent sinner; it is very fitting, then, that I should have recourse to you. You are the Mother of Compassion; then you will surely be moved with pity for my many miseries. You are my best hope after Jesus, so accept the loving confidence that I have in you.

PRAYER FOR THE FIRST DAY

Behold me at your feet, O Immaculate Virgin, I rejoice with you, because from all eternity you were elected to be the Mother of the Eternal Word, and was preserved stainless from the taint of original

151

sin. I praise and bless the Most Holy Trinity, who poured out on your soul in your Conception the treasure of that privilege. I pray to you to obtain for me the grace to effectively overcome the effects produced in my soul by original sin.

CONCLUDING PAYER (SAID EACH DAY)

In your conception, O Virgin, you were immaculate.

Pray for us to the Father, whose Son was born of you.

Let us pray: O God, who through the Immaculate Conception of a virgin did prepare a worthy dwelling for your Son, we ask you, who by the death of that Son, foreseen by you, did preserve her from all stain of sin, grant that by her intercession we also may be purified, and so may come to you. Through Christ, our Lord. Amen.

Continue through the next eight days, observing the order above and substituting each of the following prayers.

PRAYER FOR THE SECOND DAY

Mary, unsullied lily of Purity, I rejoice with you, because from the first moment of your conception, you were filled with grace, and had given unto you the perfect use of reason. I thank and adore the ever blessed Trinity, who gave you these gifts. Behold me at your feet overwhelmed with shame to see myself so poor in grace. O you who was filled with a heavenly grace, grant me a portion of that same grace, and make me a partaker in the treasures of your Immaculate Conception.

PRAYER FOR THE THIRD DAY

Mary, mystic rose of purity, I rejoice with you at the glorious triumph you gained over the serpent by your Immaculate Conception, in that you were conceived without original sin. I thank and praise with my whole heart the ever blessed Trinity, who granted you that glorious privilege; and I pray to obtain for me courage to overcome every snare of the great enemy, and never to stain my soul with mortal sin. Always come to my aid, and enable me, with you protection, to obtain victory over all of the enemies of our eternal welfare.

PRAYER FOR THE FOURTH DAY

Mary Immaculate Virgin, mirror of holy purity, I rejoice exceedingly to see how from your Immaculate Conception there were infused into your soul the most sublime and perfect virtues with all the gifts of the most Holy Spirit. I thank and praise the ever blessed Trinity who bestowed upon you these high privileges, and I beseech you, gracious Mother, obtain for me grace to practice every Christian virtue, and so to become worthy to receive the gifts and graces of the Holy Spirit.

PRAYER FOR THE FIFTH DAY

Mary, bright moon of purity, I congratulate you in that the mystery of your Immaculate Conception was the beginning of salvation to the human race, and was the joy of the whole world. I thank and bless the ever blessed Trinity who did so magnify and glorify your person. I entreat you to obtain for me grace so as to profit by the death and passion of your dear Son, that his Precious Blood may not have been shed upon the Cross for me in vain, but that after a holy life I may be saved.

PRAYER FOR THE SIXTH DAY

Mary Immaculate, brilliant star of purity, I rejoice with you, because your Immaculate Conception brought exceeding joy to all the angels of Paradise. I thank and bless the ever blessed Trinity, who enriched you with this privilege. Enable me also one day to take part in this heavenly joy, praising and blessing you in the company of angels, world without end.

PRAYER FOR THE SEVENTH DAY

Mary Immaculate, rising morn of purity, I rejoice with you, and I am filled with admiration at beholding you confirmed in grace and rendered sinless from the first moment of your conception. I thank and praise the ever blessed Trinity, who elected you alone from all human beings for this special privilege. Holiest Virgin, obtain for me so entire and lasting a hatred of sin, the worst of all evils, that I may rather die than ever again commit a mortal sin.

PRAYER FOR THE EIGHTH DAY

Mary, Virgin, sun without stain, I congratulate you and I rejoice with you, because God gave you in your conception a greater and more abundant grace than he gave to all his angels and his saints together, even when their merits were most exalted. I thank and admire the immense generosity of the ever blessed Trinity, who has dispensed to you alone this privilege. Oh, enable me to correspond with the grace of God, and never more to receive it in vain; change my heart, and help me to begin in earnest a new life.

PRAYER FOR THE NINTH DAY

Immaculate Mary, living light of holiness, model of purity, Virgin and Mother, as soon as you were conceived, you did profoundly adore your God, giving him thanks, because by means of you the ancient curse was blotted out, and blessing has again come upon the sinful sons and daughters of Adam. Let this blessing kindle in my heart love toward God; and do you inflame my heart still more and more, that I may ever love him constantly on earth, and afterwards eternally in heaven, there to thank and praise him for all the wondrous privileges conferred on you, and to rejoice with you in your crown of glory.

2. Novena to Our Mother of Perpetual Help

INTRODUCTORY PRAYER

O Mary, Mother of Jesus and our Mother of Perpetual Help, during these nine days I am going to look to you to discover what you want to teach me about your Son and our God, father and mother of all love.

O Holy Virgin Mary who to inspire us with boundless confidence has taken the sweet name of Our Mother of Perpetual Help, I implore you to come to my aid always and everywhere in my temptations, after my falls, in my difficulties, in all the miseries of life and, above all, at the hour of my death. Give me, O loving Mother the desire and the habit to always have recourse to you, trusting that you will come to my assistance. Obtain for me, then, this grace of graces, the grace to pray to you without ceasing and with childlike confidence that I may ensure your perpetual help and final perseverance. O Mother of Perpetual Help, pray for me now and at the hour of my death. Amen.

(Say the Hail Mary three times)

PRAYER FOR DAY ONE

In Nazareth you raised Jesus in an atmosphere of simplicity and work. You, Mother, used to take Jesus' hands in yours to teach Him to pray. You taught Him the psalms and prayers of your people.

Dearest Mother, servant of the Lord and caretaker of the house at Nazareth, teach us to love our homes and fill them with joy and understanding. Help us to build a society that is both just and brotherly, where there is bread and work for all.

(Say the Hail Mary three times)

PRAYER FOR DAY TWO

Dear Mother, let the Archangel Michael, leader of angelic armies and defender of the Lord's glory, remind us that only God is Lord of the Universe and that his kingdom is one of justice, love, and peace.

O Mother of Perpetual Help, give us faith in the power of your Son, victor over sin and death. Give us faith in the restoring power of his sacred blood. He gave his life for everyone because his strength was anchored in love. Help us, disgraced sinners, to anchor ourselves in your love.

(Say the Hail Mary three times)

PRAYER FOR DAY THREE

Mother of the Son of God made man, Jesus Christ, be also our Perpetual Help, our certain, tireless intercessor.

There are many mothers with illustrious sons, but you are the one we praise, we venerate, and we rejoice in above all creatures. God continues to show us his mercy through you who we call "Blessed." Holy Mary, "blessed among all women," pray for us.

(Say the Hail Mary three times)

PRAYER FOR DAY FOUR

As you presented your Son in the Temple, Simeon told you that a sword would pierce your soul. From that moment on, Mary, not a day passed without your thinking of the meaning of those words. You cherished the first words of baby Jesus, his first faltering steps and, later on, his independence. But you always saw in him the shadow of a sword hanging over his head, a sword that was to pierce your own heart and soul with sorrow.

Mother of Perpetual Help, you hold Jesus against your heart. Sustain us in our weaknesses. We look to the future and perhaps see it darkened by sickness and pain. We trust in your protection, because your very title of Perpetual Help is an invitation to confidence and hope.

(Say the Hail Mary three times)

PRAYER FOR DAY FIVE

Our heavenly Father said at the moment of the Transfiguration: "This is my beloved Son, listen to Him." Mary, you are the sign that allows us to identify the loving and comforting presence of Jesus. Where he is, you are, inseparable. You tell us, Mary, Mother and first disciple of Jesus, that to be a Christian consists of following your Son and that you will take us by the hand to him.

Thank you, Mother, for lighting our way to our Father's house. Strengthen our faith and enliven our hope when we tire on life's journey.

(Say the Hail Mary three times)

PRAYER FOR DAY SIX

Good Mother, enlighten us to recognize the presence of our heavenly Father even in the fatigue of our daily life. He never lets go of our hand, even when our faith seems to falter or we are overcome by difficulties. Strengthen us so that, full of confidence, we can ask him, as Jesus taught us, for our daily bread, and not to let us fall into temptation and despair.

(Say the Hail Mary three times)

PRAYER FOR DAY SEVEN

O gracious Mother, crowned with stars, like the star of Bethlehem, guide us to Jesus—in his word, in his Eucharist, in the silence of prayer, and in our brothers and sisters. Holy Mary, Star of Evangelization, help us to fulfill our mission as followers of your Son. Bless the efforts of all who proclaim the Good News.

(Say the Hail Mary three times)

PRAYER FOR DAY EIGHT

O Mother of the Redeemer, imbue us with the golden light of your presence as a created yet immaculate person. Give me the grace, through your Son, to live my life with optimism, and to persevere through the living and the dying that goes on each day. Help me to understand more of the mystery of our salvation that passes through the pain of the cross to reach the triumph of the Resurrection.

(Say the Hail Mary three times)

PRAYER FOR DAY NINE

Our Lady of Perpetual Help, watch over us with love and protect us perpetually, whatever our situation may be, whatever our detours, our absences, our sins, and our returns. Since you are forever at the side of your Son as our faithful intercessor, grant us your help and mediate for us God's inexhaustible reservoir of grace. Do this, despite the immensity of our faults. Grant us the favor of a response and enable us always to come to you in hopeful and persevering prayer.

(Say the Hail Mary three times)

CONCLUDING PRAYER

O Virgin of Perpetual Help, great sign of our hope, Holy Mother of the Redeemer, we invoke your name. Help your people who desire to be renewed. Give us joy as we walk toward the future in conscious and active solidarity with the poorest of our brothers and sisters, announcing to them in a new and courageous way, the Gospel of your Son, the beginning and end of all human relationships that aspire to live a true, just, and lasting peace. As does the Child Jesus, whom we admire as you hold him in your arms, so we also want to hold your hand. You have both the power and the goodness to help us in every need and circumstance of life. Come, then, and help us; be for us our refuge, our strength, and our hope. Amen.

3. Novena for the Assumption of Our Blessed Virgin Mary

FIRST DAY

Most holy Virgin, who in order to prepare yourself for a holy death, did live in continual desire of the beatific vision, take from us all vain desires for the frail things of earth.

Most holy Virgin, who in order to prepare yourself for a holy death did in life ever sigh to be united to your son Jesus, obtain for us fidelity to Jesus even unto death.

Most holy Virgin, who, in preparation for a holy death, did attain an unapproachable height of merit and of virtue, intercede for us that we may know that virtue and the grace of God alone will lead us to salvation.

Let us pray: We beseech you, O Lord, to pardon the shortcomings of your servants; that we who by our own works are not able to please you, may be saved by the intercession of the Mother of your Son, our Lord Jesus Christ.

SECOND DAY

Glorious Virgin, who for your consolation did merit to die in the blessed company of apostles and saints: obtain for us, that when we breathe forth our souls we may feel your presence and that of our holy patrons, assisting us always.

Glorious Virgin, who at the moment of your death was comforted by the sight of your dear son Jesus: pray for us, that at that moment we too may be comforted by receiving Jesus in the holy sacrament of healing.

Glorious Virgin, who did surrender your spirit into the arms of Jesus, assist us, that we also, in life and in death, may surrender our souls into the arms of Jesus, and that we may always desire that his most Holy Will be done.

Come then, let us magnify the glory of Mary, assisted at her death by her son Jesus and his apostles, and join in jubilee at her triumph, with the second choir of the heavenly host.

THIRD DAY

Mary, most happy Virgin, make it your care that in our hearts there will be lit up the living fire of his love.

Mary, most happy Virgin, whose love did teach us what our love of God ought to do; pray for us, that we may never abandon our God in life or death.

Mary, most happy Virgin, whose heart burned with the love of God, obtain for us at least a spark of that same fire and give us true sorrow for our sins.

FOURTH DAY

O Lady, most pure, who by reason of your virginal purity did merit the glory of being so bright and so majestic in your body after death, obtain for us the strength to detach ourselves from every spirit of impurity.

O Lady, most pure, who by reason of your rare virtue did from your dead body spread around the sweetness of Paradise, make it your care that we may edify our neighbor by our life, and never by our bad example become a stumbling block to others.

O Lady, most pure, in whose presence bodily infirmities were cured, intercede for us, that by your prayers all our spiritual ills may be healed.

FIFTH DAY

O Lady exalted, to whose risen body was given the gifts of brightness and subtlety, by reason of the bright example and humility of your life on earth, pray for us, that all contemptuous affectation may be taken from us so that our souls, being freed from all self-love, may be adorned with humility.

O Lady exalted, whose risen body was glorified by reason of your spiritual zeal and patience while on earth, obtain for us valiant courage to curb all our inclinations to sin.

SIXTH DAY

Great Queen, who was assumed so royally into the Kingdom of eternal peace, obtain for us that all earthly thoughts be taken away from us, and our hearts be fixed upon the contemplation of the unchangeable happiness of Heaven.

Great Queen, who was assumed to Heaven amid a company of the angels, obtain for us strength to overcome the wiles of all our enemies, that we may lend a listening ear to the counsels of that good angel who continually assists and governs us.

Great Queen, who was assumed to Heaven most gloriously, in the company of souls drawn by your merits out of Purgatory, free us from the slavery of sin, and make us worthy to praise you for all eternity.

SEVENTH DAY

Sovereign Queen of the universe, who for your incomparable merit was raised to such high glory in the heavens, in your pity, look upon our miseries, and rule us with the gentle sway of your protection.

Sovereign Queen of the universe, who is ever receiving worship and homage from all the heavenly host, accept, we pray you, these our invocations, offered with such reverence as befits your dignity and greatness.

Sovereign Queen of the universe, by that glory which you possess by reason of your high place in heaven, take us into the number of your servants, and obtain for us grace that with quick and ready will we may faithfully keep the precepts of God our Lord.

EIGHTH DAY

Queen unrivaled, who in heaven above enjoys the high glory of being crowned by your divine Son, help us to share your matchless virtues, and ask for us that, purified in heart, we may be made worthy to be crowned with you in paradise.

Queen unrivaled, in the full knowledge granted you of all things on earth, for your own glory's sake, obtain pardon for our past misdeeds, that we may never offend again by tongue, by thought, or by deed.

Queen unrivaled, whose desire it is to see all people pure and clean of heart, so they may be worthy of seeing God, obtain for us forgiveness of our sins, and help us, that all our looks, words, and deeds may please his heavenly majesty.

Let us then purify our hearts, in order that we may be worthy to give praise to Mary, and to the glory she possesses in that bright crown which adorns her royal brow, let us add humble tokens of our love and rejoicing.

NINTH DAY

Mary, our most powerful patroness, whose glory it is in heaven to be the advocate of all people, take us from the hands of the enemy and place us in the arms of our God and Creator.

Mary, our most powerful patroness, who in heaven is the advocate of all people and would wish that all be saved, make it your care that none of us succumb at the thought of our past relapses into sin.

Mary, our most powerful patroness, who to fulfill your office continually invoked by all people, obtain for us such true devotion that we may ever call upon you in life and, above all, at the moment of our death.

4. Novena to Our Lady of Lourdes

Mary, Mother of God, I firmly believe in the doctrine of Holy Mother Church concerning your Immaculate Conception: namely, that you were, in the first instant of your conception, by the singular grace and privilege of God, in view of the merits of Jesus Christ, the Savior of the human race, preserved immune from all stain of original sin.

Alone of all the children of Adam, you were gifted with the fullness of sanctifying grace that made you the object of a very special love on the part of God. How wonderful were the workings of divine power to make you a fitting dwelling for the Redeemer of the world! With no tendency to evil, but with a deep yearning for the highest virtue, you glorified God more than all his other creatures. At the very instant of your conception, your mind was filled with the light of God, and your will was entirely conformed to the divine Will. You were always intimately united with God.

I thank God with you for these wonderful blessings. Help me to imitate your holiness to some degree. Your holiness was not the result of the privilege of your Immaculate Conception and sanctifying grace alone, but followed from your gift of yourself to God and your constant cooperation with his graces. Help me to be generous with God by turning to good account the graces that he ever bestows on me, and by rising promptly when I fall, with renewed confidence in his mercy.

Ever Immaculate virgin, Mother of mercy, health of the sick, refuge of sinners, comfort of the afflicted, you know my wants, my troubles, my sufferings. Please cast upon me a look of mercy.

By appearing in the Grotto of Lourdes, you were pleased to make it a privileged sanctuary, from which you dispense your favors; and already many sufferers have obtained the cure of their infirmities, both spiritual and corporal. I come, therefore, with the most un-bounded confidence to implore your maternal intercession.

Obtain, O loving Mother, the granting of my requests. Through gratitude for your favors, I will endeavor to imitate your virtues that I may one day share your glory.

Through your loving compassion shown to thousands of pilgrims who come to your shrine at Lourdes, and through your special love for your devoted Bernadette, I ask for this grace if it be the will of God: *(Here mention your request).*

Our Lady of Lourdes, aid me through your prayer with your divine Son, to be a true child of yours, as Bernadette was, and to grow daily into your likeness.

CONCLUDING PRAYER TO SAINT BERNADETTE

Saint Bernadette, little shepherd of Lourdes, favored with eighteen apparitions of the Immaculate Virgin Mary and with the privilege of conversing with her, now that you are eternally enjoying the beauty of the Immaculate Mother of God, do not forsake me, your devoted client, who still resides in this valley of tears.

Intercede for me that I, too, may walk the simple paths of faith. Help me to imitate your example, at our heavenly Queen's request, by saying the rosary daily and by doing penance for sinners.

Teach me to imitate your wonderful devotedness to God and our Lady, the Immaculate Conception, so that, like you, I may be blessed with the grace of lasting faithfulness and enjoy the happiness in heaven of the eternal vision of God the Father, Son, and Holy Spirit. Amen.

CONCLUDING PRAYER

God of infinite mercy, we celebrate the feast of Mary, Our Lady of Lourdes, the sinless Mother of God. May her prayers help us to rise above our human weakness. We ask this through our Lord Jesus Christ, your son who lives forever. Amen.

5. Novena to Our Lady of the Miraculous Medal

OPENING PRAYER TO BE SAID EACH DAY

Come, O Holy Spirit, fill the hearts of your faithful, and kindle in them the fire of your divine love. Send forth your Spirit, and renew the face of the earth.

O God, you instructed the hearts of the faithful by the light of the Holy Spirit. Grant us in the same Spirit to be truly wise and ever to rejoice in his consolation, through Jesus Christ, our Lord. Amen.

O Mary, conceived without sin, pray for us who have recourse to you.

Lord Jesus Christ, you have been pleased to glorify by numberless miracles the Blessed Virgin Mary, immaculate from the first moment of her conception. Grant that all who devoutly implore her protection on earth may eternally enjoy your presence in heaven, who, with the Father and the Holy Spirit, live and reign, God, forever and ever. Amen.

Lord Jesus Christ, for the accomplishment of your works, you have chosen the weak things of the world, and for a better and more widely spread belief in the Immaculate Conception of your mother, you have wished that the Miraculous Medal be manifested to Saint Catherine Labouré. Grant, we beseech you, that filled with humility, we may glorify this mystery of the Immaculate Conception by word and work. Amen.

NOVENA PRAYER TO BE SAID EACH DAY

Immaculate Virgin Mary, mother of our Lord Jesus Christ and our mother, penetrated with the most lively confidence in your all-powerful and never-failing intercession, manifested so often through the Miraculous Medal, we your loving and trustful children implore you to obtain for us the graces and favors we ask during this novena, if they be beneficial to our immortal souls, and the souls for which we pray. *(Here mention your intention)*

You know, Mary, how often our souls have been the sanctuaries of your Son who hates sin. Obtain for us then an abiding hatred of evil and that purity of heart which will attach us to God alone so that our every thought, word, and deed may proclaim his greater glory.

Obtain for us also a spirit of prayer and self-denial that we may recover by penance what we have lost by sin and at length reach that blessed home where you are the Queen of Angels and of all people. Amen.

Virgin Mother of God, Mary Immaculate, we dedicate ourselves to you under the title of Our Lady of the Miraculous Medal. May this medal be a sure sign of your affection for us and a constant reminder of our duties toward you and your Son. Ever while wearing it, may we be blessed by your loving protection and preserved in grace.

Most powerful virgin, Mother of our Savior, keep us close to you every moment of our lives. Obtain for us, your children, the grace of a happy death; so that, in union with you, we may enjoy the blessing of heaven forever. Amen.

Mary, conceived without sin, pray for us who have recourse to you.

Devotions to Our Blessed Virgin Mary

D evotions or devotional prayers are forms of prayer—sometimes joined with readings, song, symbol, and ceremony—directed towards nourishing the worship needs of the faithful outside of the liturgy, but preparing them for it and trying to make it more effective in their everyday life. Devotional prayer is often called *paraliturgical* prayer.

There are three types of devotional prayer: first, prayer activities under the direct supervision of a local bishop; second, prayer forms used at gatherings of the faithful, usually with a priest or deacon; and finally, all the prayers and activities that an individual might use alone or within the private circle of family or friends. It is this last form of paraliturgical prayer which is of most interest to us here in the following section of this book.

Vatican II, in its document *Constitution on the Sacred Liturgy* (§13), calls for the renewal of popular devotions. Here are some guidelines that can help position devotional prayer, both ancient and recent, in a new light:

1. God the Father has created all things so that they can be given over to Christ, as their Savior and Lord. Genuine devotions should always demonstrate this essential relationship ("through Christ our Lord"), especially in prayers to the Blessed Virgin and saints.

2. Prayers and devotions are rightly offered to the Father, Son, and Holy Spirit. This Trinitarian aspect should be consciously included.

3. The Bible is the word of God, and as such, it should be used as the springboard and inspiration for the composition of prayers or additions to them.

4. Since prayer and devotional activity should be inspired by the liturgy and flow back to it, guidance and examples from good liturgy can be applied to all forms of prayer, being careful, of course, not to undermine the liturgy itself.

5. Devotions should bear a relationship to the community of the Church, since that is the vehicle for our salvation. Overly individualistic devotions should be disregarded in favor of those that give reference to the Mystical Body of Christ, the people and family of God, or the Church as an institution.

6. Preserve meaningful ancient practices but use them with the proper attitudes of praise and thanksgiving to God.

7. Harmonize prayers to Our Blessed Virgin with the liturgical year.

Private devotion to Our Lady has been extensive both through the centuries and all over the world. The *Dogmatic Constitution on the Church* has this to say about devotions to Our Lady: "The various forms of piety towards the Mother of God, which the Church has approved within the limits of sound and orthodox doctrine, according to the dispositions and understanding of the faithful" (§66).

1. The Rosary of Saint Dominic

This rosary is composed of fifteen decades, divided into three parts, each containing five decades. The first part consists of five joyful events in the life of Jesus and Mary, the second part recalls five sorrowful events, and the third part considers five glorious events.

We begin by making the Sign of the Cross.

Then we say the Apostles' Creed, one Our Father, three Hail Marys, and one Glory to the Father on the small chain. Then we recall the first mystery, say one Our Father, ten Hail Marys, and one Glory to the Father. This completes one decade. All the other decades are said in the same manner with a different mystery meditated upon during each decade. At the end of the rosary, the prayer Hail, Holy Queen may be recited.

The mysteries of the rosary are scenes from the lives of Jesus and Mary. By meditating on these sublime truths, we come to a better understanding of our faith: the Incarnation of the Lord, the Redemption, and the Christian life—present and future. The following are the mysteries of the rosary. The Scripture quotations listed in parentheses that follow each mystery can be used as a basis for meditating on that particular event. A suggested intention is given within the second set of parentheses.

THE JOYFUL MYSTERIES

1. The Annunciation (Luke 1:26–38) (For the love of humility)
2. The Visitation (Luke 1:39–56) (For charity toward one's neighbor)
3. The Birth of Christ (Luke 2:1–19) (For the spirit of poverty)
4. The Presentation (Luke 2:22–40) (For the virtue of obedience)
5. The Finding in the Temple (Luke 2:41–52) (For the virtue of piety)

THE SORROWFUL MYSTERIES

1. The Agony in the Garden (Luke 22:39–46) (For true contrition)
2. The Scourging at the Pillar (John 19:1–3) (For the virtue of purity)
3. The Crowning With Thorns (Matthew 27:27–31) (For moral courage)
4. The Carrying of the Cross (Matthew 27:32–34) (For the virtue of patience)
5. The Crucifixion (Matthew 27:35–37) (For final perseverance)

THE GLORIOUS MYSTERIES

1. The Resurrection (Mark 16:1–14) (For the virtue of faith)
2. The Ascension (Luke 24:50–53) (For the virtue of hope)
3. The Descent of the Holy Spirit (Acts 2:1–12) (For the love of God)
4. The Assumption of Mary Into Heaven (Judith 13:23–31) (For devotion to Mary)

5. The Coronation of the Blessed Virgin Mary (Revelations 12) (For eternal happiness)

2. Fifteen Promises of Mary to Those Who Recite the Rosary

These promises were given by Our Lady in an apparition to Saint Dominic and Alan de la Roche.

1. Whoever recites the rosary shall receive singular graces.
2. I promise special protection and graces to those who recite the rosary.
3. The rosary will destroy vice, decrease sin, and defeat heresies.
4. The rosary will cause virtue and good works to flourish; it will obtain for souls the abundant mercy of God; it will withdraw the hearts of people from the love of the world and its vanities, and will lift them to the desire of eternal things.
5. The souls of those who recite the rosary shall not perish.
6. Those who recite the rosary devoutly shall never be conquered by misfortune. God will not chastise them in his justices; they shall not perish by an unprovided death; if they be just, they shall remain in the grace of God and become worthy of eternal life.
7. Those who have a true devotion to the rosary shall not die without the sacraments of the Church.
8. Those who are faithful in the recitation of the rosary shall have, during their life and at their death, the light of God and the plenitude of his graces; at the moment of death, they shall participate in the merits of the saints in paradise.
9. I shall deliver from purgatory those who have been devoted to the rosary.
10. The faithful children of the rosary shall merit a high degree of glory in heaven.

11. You shall obtain all that you ask of me by the recitation of the rosary.

12. All those who propagate the holy rosary shall be aided by me in their necessities.

13. I have obtained from my divine Son that all the advocates of the rosary shall have for intercessors the entire celestial court during their life and at the hour of death.

14. All who recite the rosary are my children, and brothers and sisters of my only Son, Jesus Christ.

15. Devotion to my rosary is a sign of predestination.

3. Group or Family Rosary

The rosary can be fruitfully said by an assembly, either a family or a prayer group. In this case, the saying of the rosary may be preceded by a Scripture reading, an introductory prayer, and a hymn. Silence is often observed between the decades as an opportunity for further meditation. The rosary is concluded by spontaneous or a summarizing prayer. The meditations for each decade may be given by a different member of the group, as may the function of the prayer leader alternate among those present.

PRAYER BEFORE THE FAMILY ROSARY

Most Holy Trinity, Father, Son, and Holy Spirit, we, the members of this family, place ourselves under your protection. Through the mysteries of the rosary may we know your plan of salvation and learn how much you love us. May your kingdom come in our family so that we may one day share in your heavenly home hereafter. Amen.

PRAYER AFTER THE FAMILY ROSARY

Holy Mary, Mother of God, be a mother to each one in this home. As in Cana you watched over the needs of a married couple, watch now over the needs of this family. And as you stood by the cross of your

Son and saw him die, stand by each one of us, father, mother, children, and lead us at the hour of death to our true home in heaven. Amen.

4. The Franciscan Crown or the Rosary (Chaplet) of the Seven Joys

Devotion to the Seven Joys or Seven Delights of Mary was encouraged by the Franciscans as far back as the founding of that order in the thirteenth century. Saint Bernardine of Siena (d. 1444) and his followers promoted this devotion as the Chaplet of the Seventy-two Hail Marys.

This devotion is often used as a seven-decade rosary in which each joy is meditated on during the recitation of each decade of Hail Marys. At the end of the rosary, two Hail Marys are added in order to commemorate the traditional seventy-two years of Mary's life. These are followed by the Our Father, the Hail Mary, and a Glory to the Father. One form of the Seven Joys of Our Lady is as follows:

1. The Annunciation by the Angel Gabriel
2. Mary's visit to her cousin Elizabeth
3. The birth of Christ
4. The adoration of the Magi
5. Finding Jesus in the Temple
6. The Resurrection of Christ
7. The Assumption of Mary into heaven

5. The Rosary (Chaplet) of the Seven Sorrows of the Blessed Virgin Mary

Devotion to the Seven Sorrows of Mary probably originated under the influence of the Dominican Order and Blessed Henry Suso (d. 1366) in the fourteenth century. It spread throughout the Church and seemed to have reached its present form in 1482 under the influence of a parish priest of Flanders, John de Coudenberghe. The Seven Sorrows of Mary are as follows:

1. The prophecy of Simeon (Lk 2:34–35)
2. The flight into Egypt (Mt 2:13–21)
3. The loss of the boy Jesus for three days (Lk 2:41–50)
4. The way of the Cross (Jn 19:17)
5. The crucifixion and death of Christ (Jn 19:18–30)
6. Jesus taken down from the Cross (Jn 19:38)
7. Jesus laid in the tomb (Jn 19:42)

The Seven Sorrows of Mary can be prayed as a seven-decade rosary during which each of Mary's sorrows is meditated on as the ten Hail Marys of each decade are prayed. This rosary is preceded by an act of contrition asking for true sorrow for sins. Each set of Hail Marys is interspersed with an Our Father, an additional Hail Mary, and a Glory to the Father. It is concluded by three additional Hail Marys in memory of the tears of Our Blessed Virgin and by this closing prayer:

O Mother, pray that my love may rest with you and your Son, Our Savior, who shed his blood for my salvation. May the memory of your sorrows abide in my own soul, that my heart may burn with love for you and your Son. To him be honor, glory, and thanksgiving forever and ever. Amen.

FOUR GRACES GIVEN TO THOSE WHO ARE DEVOTED TO OUR LADY OF SORROWS

According to Saint Alphonsus Liguori, the following four special graces were revealed by Christ to Saint Elizabeth of Hungry and are granted to those devoted to the Seven Sorrows:

1. Those who before death invoke the Blessed Mother under the name of her Seven Sorrows will obtain true repentance for all of their sins.
2. Christ will protect all those devoted to Our Lady of Sorrows in all their trials and especially at the hour of death.
3. Christ will impress on the minds of all those devoted to Our Lady of Sorrows the memory of his passion.
4. Christ will commit those devoted to Our Lady of Sorrows into the hands of Mary, so that she might obtain for them all the graces she wishes to lavish on them.

6. The Rosary (Chaplet) of Saint Bridget

This rosary is said in honor of the sixty-three years which, according to tradition, the most holy Mary lived on earth. It is composed of six divisions or parts; each division consists of saying the Our Father once, the Hail Mary ten times, and the Apostles' Creed once. This sequence is repeated six times, and the prayer concludes with one additional Our Father and three additional Hail Marys. Thus the Our Father is said seven times to commemorate the Seven Sorrows and the Seven Joys of Our Lady, and the Hail Mary is said sixty-three times to honor the number of years the Blessed Virgin Mary purportedly spent on earth.

7. The Biblical Rosary

This rosary is made up of fifty descriptors of the Blessed Virgin taken from biblical passages. Begin the rosary in its usual way with the Apostles' Creed, the Our Father, three Hail Marys, and the Glory to the Father. Meditate on each one of the following biblical passages and then say the Hail Mary. Conclude the rosary in the usual way, with the Glory to the Father, the Fátima prayer, and the Hail, Holy Queen.

Greeted by the angel Gabriel: Lk 1:28

Full of grace: Lk 1:28

Mother of Jesus: Lk 1:31

Mother of the Son of the Most High: Lk 1:32

Mother of the Son of David: Lk 1:32

Mother of the King of Israel: Lk 1:33

Mother by act of the Holy Spirit: Lk 1:35, Mt 1:20

Handmaid of the Lord: Lk 1:38

Virgin, Mother of Emmanuel: Mt 1:23

You in whom the Word became flesh: Jn 1:14

You in whom the Word dwelt among us: Jn 1:14

Blessed among all women: Lk 1:41

Mother of the Lord: Lk 1:43

Happy are you who have believed in the words uttered
    by the Lord: Lk 1:43

Lowly handmaid of the Lord: Lk 1:48

Called blessed by all generations: Lk 1:48

You in whom the Almighty worked wonders: Lk 1:48

Heiress of the promises made to Abraham: Lk 1:55

Mother of the new Isaac: Lk 1:37, Gn 18:14

You who gave birth to your firstborn at Bethlehem: Lk 2:7

You who wrapped your Child in swaddling clothes and laid Him
    in a manger: Lk 2:7

Woman from whom Jesus was born: Gal 4:4, Mt 1:16, 21

Mother of the Savior: Lk 2:11, Mt 1:21

Mother of the Messiah: Lk 2:11, Mt 1:16

You who were found by the shepherds with Joseph and the
    newborn Christ Child: Lk 2:16

You who kept and meditated all things in your heart: Lk 2:19

You who offered Jesus in the Temple: Lk 2:22

You who put Jesus into the arms of Simeon: Lk 2:28

You who marveled at what was said of Jesus: Lk 2:33

You whose soul a sword should pierce: Lk 2:35

Mother who was found together with the Child by the Wise Men:
  Mt 2:11

Mother whom Joseph took into refuge in Egypt: Mt 2:14

You who took the child Jesus to Jerusalem for the Passover:
  Lk 2:42

You who searched for Jesus for three days: Lk 2:46

You who found Jesus again in His Father's house: Lk 2:46–49

Mother whom Jesus obeyed at Nazareth: Lk 2:51

Model of widows: Mk 6:3

Jesus' companion at the marriage feast at Cana: Jn 2:1–2

You who gave rise to Jesus' first miracle: Jn 2:11

Mother of Jesus for having done the will of the Father in
  heaven: Mt 12:50

Mary who chose the better part: Lk 10:42

Blessed for having heard the word of God and kept it: Lk 11:28

Mother standing at the foot of the cross: Jn 19:25

Mother of the disciple whom Jesus loved: Jn 19:26–27

Queen of the Apostles, persevering in prayer with them: Acts 1:14

Woman clothes with the sun: Rev 12:1

Woman crowned with twelve stars: Rev 12:1

Sorrowful Mother of the Church: Rev 12:2

Glorious Mother of the Messiah: Rev 12:5

Image of the New Jerusalem: Rev 21:2

8. The Angelus

The Angelus evolved into its present form around 1270 and was based on a Franciscan devotion. Traditionally, the Angelus is recited three times each day—in the morning, at noon, and in the evening. It consists of a series of invocations and responses based on Scripture verses, each followed by three Hail Marys, and concluding with a prayer. It takes its name from the Latin word for "angel," which is the first word of the beginning invocation.

V. The angel of the Lord declared unto Mary.
R. And she conceived by the Holy Spirit.
   (Three Hail Marys)

V. Behold the handmaid of the Lord.
R. Let it be done to me according to your word.
   (Three Hail Marys)

V. And the Word was made flesh.
R. And dwelt among us.
   (Three Hail Marys)

V. Pray for us, O Holy Mother of God,
R. That we may be made worthy of the promises of Christ

Pour forth, we beseech you, O Lord, your grace into our hearts: that we, to whom the Incarnation of Christ your Son was made known by the message of an Angel, may by his passion and cross be brought to the glory of his Resurrection. Through the same Christ Our Lord. Amen.

9. The Scapular

The scapular has its origins in a medieval cloak or apron worn by monks and nuns as part of their religious garb. Gradually, laypeople became affiliated with various religious orders and adopted aspects of their religious practice. The long piece of cloth which hung down in front and back with a hole in the center for the head—the scapular—became an outward sign of this affiliation on the part of lay-people. In time, a stylized scapular—two small decorated squares of cloth connected by two pieces of ribbon or cord—came into use. There are eight Marian scapulars approved by the Church:

1. The white Scapular of the Hearts of Jesus and Mary
2. The blue Scapular of the Immaculate Conception
3. The white Scapular of the Immaculate Heart of Mary
4. The white Scapular of Our Lady of Good Counsel
5. The white Scapular of Our Lady of Ransom
6. The black Scapular of our Lady of Sorrows
7. The green "Scapular" of Our Lady
8. The brown Scapular of Our Lady of Mount Carmel

The last named, the brown scapular, is perhaps the oldest and most widely practiced of the scapular devotions to Our Lady. It is often ornamented with pictures and originated in a vision of Our Blessed Virgin to Saint Simon Stock, an English Carmelite. In this vision, Our Lady showed him a large scapular and gave it to him as a sign of great blessings for his order of Carmelites. She promised that whoever died wearing it would not suffer everlasting punishment and would quickly be released from purgatory. This grace is known as the Sabbatine Privilege. The scapular, in its cloth or medal form, may be worn by anyone as a visible sign of commitment to Marylike service and a desire of protection from Our Lady.

PRAYER TO OUR LADY OF MOUNT CARMEL

O almighty and eternal God, you willed that your only-begotten Son should be clothed in our mortal nature of the Virgin Mary. I have put on the new person in Baptism, and wish to add the scapular of Our Lady of Mount Carmel as an outward sign of my dedication to Jesus through his Mother. She will surely lead me to him. With the prayers of the Carmelite Order to assist me as I wear this scapular, may I do good, grow in the love of Jesus and Mary, and attain the reward of a blessed eternity with you forever and ever. Amen.

10. Consecration to Mary

The use of a prayer or act of consecration of the self to God through Christ or the Blessed Virgin is a re-avowal of one's baptismal vows. Besides ordinary consecration which is only a commitment to what a person is already obliged as a good Christian, some people also make an act of total consecration. This involves an intention to make an all-embracing dedication of his or her spiritual life around the Blessed Virgin in order to imitate her life which was totally dedicated to Christ. Odilo of Cluny (d. 1049) originated such an idea and it was perfected by Saint Louis Marie Grignion de Montfort (d. 1716).

CONSECRATION TO OUR LADY BY
LOUIS MARIE GRIGNION DE MONTFORT

Eternal and incarnate Wisdom, true God and true man, only Son of the Eternal Father and of Mary ever Virgin, I adore you in the splendor of your Father through all eternity.

I return to you thanks that you did sacrifice yourself to rescue me from the cruel slavery of the devil. I praise and glorify you. I dare no longer approach you alone. Therefore, I have recourse to the intercession of your most holy Mother, whom you have given me to be my intercessor. It is by this means that I hope to obtain from you the grace of contrition, the pardon of my sins, and the gift of abiding wisdom.

I salute you, then, Mary Immaculate, Queen of heaven and of earth. I salute you, secure refuge of sinners, whose mercy fails no one; graciously receive the vows which I make to you.

I, *N*, a faithless sinner, renew and ratify this day at your hands my baptismal vows. I renounce forever Satan, his works and pomps, and I give myself wholly to Jesus Christ, the incarnate Wisdom, to carry my cross after him all the days of my life, and, in order that I may be more faithful to him than I have been in the past, I choose you this day, O Mary, for my Mother and Mistress.

I deliver and consecrate to you, as a bond, my body and my soul, my possessions interior and exterior, and even the value of all my good actions, past, present and to come, leaving you the entire and full right to dispose of me and of all that belongs to me without exception, according to your good pleasure, to the greater glory of God, for time and eternity.

Receive, O loving Virgin, this offering which I make to you. O Mother most admirable, present me to your Son so that, having redeemed me through you, he may receive me from you. O Mother of mercy, obtain for me from God the gift of true wisdom, and also, the grace to place myself among the number of those who love you, and whom you cherish and protect as your children. O faithful Virgin, make me a perfect disciple in all things, imitator of your Son, so that by your intercession I may come share your glory in heaven. Amen.

CONSECRATION OF SAINT MAXIMILIAN KOLBE TO OUR LADY

O Immaculata, Queen of heaven and earth, refuge of sinners and our most loving Mother, God has willed to entrust the entire order of mercy to you.

I, *N*, a repentant sinner, case myself at your feet humbly imploring you to take me with all that I am and have, wholly to yourself as your possession and property.

Please make of me, of all my powers of soul and body, of my whole life, death, and eternity, whatever most pleases you. If it pleases you, use all that I am and have without reserve, wholly to accomplish what was said of you: "She will crush your head" and "You alone have destroyed all heresies in the whole world."

Let me be a fit instrument in your immaculate and merciful hands for introducing and increasing your glory to the maximum in all the many strayed and indifferent souls, and thus help extend as far as possible the blessed kingdom of the most Sacred Heart of Jesus. For wherever you enter you obtain the grace of conversion and growth in holiness, since it is through your hands that all graces come to us from the most Sacred Heart of Jesus.

Allow me to praise you, O sacred Virgin. Give me strength against your enemies. Amen.

11. The Little Office of the Compassion of Our Lady

This is a shorter office of Our Lady said in the thirteenth century by which laypeople participated in the Church's cycle of daily prayer. This version is from a prayer-roll and was written in Anglo-Norman verse. This translation will give a brief method of observing the daily prayer of the hours.

O Lord Jesus, who at the early hour of the morning, just after midnight (matins) did willingly suffer blows on the face and permitted yourself to be mocked, spit upon, and buffeted, and at the same hour did raise yourself from the dead, grant me pardon of my sins and patience in tribulation.

(Say five Our Fathers and five Hail Marys)

Lord Jesus Christ, who at the first hour of the morning (Prime) was through envy charged by the Jews before Pilate with a treacherous crime, and at the same hour did show yourself to Mary Magdalene, who loved you much; show me, Lord, your face, and give me the grace to do well.

(Say five Our Fathers and five Hail Marys)

Lord Jesus, I cry to you for mercy, who at the third hour of the morning (Terce) was reviled by your persecutors,'tied to a pillar, and your body scourged; and at the same hour you enlightened your apostles with the Holy Spirit; enlighten my heart with your love, that I may serve you day and night.

(Say five Our Fathers and five Hail Marys)

Lord Jesus, who at the hour of noon (Sext) was fastened to the cross with nails, amid sinners and wicked persons, and at the same hour did take the flesh of a true Virgin, the holy Mary; for that Annunciation give me pardon of my sins.

(Say five Our Fathers and five Hail Marys)

Lord Jesus, who at three o'clock in the afternoon (None) did pray for us and deliver up your soul to your Father, who is always in every place as it so pleases him; and at that some hour you ascended into heaven and confirmed our faith; bring me to heaven, that I may there enjoy you.

(Say five Our Fathers and five Hail Marys)

Lord Jesus, who at evensong (Vespers) was with love and reverence taken down from the cross by Joseph of Arimathea, and at the same hour did give your flesh in the sacrament of your holy supper; for that holy sacrament deliver me from the encumbrances of sin.

(Say five Our Fathers and five Hail Marys)

Lord Jesus, who at the hour of nine o'clock in the evening (Compline) did, when you prayed, sweat drops of blood, and did waken your disciples and tell them of the treason of Judas who betrayed you for thirty pieces of silver; and at that same hour was devoutly laid in the tomb; for the holy sepulcher, defend me from purgatory.

(Say five Our Fathers and five Hail Marys)

12. Prayer Sequence Commemorating the Privileges of Our Lady

In the name of the Father, and of the Son, and of the Holy Spirit. Amen.

O God, come to my assistance.

O Lord, make haste to help me.

Glory to the Father, and to the Son, and to the Holy Spirit. Amen.

Hail to you, purest, holiest Mother of Jesus. We humbly pray you, by your predestination, whereby you were even from all eternity elected mother of God; by your Immaculate Conception, whereby you were conceived without stain of original sin; by your most perfect resignation, whereby you were ever conformed to the will of God; and, lastly, by your consummate holiness, whereby throughout your whole life you never committed one single fault: we pray you to become our advocate with our Lord, that He may pardon our many sins, which are the cause of his wrath. And you, O Father Almighty, by the merits of these privileges vouchsafed to this your well-beloved Daughter, hear her supplications for us and pardon us, her clients.

Spare, O Lord, spare your people.

(Say one Our Father, one Hail Mary and one Glory to the Father)

By your holy and Immaculate Conception deliver us, glorious Virgin Mary.

Hail to you, purest, holiest Mother of Jesus. We humbly pray you, by the most holy Annunciation, when you conceived the Divine Word in your womb; by your most happy delivery, in which you experienced no pain; by your perpetual virginity, which you did unite with the fruitfulness of a mother; and, lastly, by the bitter martyrdom which you underwent Savior's death: we pray you become our mediatrix, that we may reap the fruit of the Precious Blood of your Son. And you,

185

O Divine Son, by the merit of these privileges granted to your well-beloved Mother, hear her supplications, and pardon us, her clients.

Spare, O Lord, spare your people.
   (*Say one Our Father, one Hail Mary and one Glory to the Father*)
   By your holy and Immaculate Conception deliver us, glorious Virgin Mary.

Hail to you, purest; holiest Mother of Jesus. We humbly pray you, by the joys which you felt in your heart at the Resurrection and Ascension of Jesus Christ; by your Assumption into heaven, whereby you were exalted above all the Choirs of the Angels; by the glory which God has given you to be Queen of all Saints; and, lastly, by that most powerful intercession, whereby you are able to obtain all that you desire: we pray you, obtain for us true love of God. And you, O Holy Spirit, by the merits of these privileges of your well-beloved Spouse, hear her supplications, and pardon us, her clients. Amen.

Spare, O Lord, spare your people.
   (*Say one Our Father, one Hail Mary and one Glory to the Father*)
   By your holy and Immaculate Conception deliver us, O glorious Virgin Mary.

Antiphon: Your conception, Virgin Mother of God, brought joy to the whole world, for of you was born the Sun of Justice, Christ our God, who, loosing the curse, bestowed the blessing, and, confounding death, gave unto us eternal life.

V. In your Conception, Virgin Mary, you were Immaculate.
R. Pray to the Father for us, whose Son Jesus, conceived by the Holy Spirit, you brought forth. Let us pray.

God of mercy, God of pity, God of tenderness, who, pitying the affliction of your people, said to the angel smiting them, "Withhold your hand"; for the love of your glorious Mother, at whose precious breast you found an antidote to the venom of our sins, bestow on us the help of your grace, that we may be freed from all evil, and mercifully protected from every onset of destruction. Who lives and reigns forever and ever. Amen.

13. Prayer Sequence in Honor of the Sorrowful Heart of Mary

V. O God, come to my assistance.

R. O Lord, make haste to help me.

Glory be to the Father, the Son, and the Holy Spirit. Amen.

I share your sorrow, O Mary, in the affliction of your tender heart at the prophecy of the holy man Simeon. Dear Mother, by your heart then so afflicted, obtain for me the virtue of humility and the gift of holy fear of God. Ave Maria.

(Say one Hail Mary)

I share your sorrow, O Mary, in the anxiety which your sensitive heart underwent in the flight and sojourn in Egypt. Dear Mother, by your heart then made so anxious, obtain for me the virtue of generosity, especially toward the poor, and the gift of pity.

(Say one Hail Mary)

I share your sorrow, O Mary, in the trouble of your anxious heart, when you lost your dear son Jesus. Dear Mother, by your heart then so troubled, obtain for me the virtue of holy chastity and the gift of knowledge.

(Say one Hail Mary)

I share your sorrow, O Mary, in the shock your maternal heart underwent when Jesus met you carrying his cross. Dear Mother, by your loving heart then so overwhelmed, obtain for me the virtue of patience and the gift of fortitude.

(Say one Hail Mary)

I share your sorrow, O Mary, in the martyrdom your generous heart bore so nobly while you stood by Jesus in his agony. Dear Mother, by your heart then so martyred, obtain for me the virtue of temperance and the gift of counsel.

(Say one Hail Mary)

I share your sorrow, O Mary, in the wound of your tender heart when the sacred side of Jesus was pierced with the lance. Dear Mother, by your heart then so transfixed, obtain for me the virtue of love and the gift of understanding.

(Say one Hail Mary)

I share your sorrow, O Mary, in the pang felt by your loving heart when the Body of Jesus was buried in the grave. Dear Mother, by all the bitterness of desolation you then experienced, obtain for me the virtue of diligence and the gift of wisdom.

(Say one Hail Mary)

V. Pray for us, Virgin most sorrowful.
R. That we may be made worthy of the promises of Christ.

14. Saint Alphonsus Liguori's Prayers to Mary for Each Day of the Week

PRAYER FOR SUNDAY

Mother of my God, look down upon a poor sinner, who has recourse to you. I am not worthy that you should even cast your eyes on me; but I know that you, beholding Jesus your Son dying for sinners, yearns exceedingly to save them. O Mother of Mercy, look on my miseries and have pity upon me. You are the refuge of the sinner, the hope of the desperate, the aid of the lost; be, then, my refuge, hope, and aid. It is your prayers which must save me. For the love of Jesus Christ reach forth your hand to poor fallen sinners who commend themselves to you. By my sins I have forfeited the grace of God and my own soul. I place myself in your hands; tell me what to do that I may regain the grace of God, and I will do it. My Savior bids me to go to you for help; so that, not only the merits of your Son, but your own prayers, may unite to save me. Make me experience what great good you can do for one who trusts in you. Be it done unto me according to my hope. Amen.

(Say the Hail Mary three times)

PRAYER FOR MONDAY

Most holy Mary, Queen of Heaven, I who was once a slave to evil now dedicate myself to your service forever. Accept me as your servant, and do not cast me away as I deserve. In you, O my Mother, I place all my hope. All thanksgivings be to God, who in his mercy gives me this trust in you. True, in the past, I have fallen miserably into sin; but by the merits of Jesus Christ, and by your prayers, I hope that God has pardoned me. But this is not enough, my Mother. One thought appalls me: that I may yet lose the grace of God. Danger is ever close; fresh temptations assail me. Protect me, then, my Queen; help me against the assaults of my spiritual enemy. Never suffer me to sin again. Let me not by sin lose my soul, heaven, and my God. This one grace, Mary, I ask of you. Such is my hope. Amen.

(Say the Hail Mary three times)

PRAYER FOR TUESDAY

Most holy Mary, Mother of Goodness, Mother of Mercy, when I reflect upon my sins and upon the moment of my death, I am confounded. O my Mother, in the Blood of Jesus, and in your intercession, are my hopes. Comforter of the sad, abandon me not. Fail not to console me in that affliction. Even now I am tormented by remorse for the sins I have committed, the uncertainty of my pardon, the danger of a relapse, and the strictness of the Final Judgment. O my Mother, before death overtakes me, obtain for me great sorrow for my sins, a true amendment, and constant fidelity to God for the remainder of my life. And when at length my hour arrives, then Mary, my hope, be my aid in those great troubles which will encompass my soul. Strengthen me, that I may not despair when the enemy sets my sins before my face. Obtain for me at that moment grace to invoke you often. This is my hope and my desire. Amen.

(Say the Hail Mary three times)

PRAYER FOR WEDNESDAY

Mother of God, most holy Mary, how often by my sins have I merited hell! How often should I have fallen in the dangers which beset my steps had you not preserved me by your graces and prayers. But what will your pity and favors avail, if after all I perish in the flames of hell? Wherefore, suffer me not to turn my back upon you and upon my God, who through you has granted me so many mercies. Surely you will never desire to see any servant lost who loves you. Yet lost I will assuredly be if I abandon you. But who could ever have the heart to leave you? Who can ever forget your love?

Only leave me not, my Mother, in my own hands, or I am lost! Let me but cling to you. Save me, my hope! save me from hell; or, rather, save me from sin, which alone can condemn me to hell. Amen.

(Say the Hail Mary three times)

PRAYER FOR THURSDAY

Queen of heaven, who sits enthroned above all the choirs of the angels closest to God, from this valley of miseries I, a poor sinner, say to you, "Hail, Mary," praying that you would turn your gracious eyes toward me. See, Mary, the dangers among which I dwell; I may yet lose my soul, paradise, and God. In you, Lady, is my hope. I love you; and I sigh after the time when I shall see and praise you in Paradise.

O Mary, how soon will the happy day come when I shall see my-self safe at your feet? When shall I grasp that hand, which has dis-pensed to me so many graces? Alas, it is too true, my Mother, that I have been ungrateful during my whole life; but if I get to Heaven, then I will love you there every moment of a whole eternity, and make reparation to you for my ingratitude. Thanks be to God, for he has promised the hope of your powerful intercession. This has been the hope of all your true lovers; and no one of them has been de-frauded of hope, and neither shall I be defrauded of mine.

O Mary, pray to your son Jesus, as I too pray to him, by the merits of his Passion, to strengthen and increase this hope. Amen.

(Say the Hail Mary three times)

PRAYER FOR FRIDAY

O Mary, you are the noblest, highest, purest, fairest creature of God; the holiest of all creatures! Yet great is my consolation, Mary, that there are blessed souls in the courts of heaven, and just souls still on earth, who love you as you deserve to be loved. But above all I re-joice in this, that our God himself loves you alone more than all people and angels together. I, too, O loveliest Queen, a miserable sinner, dare to love you, though my love is too little; would that I had a greater love, a more tender love. Moreover, O my Mother, when I reflect upon the debt I owe your Son, I see that he deserves of me an immeasurable love. Do you, then, who desires nothing more than to see him loved, pray that I may have this grace—a great love for Jesus Christ. Obtain this grace for me.

I do not covet goods of the earth, nor honors, nor riches, but I do desire that which your own heart desires most—to love my God alone. Will you not aid me in a desire so acceptable to you? Even now I feel your help. Pray for me, Mary, pray; nor ever cease to pray, till you see me safe in paradise, where I shall be certain of possessing and of loving my God and you, my dearest Mother. Amen.

(Say the Hail Mary three times)

PRAYER FOR SATURDAY

Most holy Mary, I know the graces which you have obtained for me, and I know the ingratitude which I have shown to you. Yet for all this I will not distrust your mercy. O my great Advocate, have pity on me, for you, Mary, are the stewardess of every grace which God chooses to give to me.

In your hands I place my eternal salvation; to you I consign my soul. I wish to be associated with those who are your special servants: reject me not. Speak for me, Mary for your Son grants what you ask. Take me beneath your shelter, for with you to guard me I fear no ill—no, not even my sins, because you will obtain God's pardon for them; no, nor evil spirits, because you are far mightier than hell; no, nor my judge Jesus Christ, for at your prayer he will lay aside his wrath. Protect me, then, my Mother; obtain for me pardon of my sins, love of Jesus, holy perseverance, a good death, and heaven. It is true that I do not merit these graces; yet you have only ask them of our God and I will obtain them. Pray, then, to Jesus for me. Mary, my Queen, in you I trust; in this trust I rest, I live; and in this trust I may I die. Amen.

(Say the Hail Mary three times)

15. Observance of the Five Consecutive First Saturdays

This observance was requested to be introduced to the Church by the Blessed Virgin during one of her appearances at Fátima in 1917. This devotion can be practiced individually or as a group. The observances requested by Our Lady of Fátima are practiced as follows:

1. Make a good confession and receive holy Communion on each of five consecutive first Saturdays of the month.
2. Recite five decades of the rosary, adding at the end the Fátima prayer taught to the children by Our Lady herself: O My Jesus, forgive us our sins, deliver us from the fires of hell, draw the souls of all to heaven, especially those in greatest need.
3. Keep Mary company for fifteen minutes while meditating of the fifteen mysteries of the rosary with the intention of making reparation for sins.
4. Conclude with a recitation of the following prayer:

Immaculate Heart of Mary, full of love of God and all people, I consecrate myself entirely to you. I entrust to you the salvation of my soul. With your help may I hate sin, love God and my neighbor, and reach eternal life together with those whom I love.

Mediatrix of Grace and Mother of Mercy, your divine Son has merited boundless treasures of grace by his sufferings, which he has confided to you for us, your children. Filled with confidence in your motherly heart, I come to your with my pressing needs. For the sake of the Sacred Heart of Jesus, obtain for me the favor I ask. (*Here mention your request*)

Dearest Mother, if what I ask for should not be according to God's will, pray that I may receive that which will be of greater benefit to my soul. May I experience the kindness of your motherly heart and the power of your intercession with Jesus during life and at the hour of my death.

V. Immaculate Heart of Mary
R. Pray for us, who have recourse to you.

Let us pray: O God of infinite goodness and mercy, fill our hearts with a great confidence in our Most Holy Mother, whom we invoke under the title of the Immaculate Heart of Mary, and grant us by her most powerful intercession all the graces, spiritual and temporal, which we need. Through Christ our Lord. Amen.

16. The Devotion of the Three Hail Marys

This devotion, also called "A Little Key to Heaven" consists simply of saying three Hail Marys each day, usually in the morning and at night, to obtain a happy death. This devotion arose from a vision to Saint Matilde of Hacehborn, Germany, of Our Lady, who said to her, "I have a little key that will open the door of heaven for you when you die. All you have to do is to say, in my honor, three Hail Marys, every day."

A Glossary of Important Terms Regarding the Blessed Virgin Mary

A

Ad Caeli Reginam (ahd chay-lee reh-gee-nam)   An encyclical issued by Pope Pius XII proclaiming the Queenship of Mary and establishing it as a feast.

Ad Diem Illum (ahd dee-em ill-uhm)   An encyclical issued by Pope Pius X setting out the theological foundation for Mary's role as mediatrix of grace.

Admirable Heart of Mary, The   The first full-length book on the Heart of Mary written by Saint John Eudes.

Admirable Secret of the Most Holy Rosary   An influential book by Saint Louis Marie Grignion de Montfort (d. 1716) in which he stressed the power of the rosary in daily life. He summarized its benefits as these: (1) It gradually gives us a perfect knowledge of Jesus Christ; (2) It purifies our souls, washing away sin; (3) It gives us victory over all enemies; (4) It makes it easy for us to practice virtue; (5) It sets us on fire with love of our Blessed Lord; (6) It enriches us with graces and merits; and (7) It supplies us with what is needed to pay all our debts to God.

Ágreda, Mary of (1602–1665)   A mystic and writer who joined the Poor Clares in Spain. Her mother and her sister entered the convent along with her; her father took up the Franciscan habit at the same time. Mary of Ágreda's most important work was the life of Our Lady as communicated to her in visions. Her work is entitled in English *The Mystical City of God and the Divine History of the Virgin Mother of God*. Though Mary of Ágreda's spiritual life was exemplary, opponents attacked her book and it was placed on the Index in 1681. After further examination, the *Mystical City of God* was approved in 1729, and in 1929 the Congregation of Rites permitted its reading.

Akathist hymn (ah-kah'-thist)   An ancient office or prayer in honor of Mary sung in Byzantine Rite churches, in part on the first four Saturdays of Lent and in its entirety on the fifth Saturday. It consists of twelve sections, each of which is followed by litanylike stanzas in praise of Mary, phrased in such words as "container of God's wisdom," "ship of salvation," "mirror of angelic life," and so on.

When the Akathistos (meaning "not sitting") is sung in churches in its entirety, the faithful remain standing and sit only during the interludes between the parts of the hymn. During other times of the year, the Akathistos is used for private devotions in a way similar to the rosary or the Litany of Our Lady.

Historically, the Akathist hymn is associated with the liberation of Constantinople from the Avars in 626 when the Patriarch Serge consecrated his city to Mary and made the Akathist hymn a song of thanksgiving.

Alan de la Roche (1428–1474)   Dominican preacher and promoter of the rosary. He founded the first confraternity of the rosary at Douai in 1470. His writings and their adaptations by others helped spread the prayer, including the legend of the origin of the rosary in Saint Dominic's life.

***Alma Redemptoris Mater* (al-mah' reh-demp'-tor-us mah'-ter)**   A Marian hymn sung at the conclusion of Evening Prayer in the Liturgy of the Hours from the first Sunday of Advent to the feast of the Purification. Its title is taken from the first line of the anthem and means "Loving Mother of the Redeemer."

The hymn was most probably composed by the tenth-century monk Hermann the Cripple who was so physically disabled as to be almost helpless. The antiphon is mentioned by the author of the *Ancren Riwle* who recommends it to the women hermits for whom he wrote and by Geoffrey Chaucer in one of his stories that form *The Canterbury Tales*.

Alphonsus Liguori, Saint (1696–1789)   Founder of the order known as the Redemptorists, Doctor of the Church, and author of *The Glories of Mary*, first published in 1750. The saint promoted devotion to Mary and treated Mary's role in theology in many of his spiritual writings.

Angelical Salutation   A little used name for the prayer we commonly know as the Hail Mary.

Angelico, Blessed Fra (1400–1455)   A Florentine painter of the Middle Ages whose radiant paintings of the Blessed Virgin reflect his prayerful devotion to Our Lady. Born Giovanni de Fiesole, he became a Dominican monk and though he was called to decorate the Vatican, his greatest works are frescoes that grace the monastery cells at San Marco in Florence. Fra Angelico's other works include the *Annunciation* (painted in 1434) and the *Descent from the Cross* (also painted in 1434).

Angelus   A prayer comprised of four short sentences that are said by the officiator and four responses interspersed with Hail Marys and concluding with a petition for God's grace through the Incarnation. Its name comes from the opening words in Latin of the first sentence: *Angelus Domini* ("Angel of the Lord").

In present times, this devotion is said morning, noon, and evening and accompanied by the tolling of bells. Following the custom of his predecessors, Pope John Paul II recites the *Angelus* every Sunday from the window of the Apostolic Palace and concludes this recitation with his blessing.

Historically, the *Angelus* is associated with peace as when Pope Callistus III ordered the daily ringing of bells at midday with the praying of three Hail Marys for the success of the Crusade.

Finally, Pope Benedict XIV stipulated that the *Angelus* be replaced by a similar devotion, the *Regina Coeli*, throughout Eastertide. Further, Pope Paul VI permitted an alternative concluding prayer from the feast of the Annunciation to be used at the end of the Angelus.

Angelus bell   The bell rung to mark the time of the *Angelus*, usually around six A.M., noon, and six P.M. This ringing consists usually of nine peals in groups of three, sometimes followed by a series of even peals.

Anne and Joachim, Saints   Sacred Scriptures tell us nothing about the parents of Mary, not even their names. Many of the details of Mary's life come from the apocrypha, or the uncanonical writings, particularly of the second-century

In the *Protoevangelium of James*, the story is told of Joachim (whose name means "the Lord prepares"), a rich but childless man, who thus went off to the wilderness to fast and pray. At the same time as his wife Anne (whose name means "grace") sat praying beneath a laurel bush, an angel appeared to her and promised that she would conceive. When it came to pass that Mary was born, her mother promised her to God. The joint feast day of Saints Anne and Joachim is celebrated on July 26.

Annonciade (an-on'-cee-add)   An old-form French word for the Annunciation. It still is used by certain religious orders of women, notably the Annonciades of Bourges founded by Saint John of Valois in 1501 and the Sky-Blue Annonciades.

Annunciation   The announcement to Mary that she would be the mother of Jesus, the account of which is told in Luke 1:26–38. In this account the angel Gabriel sent by God appears to Mary, a young virgin who is betrothed to Joseph. Gabriel reveals the approaching birth of Jesus (whose name means "the Lord saves"), his status as the Son of God, and his destiny to rule without end. Mary is given the favor of God but is troubled as to how she will conceive. Gabriel responds by assuring Mary that the power of the Holy Spirit will overshadow her. Finally, Mary vows her complete submission to God's will: "Behold I am the handmaid of the Lord: let it be to me according to your word."

The Annunciation is one of the earliest of Mary's feasts, certainly celebrated in Palestine before A.D. 500. It is celebrated on March 25, nine months before the birth of Jesus. (*CCC* §484–486)

Annunciata, The   A painting of the Annunciation commissioned in 1252 for the house in Florence of the Friar Servants of Mary. The painter fell asleep at his easel and, according to tradition, he awoke to see the picture completed. Saint Aloysius Gonzaga made his vow of chastity before this image in 1579. The original small chapel of the Servites was rebuilt in the fifteenth century and decorated by Andrea del Sarto.

antiphons of Our Lady   Marian antiphons, or anthems, are short scriptural texts sung at the conclusion of the Evening Prayer in the Liturgy of the Hours and varied according to the season of the Church's liturgical year. The major antiphons of Our Lady are *Alma Redemptoris Mater* for the season of Advent until the feast of the Purification; the *Ave Regina Caelorum* from Purification until Holy Thursday; the *Regina Caeli* for Eastertide until Trinity; and the *Salve Regina* for the rest of the year. These solemn melodies are sung daily in some monasteries, notably by the Carthusians and the Carmelites. Other religious orders customarily sang these antiphons, especially the *Salve*, before the Blessed Virgin's statue every evening.

apocryphal writings and Mary   Early popular literature written in imitation of the books of the New Testament. These works are not accepted as part of the sacred writings of the Church and cannot be read during the liturgy. Whether the information contained in the apocryphal writings is true or false must be decided by study and critical examination. Our Blessed Virgin Mary plays a large part in the following apocryphal writings: the *Protoevangelium of James*, the *Gospel of Pseudo-Matthew,* the *Nativity of Mary*, and the *Passing of Mary*.

Apostolic Rosary   A colloquial term for rosary beads which have been blessed by the Holy Father and which are carried on one's person or kept in a suitable place at home as an object of devotion. More precisely, a reference is apostolic indulgences which are actually attached to any small object of devotion. This indulgence may be given by any priest who has been granted the necessary permission, and may be gained only by the performance of the good works prescribed by the pope at the beginning of his reign.

apparitions of the Blessed Virgin Mary   Visions or appearances of the Mother of God that occurred after her death. Most apparitions of the Blessed Virgin Mary are bodily visions wherein Mary miraculously becomes visible to the human eye. Since the fourth century, there has been a large number of reported appearings of Mary in different parts of the world. Among the most celebrated examples are the apparitions of the Miraculous Medal, Lourdes, Fátima, Guadalupe, La Salette, Banneaux, and Beauraing.

It is the duty of ecclesiastical authority to determine the authenticity of any apparitions. The Church is not so much concerned with the miraculous aspects of these supernatural visions as with the orthodoxy of the messages pointed out by Mary and the integrity of the devotions associated with the apparition. When an apparition is recognized as authentic, such recognition does not bind Catholics to believe in an appearance; rather it only means that the Church does not regard such belief as harmful to the faithful.

archaeology and Mary   The study of ancient peoples and their culture through the analysis of their remains, especially those that have been excavated. Archaeologists sometimes unearth sites that offer evidence that increases our knowledge of Mary and our devotion to her. For example, excavations at the site of the Church of the Annunciation have uncovered evidence of a much earlier and a much attended shrine to Mary on that very spot. Inscriptions uncovered from the second-century catacombs under St. Peter's Basilica portray Mary as a protector of the Christian dead and their mediator with Christ. An inscription from a Jewish burial site in Egypt affirms the tradition of Mary's perpetual virginity.

Assumption of Our Lady   The dogma of faith, infallibly defined by Pope Pius XII in 1950, that Mary, "Immaculate Mother of God ever Virgin, after finishing the course of her life on earth, was taken up in body and soul to heavenly glory." The Church's solemn definition of the Assumption requires the belief of the faithful. In these words, Pius XII leaves open the question of whether Mary died before being taken up, though opinions favor her death and burial, probably in Jerusalem. Many saints and scholars hold that, though buried, Mary's body did not decompose, but was assumed undecayed.

The dogma of the Assumption is distinct from that of Christ's Ascension: Christ rose into heaven through his own power; Mary is given the privilege of being taken up into heaven by means of God's divine power.

When the dogma was declared in 1950, there was no question of new Revelation. The Church teaches that this truth is contained in tradition from the very beginning, its foundation being sacred Scripture and witness of the faithful, especially by means of their devotions and their celebration of the liturgy. The Christians of the East celebrated the Memorial of Mary on August 15 as early as the fifth century; and this feast became known as the Dormition, or falling asleep, of Mary. The Church of Rome established the feast of the Dormition of Mary on August 15 in the seventh century, though its title was changed to Assumption by Pope Saint Adrian soon after.

Vatican II calls Mary's Assumption "...a sign of certain hope and comfort to the Pilgrim People of God." Once Mary is taken up into heaven, she is still united with Christ who became incarnated in her and, through this union, she extends her maternal love to all creatures whom God loves. (*CCC* §966)

Ave Maria   The Latin words that begin the Hail Mary and the name of Marian hymn popular in the first part of the twentieth century. This hymn was composed by Charles Gounod (1818–1893) and is based on a prelude by Johannes Sebastian Bach. Earlier Franz Schubert (1797–1828) also wrote music to which the words of the *Ave Maria* have been set.   See **Hail Mary.**

***Ave Maris Stella* ("Hail Star of the Sea")**   This hymn is widely used at Vespers on feasts of Our Lady. It was first found in a manuscript as early as the ninth century; its author is unknown, though it has been attributed to Saint Bernard. In this hymn, Mary is called "star of the sea," "Mother of God," "ever Virgin," and "gate of heaven."

B

Banneaux (bahn-oh)   Town in Belgium where Our Lady appeared to twelve-year-old Mariette Beco eight times between January and March 1933. The Bishop of Liège verified the apparitions in 1949. Many pilgrims, including the sick, come to pray to Our Lady of Banneaux.

beads   A set number of knots or beads on a string or chain used to keep count of prayers in those devotions that involve repeated recitation. The Middle English word *bede* originally meant "prayer," and so the phrase "saying one's beads" colloquially refers to saying the rosary. Rosary beads may be made of any solid durable material, such as wood, precious stones, or metal.

Birthday of Our Lady, Feast of the   Now observed on September 8, this is one of the three feasts of the liturgical cycle that commemorates a temporal birth—the others being that of John the Baptist and Jesus. The feast of Mary's birthday is thought to have originated in Jerusalem about the sixth century. It made its way to Rome in the seventh century when Pope Sergius I proclaimed its observance by a solemn procession leading to St. Mary Major from the Roman Forum.

Scripture does not give an account of the birth of Mary but an apocryphal *Nativity of Mary* holds that her birthplace is Jerusalem, in a house located near what is now St. Stephen's Gate.

Beaupré, Sainte Anne de   Shrine dedicated to Sainte Anne, the mother of Mary, located in Quebec City, Canada.

Bernadette of Lourdes, Saint   A young woman (1844–1879) of Lourdes, France, to whom Our Lady appeared beginning in February 1858. These visions made Lourdes a worldwide pilgrimage site for visitors in search of cures and information on Our Lady. In these apparitions, Our Lady declared herself to be the Immaculate Conception.

Beauraing (boh-rang)   Town in Belgium where five children claimed to have seen more than thirty apparitions of the Blessed Virgin during the period from November 1932 to January 1933. The Immaculate Heart of Mary figures prominently in the last six evenings that Mary appeared.

Bernard, Saint (1090–1153)   Often held to be the author of the *Memorare*, Saint Bernard is a Doctor of the Church whose writings on Mary are considered of immense influence. He wrote a collection of sermons entitled "In Praise of the Virgin Mother," and other homilies for the Purification, Annunciation, and Assumption, plus a sermon entitled the "Aqueduct" for the feast of Mary's birth. His distinctive language about Mary also is found in a number of his other writings.

Bethlehem Now a suburb of Jerusalem, Bethlehem is home to the shrine that holds the cave where Jesus Christ was born of Mary. It is under the eastern end of the church of the Nativity. The present basilica was originated by Emperor Constantine in the fourth century and restored by Justinian around A.D. 545.

Black Madonna or Virgin A statue or picture of Our Lady that is black either because of the way it was painted or because of age. The most famous of the Black Madonnas are Our Lady of Czestochowa in Poland, Our Lady of the Pillar at Chartres in France, Our Lady of Montserrat in Spain, and the black statue of Our Lady at Einsiedeln, in Switzerland.

Blue Army, The An association inspired by the apparitions of Our Lady at Fátima and founded in New Jersey in 1947 by the Rt. Rev. Monsignor Harold V. Colgan. Members of The Blue Army pledge themselves to carry out Our Lady's requests made at Fátima for the conversion of Russia and for world peace. They pledge to say the rosary daily and to practice self-denial.

Bridget of Sweden, Saint (1303–1375) A mystic and founder of a religious order, Saint Bridget is known for her *Revelations* which record her visions and spiritual experiences. Many of these revelations concern Mary's place in the divine plan. Saint Bridget also composed twenty-one readings covering the life of Mary and which were interspersed with theological comments. This work was intended for the Office of the members of her religious order.

Brigettine office A series of twenty-one readings covering the life of Mary with theology interwoven and intended to be used as the Office for the members of the religious order founded by Saint Bridget of Sweden.

Brigettine Rosary A chaplet, corona, or series of prayers, said by the Order of the Most Holy Savior, founded by Saint Bridget of Sweden. It has six decades, each consisting of the Our Father once, the Hail Mary ten times, the Apostles' Creed once, concluded by the Lord's Prayer once and the Hail Mary recited three times. Saint Bridget believed that Mary lived on earth for sixty-three years and thus the sixty-three Hail Marys of this chaplet represent the span of Our Lady's earthly life.

C

Cana, wedding feast at   The story in John's Gospel (2:1–12) in which Jesus intervenes and changes water into wine for the guests at the wedding feast. This is done, at the request of his mother, to save his host from an embarrassing situation. John's Gospel does not identify Mary by name but refers to her as "the mother of Jesus" or "woman."

Candlemas   One of the several names of a feast (celebrated on February 2) that commemorates the Purification of the Blessed Virgin. This feast has also been called the Meeting of the Infant Jesus and Simeon and the Presentation of the Lord, which it has been designated since the 1969 reform of the Church calendar. The colloquial name of Candlemas arose out of the lights and candles appearing as part of the celebration.

Casimir's Hymn, Saint   The name given to a hymn familiar in English as "Daily, daily, sing to Mary." Saint Casimir of Poland did not compose this hymn, but he recited it often and asked that a copy of it be buried with him.

Carmel, Mount, Our Lady of   A title of Our Lady that commemorates Mount Carmel in the Holy Land—the place of origin of the Carmelite order which saw Mary as its principal patroness. As the Order of Carmelites spread to Europe, they often named churches for the Annunciation, reflecting Mary's purity of heart and total dedication to God. As the Carmelites shaped their devotion to Mary around the Brown Scapular, a special feast arose to offer thanksgiving to Mary for the many graces given to the Order through her intercession. A special feast of the Solemn Commemoration of the Blessed Virgin of Mary of Mount Carmel was set for July 16 and rapidly spread through Europe. It was declared a feast of the universal Church in 1726. In the recent reform of the liturgical calendar, it is included as an optional memorial.

   This title of Mary also recalls that it was on Mount Carmel that the Old Testament prophet Elijah prayed seven times for rain to avert a long drought and then announced the sight of a little cloud rising from the sea. This little cloud of rain is seen as a symbol of Mary who brings us the saving waters of Christ's salvation.

Carmelites   A religious order founded by Crusaders who retired as hermits to Mount Carmel and who, from the very beginning, associated themselves with the Virgin Mary. About 1235, as the victories of the Saracens made religious life more difficult to live on Mt. Carmel, the hermits migrated to Europe where their rule was adapted to town life and they were officially called the Order of the Blessed Virgin Mary of Mt. Carmel (O. Carm.). A contemplative order of Carmelite nuns was founded in 1452 by John Soreth.

As the Middle Ages waned, a stricter and autonomous branch of the Carmelite Order was founded in 1562 by Saint Teresa of Ávila and Saint John of the Cross. Known as the Discalced Carmelites (O.C.D.), this order has as its aim the contemplative and apostolic life, missions among the unbaptized, and devotion of Our Lady of Mt. Carmel.

The vibrancy of the Carmelites in modern times is witnessed to by Thérèse of Lisieux (d. 1897), Elizabeth of the Trinity (d. 1906), and Edith Stein and Titus Brandsma, both killed in 1942 in Nazi concentration camps.

Today both orders have congregations of friars, nuns, as well as laity affiliated with them.

chaplet From the French word for a garland of flowers, a chaplet is any string of beads used to count off prayers. A five-decade rosary was thought of as a chaplet, while the complete rosary is made up of fifteen decades.

Christian Life Communities Small associations of laypersons who unite for prayer and personal piety, as well as for scripture study and ecumenism. Christian Life Communities were called Sodalities of Our Lady prior to 1971 when Pope Paul VI promulgated revised norms for these associations.

Children of Mary A name given to various pious unions founded to encourage a personal sanctity through devotion to the Blessed Virgin Mary. The most widespread sodality of the Children of Mary originated from the apparitions of Our Blessed Lady to Saint Catherine Labouré in 1830. After Vatican II, these sodalities adopted rules and practices in accordance with the Council and became part of a new designation known as "Christian Life Communities."

Claretians The official title of the Claretian Fathers is the Congregation of the Missionary Sons of the Immaculate Heart of the Blessed Virgin Mary. This congregation was founded in 1849 in Spain by Saint Anthony Mary Claret for purposes of preaching and catechizing. At their religious profession, members make a solemn promise to propagate the devotion to the Immaculate Heart of Mary.

colors of Mary The color traditionally associated with the Blessed Virgin Mary in modern times is blue, perhaps because Saint Bernadette states that Mary appeared to her at Lourdes wearing a blue sash. Blue is not used for liturgical vestments except in Spain and Spanish Latin America where its use is permitted. The color white (including gold and silver) is used for vestments for feasts of Our Blessed Virgin Mary. The custom of fixing colors for liturgical vestments is somewhat recent; in twelfth-century Jerusalem, Augustinian canons assigned black to Our Blessed Lady.

confraternity An association of the Christian faithful which strives to promote a more perfect life, which fosters some kind of public worship, or undertakes some kind of apostolic works. Such groups are now classed as "associations of Christian faithful" under the present Code of Canon Law. These associations are groups of persons who are not under vow—by contrast to religious orders and congregations, for example.

congress, Marian A series of over 150 meetings that have been held since 1895 for the purposes of deepening our devotion to and understanding of Mary. A Marian congress is similar to a Eucharistic congress in scope and intent.

consecration to Mary A sacred designation of a person to the service of God through his Blessed Mother. This word is associated with the consecration to the Blessed Virgin as outlined by Saint Louis Grignion de Montfort. The external practice indicating a consecration to Mary was the frequent saying of the *Magnificat*. The internal focus was the intent that all things should be done through Mary, with Mary, in Mary, and for Mary.

Saint Louis saw this dedication as a form of holy slavery. Thus in his form for consecration, the following prayer is said: "As your slave, I give up and consecrate to you my body and soul, all my goods, interior and exterior, and the worth of my good deeds, past, present, and to come. I give you full and complete right to dispose of me and of everything whatever that belongs to me according to your good pleasure, for the greatest glory of God, now and forever."

Pope John Paul II in his prayers of consecration of the world to Our Lady uses the word *entrustment* as a form of consecration.

coredemptrix A title which celebrates Mary's human part in the Redemption. Mary is seen to participate in the world's salvation in these ways: (1) She indirectly cooperated in the Redemption by knowingly and willingly giving birth to Jesus Christ; (2) She distributes to us the graces of Christ's Redemption which has already been accomplished; (3) She joins her sinless suffering to that of Christ's on the cross and thereby actively shares in the Savior's redeeming sacrifice on Calvary.

This title is not interpreted to mean that Mary is essential to Christ's act of Redemption, for Christ alone is our Redeemer and Mary is his willing cooperator.

Crosier Rosary Informal name for the rosary beads or chaplets blessed by the Crosier Fathers, resulting in an indulgence of five hundred days each time an Our Father or Hail Mary is said on beads so blessed.

Crown of Our Lady, Little A devotion to Our Lady consisting of praying the Lord's Prayer three times and the Hail Mary twelve times in honor the Blessed Virgin's twelve privileges, from her Immaculate Conception to her power of intercession. This devotion is recommended by Saint Louis Marie de Montfort in the *True Devotion to Our Blessed Virgin*.

Crown of the Seven Decades A devotion consisting of seventy-two Hail Marys which originated in the fifteenth century and was popularized by Saint Bernardine of Siena. At first the seventy-two Hail Marys recalled the traditional seventy-two years of Our Lady's life on earth; subsequently, this devotion evolved into the Rosary of the Seven Joys of Our Lady.

Crown of Twelve Stars A devotion derived from the idea of the twelve stars of the Apocalypse. Among the "stars" are the Immaculate Conception, Mary's birth, her marriage, the Incarnation, Christ's birth, his upbringing by Mary, his revelation to her of the mystery of the Redemption, Mary as virgin yet mother, Mary as the living temple of God.

Czestochowa, Our Lady of (ches-tah-koh'-vah) Icon in the Monastery of Jasna Gora which is seen as a symbol of Poland and its devotion to Mary. The icon was held originally by Russian princes until, in 1382, Duke Ladislas of Opole sent it from the Ukraine to Czestochowa and built a monastery of Pauline monks to care for the image. In 1665, Charles Gustave and his Swedish army met defeat at the heads of a small military force led by the Prior of Czestochowa's monastery. In gratitude, King Casimir proclaimed Our Lady "Queen of the Crown of Poland."

D

Daughter of Zion In the Old Testament the title Daughter of Zion is seen to represent Jerusalem, the suffering virgin Israel who awaits the coming of the Lord. The idea that Mary was the Daughter of Zion is suggested in the words Gabriel speaks to Mary and the texts in Revelation 12. The Vatican II document *Lumen Gentium* calls Mary the "exalted Daughter of Zion."

death of Mary Theologians dispute whether Mary died before being assumed into heaven or whether she was assumed into heaven, her body intact, and without having experienced a human death. In the Apostolic Constitution announcing the dogma of the Assumption, Pius XII says only that Mary "completed the course of her life"; he did not say that she had died.

decade A section of the rosary of Our Lady, made up of one Our Father, ten Hail Marys, and one Glory to the Father. These prayers are said while meditating on the mystery assigned to that decade.

Deipara (day-ee-pahr'-ah) A Latin translation of the Greek *Theotokos* or "God-bearer," the title given to Mary at the Council of Ephesus in 431 to attest that she is truly the Mother of God.

devotions, Marian In the celebration of the Eucharist, Mary is remembered along with the apostles, martyrs, and all the saints. As the liturgical year progresses, starting from the first Sunday of Advent, the Church also pays respect to Mary in a number of feasts, solemnities, and memorials.

In addition to her recollection in the eucharistic liturgy, Mary is remembered by acts of personal piety, such as prayers, the rosary, pilgrimages, icons, images such as the Miraculous Medal, and practices associated with special Marian titles. Whatever diversity the forms of devotion to Our Lady take, the Church makes it clear that honoring Mary should not overshadow the basic truths of the creed, Christ's preeminent place in salvation history, and should be based on the Scriptures. Though respectful of the "inclinations of the faithful," the Church still condemns excesses, for example, devotion to the Queen of the Sacred Heart or to Mary's Virgin Priesthood.

Doctors of the Church, Marian Of those holding the title of Doctor of the Church, many have dealt with Our Lady in their writings and sermons. Marian Doctors are persons whose devotion to Mary was a strong feature of their spirituality and writings. The Doctors of the universal Church most prominently associated with Mary are Saint Ephraem, Saint Ambrose, Saint Jerome, Saint Augustine, Saint Cyril of Alexandria, Saint John of Damascus, Saint Anselm, Saint Bernard, Saint Albert the Great, Saint Thomas, Saint Peter Canisius, Saint Lawrence of Brindisi, and Saint Alphonsus Liguori.

Dolors, Seven See Sorrows of Our Lady.

Dormition of Mary This is a feast still celebrated in the Oriental liturgies. Dormition figuratively refers to Mary's death and means "the falling asleep." This feast celebrates Mary's peaceful journey to God in heaven and implicitly reaffirms the doctrine of the Assumption. The death of Mary is not mentioned in the New Testament, but details about her death are contained in the apocryphal literature in which Mary's last hours are described in detail. See **death of Mary.**

Dowry, Our Lady's A title for England derived from an image of Saint Edmund, King of England, who is portrayed as lifting up his hands to Our Blessed Lady and asking her to "defend and preserve England, thy dowry, and hold it in all prosperity."

E

Einsiedeln, Our Lady of (in'-tseed-uhn) After the death of the hermit Saint Meinrad who built his cell at a spot just a few miles from the Swiss city of Zurich, a Madonna chapel was built over the place of his oratory. An ancient statue of the Madonna and Child, known as the Black Virgin, was enshrined in this chapel. This Abbey of Our Lady of the Hermits is a popular pilgrimage site.

Entreaty of the Mother of God A service of the Byzantine Rite which asks in part that Mary, the Mother of God, pour out her compassion. The rite also contains litanies, chants, a Gospel reading, as well as petitions to Mary, and is sung every evening on the fourteen days of fasting before the feast of the Assumption.

Ephesus An ancient city in Asia Minor near Smyrna where Saint John the Evangelist is thought to have died. Since Jesus had committed his mother to John as he was dying on the cross, the idea grew up that Mary, too, lived and possibly died in Ephesus.

Ephesus, Council of The third ecumenical council of the Church held in 431, which declared Mary the Mother of God.

Ephraem the Syrian, Saint (306–373) A Doctor of the Church who also wrote poetry. He insisted on Mary's sinlessness, upheld the parallel and contrast of Mary to Eve, strongly exalted Mary's total virginity, and was the first to call her the "Bride of Christ."

F

family rosary The devotion to Mary exemplified by the praying of the family rosary based on the belief that the "family that prays together, stays together." This crusade, organized by Irish-born priest Father Patrick Peyton, C.S.C., had wide impact during the middle of the twentieth century in the United States and in other countries.

Fátima Location of one of the most famous of modern shrines to Our Lady. In this town north of Lisbon, Portugal, the Blessed Virgin Mary appeared to three children a total of six times between April and November 1917. In these visions she revealed that she was the Lady of the Rosary, and she made an appeal for devotion to her Immaculate Heart, for increased prayer and penance, and for the consecration of Russia to her Immaculate Heart. She spoke of wars and persecutions and on October 13 the miracle which she had promised—the dance of the sun—occurred. In 1930, Pope Pius XI authorized devotion to the Lady of Fátima; in 1982, Pope John Paul II visited Fátima in thanksgiving for having survived an attempt on his life.

Fifteen Saturdays A devout practice encouraged originally in the seventeenth century by the Dominicans. It was popular in France, Belgium, and Italy. It consists of offering various acts of devotion to Our Lady on the fifteen Saturdays preceding the feast of the Holy Rosary. The practice was indulgenced by Pope Alexander (d. 1691), Pope Pius IX (d. 1878) and Pope Leo XIII (d. 1903) if the following conditions are met: reception of the sacrament of reconciliation within the week, holy Communion on each Saturday, and recitation of the five decades of the rosary.

First Saturdays devotion A devotion whose origins are in the seventeenth century and which consists of the setting aside of the first Saturday of each month as a day of reparation for all the acts of blasphemy committed against the Blessed Virgin Mary. A form of this devotion was promoted first in Italy and consisted of receiving holy Communion, receiving the sacrament of reconciliation, and performing some act of reparation in honor of Our Lady. Pope Pius X (d. 1914) decreed that all the faithful could receive a plenary indulgence for the souls in purgatory provided they accomplished the preceding conditions.

Five Psalms, The A devotion popularized by Blessed Jordan of Saxony (d. 1237) which consists of the saying of a canticle and four psalms whose first letters in Latin spell out the name of Mary (Maria), for example: *Magnificat* (Lk 1:46–55); *Ad Dominum cum tribularer* (Ps 119); *Retribue servo tuo* (Ps 119:17–176); *In convertendo* (Ps 125); and *Ad te levavi* (Ps 122).

flower names, Marian The association of flowers with Our Lady seems obvious. She is a "lily among thorns," the "mystical rose," and the "flower of flowers." Many wildflowers have been given common names in her honor: Lady's mantle, Lady fern, Lady's slipper, marigold, madonna lily, and so on. Some gardeners construct entire Mary gardens using only those flowers with names associated with hers.

Franciscan Crown Another name for the Seraphic Rosary, or the Rosary of the Seven Joys of Our Lady. Each decade highlights one of Mary's joys and begins with the Our Father followed by ten Hail Marys. Two Hail Marys are added after the seventh decade to make a total of seventy-two, a number that some traditions claim represents the years that Mary lived on earth.

This chaplet dates to the fifteenth century when a young Franciscan received a vision of the Blessed Virgin Mary who instructed him to say the Rosary of the Seven Joys, so that instead of weaving a crown of flowers for her image, he would weave a crown of prayers for her heart.

fullness of grace, Mary's A basic concept holding that Mary's dignity is above that of all created persons and angels by virtue of Mary's role as the Mother of God. Pope Pius IX declared in the encyclical *Ineffabilis Deus* that God gifted Mary with "more than all the angels and saints, with such an abundance of heavenly gifts that she was always wholly free from sin; so that, perfect and all-beautiful, she shone in such complete innocence and holiness that no greater holiness can be imagined except that of God himself."

G

Gabriel   Archangel whose name means "man of God." He was sent to announce the birth of Jesus to the Blessed Virgin.

Gabriel bell   In England of the Middle Ages, a special bell set aside to mark the Hail Marys said in the morning and the evening. Many bells in England were dedicated to Mary and were inscribed with sayings in her honor, such as "Hail Mary say, when you pass this way."

Gabriel of the Sorrowful Mother (Francesco Possenti) (1838–1862)   As a young man known for his vanity and love of dancing, Francesco twice promised to enter the priestly life if he were saved from a grave illness, and twice he failed to fulfill his promise. But after watching a religious procession, his vocation called once more and he joined the Passionists, taking the religious name Gabriel of Our Lady of Sorrows. Saint Gabriel was noted for his spirit of penance and his devotion to the Blessed Virgin Mary—the source of his spiritual life.

Garabandal   A mountain village in Spain where four young girls reported that the Blessed Virgin Mary appeared to them almost two-thousand times between 1961 and 1965. The authenticity of these apparitions has not been determined.

genealogy of Mary   No genealogy of Mary exists in the New Testament; however, it has always been taught that Mary was of the house of David based on the words spoken to her at the Annunciation: "The Lord God will give him the kingdom of David, his ancestor" (Lk 1:32). In the Middle Ages, Mary's descent from David was sometimes represented in a series of figures in a stained-glass window. This series of figures is called a Jesse Tree, since Mary's ancestry begins with Jesse the Bethlehemite, the father of David.

Girdle of Our Lady, Feast of the   An observance of the Byzantine Rite commemorating the enshrining of what was venerated as Mary's girdle or sash in a church at Constantinople. In the Byzantine rite, Our Lady's girdle or *Zona* was glorified by writers and poets.

Glorious Mysteries   See Mysteries of the Rosary.

Guard of Honor of the Immaculate Heart of Mary   An archconfraternity approved by the Holy See whose members cultivate devotion to the Blessed Virgin Mary, especially through a daily Guard of Honor of Prayer. This confraternity was established by a German Franciscan in 1932 at Saint Anne's monastery in Munich.

Glories of Mary, The   A work on Mary authored by Saint Alphonsus Liguori, published in 1750, and later distributed in over eight-hundred editions in many languages. *The Glories of Mary* was meant to revive devotion to the

Mother of God in an age when reason was more important than dependence on the divine. *Glories of Mary* is divided into two main parts, the first being a commentary on the *Salve Regina*, and the second containing discussions of various mysteries and feasts such as the Annunciation, the Sorrows of Mary, and so on. These texts are supported by quotations and examples from many different sources including Saint Thomas Aquinas, Saint Bernard, and Saint Bridget of Sweden.

Grace, Mother of   A title of Our Lady accorded to her because she is the Mother of Christ from whom all graces flow and because of Mary's own fullness of grace and her subsequent mediation of grace to the faithful. The feast of Mary, Mother of Grace, was first celebrated in Faenza, Italy, in the hope of checking an oncoming epidemic.

Guadalupe, Our Lady of   On December 9, 1521, ten years after the conquest of Mexico by the Spaniards, the Blessed Virgin appeared to Juan Diego, a native Indian, with instructions that a shrine be built to her on that very spot. When Juan Diego went to tell the bishop of this apparition, he requested a sign from Our Lady. The Blessed Virgin asked him to pick some roses at the place of the apparition, a desolate, rocky place. Juan Diego filled his cloak with roses, and as he unrolled it to show the bishop, the image of Mary had ben imprinted on the cloak. A small adobe chapel was erected at the site of the apparitions probably around 1531, and later a larger church was completed which has the rank of basilica.

Our Lady of Guadalupe became the patroness of New Spain by 1746. By 1946 she was declared the patroness of all of the Americas. The feast day of Our Lady of Guadalupe is celebrated on December 12 in all dioceses of the United States.

In January 1979, Pope John Paul II made a pilgrimage to Mexico to invoke the motherly protection on his pontificate on Our Lady of Guadalupe and repeat with her his motto: *"Totus tuus sum ego!"*

H

Hail, Holy Queen   See *Salve Regina*.

Hail Mary   A treasured prayer based on the angel's greeting to Mary at the Annunciation and on Elizabeth's greeting when Mary visited her. Though the Latin text of the Hail Mary was fixed by the fact that Pius V added it to the Roman breviary in 1568, an Egyptian potsherd found about A.D. 600— with a Greek inscription on it—was dated around A.D. 400 and had a version of the Hail Mary on it. Later it became evident that the Hail Mary needed some sort of words for completion. These words were presumably taken by lifting from another prayer. (*CCC* §2676)

Help of Christians, Our Lady   A feast in honor of this title of Mary was instituted by Pope Pius VII in 1815 for the Papal States in Italy as an act of thanksgiving for his liberation from captivity under Napoleon Bonaparte. Celebrated on May 24, the feast of Mary, Help of Christians was popularized by the Salesians after their founder, Saint John Bosco, chose it for the name of their mother-church. This feast is popular in Australia and New Zealand.

Don Bosco also revived an association or archconfraternity in honor of Our Lady Help of Christians whose members practice seven simple rules.

Holy Mary   The form of address that begins the second part of the Hail Mary.

Hodegetria   In English, "Guide of the Way," a name for a group of icons in which Mary is holding the Child Jesus in her left arm. Empress Pulcheria (d. 1453) of Constantinople is said to have acquired the first-known *Hodegetria*, sent to her from Jerusalem. Our Lady of Czestochowa is an icon of the *Hodegetria* type.

Hours of Our Lady   Another name for the Little Office of the Blessed Virgin Mary.

House of Gold   An invocation in the Litany of Loreto referring to Mary as a golden palace for the Son of God and standing next to her Son after she was assumed into heaven garbed in golden garments.

Hypapante (hai-puh-pahń-tee)   In English "meeting," the name of the Byzantine feast of the Meeting of Our Lord with Simeon. It corresponds to the feast of the Presentation of Our Lord on February 2 in the Roman Rite.

hyperdulia (hai-per-doo'-lee-ah)   The special reverence given to the Blessed Virgin Mary. The highest homage is reserved to God alone and that is termed "latria"; the honor given to angels and saints is called "dulia." The Mother of God is accorded particular and special reverence because of her unique position unlike that of any other.

I

icons, Mary and   Icons are painted images created according to strict religious rules and traditions which seek to capture an expression of the divine. Icons are considered sacramentals, and they assume great importance in the tradition of the Eastern Church.

After Jesus Christ, Our Lady is the most important subject for icon-painting. Famous icons of Our Lady include Our Lady of Perpetual Help, the Virgin kissing the Child Jesus' hand, and the Virgin Protectress, a favorite of the Russians.

Imitation of Our Lady A book written by Francis Arias, S.J. (d. 1605), following the pattern of *Imitation of Christ* by Thomas à Kempis.

Immaculate Conception The dogma defined by Pope Pius IX in 1854 that declared that the Blessed Virgin Mary was from the very first instant of her conception exempt from sin and clothed in sanctifying grace. This does not mean that Mary was exempt from redemption; rather she was given this special privilege in advance according to the divine plan by God.

The doctrine of the Immaculate Conception is not explicitly revealed in Scripture; its definition rests ultimately on God's revelation as contained in the Tradition of the Church.

A feast of the Conception of Saint Anne (the conception of Mary) was celebrated in the Greek Eastern Church and later on spread to Italy, England, and Ireland. Though the theologians of the twelfth and thirteenth centuries (Saint Bonaventure, Saint Thomas Aquinas) did not accept this doctrine, John Duns Scotus (d. 1308) brought the doctrine back into favor, and the Franciscan Order advocated the doctrine and the feast. (*CCC* §490–493)

Immaculate Conception, Archconfraternity of An association arising out of the eighteen apparitions of the Blessed Mother at Lourdes in 1858. Membership is free, and members perform prescribed devotions in honor of Our Lady.

Immaculate Conception, National Shrine of The largest church in the United States dedicated to Mary is the National Shrine of the Immaculate Conception in Washington, D.C. This edifice is surmounted by a great dome and a 317-foot bell tower and was dedicated in 1959.

Immaculate Conception, Rosary of A string of three groups of one large bead and four small beads, with a medal of the Immaculate Conception attached. An Our Father is said on each large bead and a Hail Mary is said on each small bead. Each series of beads begins with the prayer: "Blessed be the holy and immaculate conception of the Blessed Virgin Mary" and ends with the doxology.

Immaculate Heart of Mary A devotion fostered by John Eudes in seventeenth-century France through his book *The Admirable Heart of Mary* and repopularized on account of the apparitions of Mary at Fátima in 1917. On the twenty-fifth anniversary of Fátima, Pius XII consecrated the whole human race to the Immaculate Heart of Mary, and he extended the feast of the Immaculate Heart of Mary to the whole Church.

This devotion recognizes the Heart of Mary as the symbol of her maternal love which assented wholeheartedly to Jesus Christ, his coming, and his Redemption. Such love from Mary draws us ever closer to Christ.

Immaculate Heart, Rosary of A chaplet, or string of beads, divided into five groups. Each group consists of one Our Father and seven Hail Marys prayed in honor of the Immaculate Heart of Mary.

Incomparable Virgin Mary, The A work in which over 4,000 different biblical texts are quoted and which defends the Church's doctrine about Our Lady against the erosion of the Reformation. It was written by Saint Peter Canisius and first appeared in 1577.

***Ineffabilis Deus* (in-ef-ah-bil'-is day'-us)** In English, "The Ineffable God," the Papal Bull in which Pope Pius IX solemnly defined the dogma of the Immaculate Conception.

intercession of Our Lady Invocation to Mary that indicates our confidence that she will intercede for us with her son, Jesus Christ, so that, through her intercession, he will grant us what we pray for. In the Vatican II document *Dogmatic Constitution on the Church* (§69), the Council urged: "Let the entire body of the faithful pour forth persevering prayer to the Mother of God and Mother of men. Let them implore that she who aided the beginnings of the Church by her prayers may now, exalted as she is in heaven above all the saints and angels, intercede with her Son in the fellowship of all the saints."

The events at Cana are chosen to illustrate the power of Mary's interventions, and it is noteworthy that her intercession brought about the beginning of the miracles of Jesus. Mary, as Daughter of Zion and symbol of Israel, has a mediating role between God and his people, and in her *Magnificat* prayer, she is also an example of Israel in her intercessions to God.

Islam, interest in Mary In the Vatican II document on the Church's relations to non-Christian religions, the Council states that though Muslims do not acknowledge Jesus as God, "they venerate Jesus as a prophet, his virgin Mother they also honor, and even at time devoutly invoke." The sacred book of Islam, the *Koran*, tells of Mary's birth, the Annunciation, and the birth of Jesus under a palm tree. Her name is mentioned more than thirty times in the whole book. This devotion to Mary is expressed at shrines in Muslim lands, for example, at Meryemana near Ephesus in Turkey.

J

John Bosco, Saint (1815–1888) Priest-founder of the Salesians, patron saint of youth, Don Bosco was particularly devoted to Our Lady Help of Christians.

Joseph, Saint The husband of Mary, the mother of Jesus. Only the Gospels of Matthew and Luke mention Joseph by name. Both give genealogies of the saint containing the name of David—essential ancestry to establishing Jesus' place among his people; but Matthew's list starts with Abraham while Luke's goes back to Adam. From the New Testament we also know that Joseph was a carpenter, a maker of wooden objects.

Joseph is not the physical father of Jesus but is his father for purposes of fulfilling the law—as Joseph's role in the Passover and the Presentation were legal requirements. The miraculous conception of Jesus caused Joseph some anxiety which was allayed by a message in a dream.

Matthew's Gospel tells us that Joseph was a just man, one faithful to the traditions of the Old Testament and, by implication, a generous and holy protector. The New Testament does not mention the death of Joseph, and indications are that he died before Jesus began his public ministry.

Pope Pius IX proclaimed Joseph the universal patron of the Church; Pope John XXIII named Joseph as the Protector of the Second Vatican Council.

Joyful Mysteries of the Rosary See Mysteries of the Rosary.

Joys of Mary A devotion centering on the joyful events in the life of the Blessed Virgin, matching in a similar way a devotion to her sorrows. Devotion to the joys appears in an eleventh-century poem, and this practice gained in popularity through the efforts of the Franciscans, especially those of Saint Bernardine of Siena (d. 1444) and Saint John of Capistrano (d. 1456). The number of joys varied—five, seven, twelve—along with a similar variety in the subject matter. The following occurrences constitute the generally accepted Joys of Mary: the Annunciation, the Visitation, the Nativity, the Adoration of the Magi, the Finding of Jesus in the Temple, the Appearance of Risen Jesus to Mary, and the Assumption and Coronation of Mary in Heaven. There is a rosary of the Seven Joys, also known as the Franciscan Crown or Seraphic Rosary.

K

Knock A village in County Mayo, Ireland, where Our Lady is reported to have appeared to a group of villagers in the churchyard of a small parish on the evening of August 21, 1979. In the vision, she is described as being flanked by Saint John the Evangelist on one side and Saint Joseph on the other. Irish ecclesiastical authorities have held that the testimony of the several witnesses and the evidence of the physically cured is valid. Large numbers of pilgrims visit the site.

Kolbe, Saint Maximilian (1894–1941) A Polish Franciscan who founded an organization known as the Knights of Mary Immaculate, which was dedicated to spreading devotion to Our Lady. He also launched a community known as the City of the Immaculate, as well as a similar organization in Japan, called the Garden of the Immaculate. Father Kolbe was imprisoned in Auschwitz, a Nazi concentration camp, where he volunteered to take the place of another man who was condemned to die.

L

La Salette, Our Lady of Title of the Blessed Virgin arising out of her apparition to two children in a village in southeast France near Grenoble. Our Lady's message warned of dire consequences unless there was repentance and a return to God's law. After being requested to pray, each child was told a secret which they later made known to Pius IX. An inquiry into the events at La Salette was conducted by the bishop of Grenoble, and after five years in which evidence was gathered, the bishop judged that the apparition had all the earmarks of truth. The site of the apparition has become a major pilgrimage shrine.

La Salette Fathers Originally founded in 1852 to care for the pilgrims who came to the Shrine of Our Lady of La Salette in France, the Missionaries of Our Lady of La Salette (M.S.) expanded beyond this focus to the conduct of missions and retreats, parish and social work, and to the leading of people away from evil toward repentance.

Lady altar A special altar dedicated in honor of the Mother of God, generally containing a statue or other image of her in a prominent place. Sometimes, in many large churches, an entire side chapel containing the Lady altar is dedicated to the Blessed Virgin Mary. The Lady altar and the Lady chapel are situated in churches even if the entire church is dedicated in her name.

***Laudesi* (law-deh'-see)** In English, praisers who were members of guilds of medieval Italy that gathered in the evening to sing canticles or praises before a statue of Our Lady. It was just such a company of *Laudesi* who formed the nucleus that brought together the Seven Holy Founders who became the Servants of Mary, or Servites.

legends of Our Lady Collections of stories—mainly from the time of the Middle Ages—about the miracles attributed to Mary. Though sometimes purely imaginative, these stories helped spread devotion to Mary in the form of the Little Office of the Blessed Virgin, the Joys of Mary, and the idea of Mary as the Mother of Mercy. Some of the more important collections are the *Miracles of the Blessed Virgin* by Dominic of Evesham, the *Miracles of the Blessed Virgin Mary* by William of Malmesburg, and the *Miracles of the Blessed Virgin Mary* by Johannes Herolt.

Legion of Mary A lay organization of Catholics founded in Ireland by Frank Duff in 1921. This organization, founded on the principles arising from the Mystical Body of Christ and those outlined by Saint Louis Grignion de Monfort in his book *True Devotion to the Blessed Virgin Mary*, has spread all over the world.

The Legion stresses particular spiritual practices for its members: an annual consecration to Mary, participation in the apostolate of visiting homes of people to encourage study of the Bible, leading a devout Catholic life, spiritual reading, and attendance at a weekly prayer meeting.

The Legion of Mary is organized after the military divisions of ancient Rome. The smallest unit is called a *praesidium*; two or more praesidiums are called a *curia*; a *senatus* is a regional governing body, and the general headquarters in Dublin is known as the *concilium*.

litany   A litany is a prayer in the form of a series of invocations followed by a petitionary response. Introductory and concluding prayers usually accompany a litany. Examples are litanies of the Holy Name, All Saints, Sacred Heart, and so on

Litany of the Blessed Virgin Mary   A litany of the praises of the Blessed Virgin based on Scripture and the writings of the Fathers of the Church. Many different litanies to Mary existed in the fifteenth and sixteenth centuries, in some places one composed for every day of the year. Finally, Pope Clement VIII suppressed all litanies except the one customarily sung at the holy House of Loreto. Eventually special permission from the Sacred Congregation of Rites was required to add any invocation to it. Invocations such as "Queen conceived without original sin," "Queen of the most holy rosary," "Mother of good counsel," "Queen of peace," and "Mother of the Church" have been added by various popes.

When the Church promulgated a new rite for *Crowning an Image of the Blessed Virgin Mary*, it included a new Litany of the Blessed Virgin with emphasis on Mary's Queenship. In addition to the litanies in honor of Mary that are approved for liturgical use, there are other litanies that have been composed for private use. One of the most relevant Marian litanies for private use is the Biblical Litany of Our Lady, made up of Bible passages.

Litany of Loreto   The popular name of the Litany of the Blessed Virgin Mary.

Little Office of the Blessed Virgin Mary   A shortened form of the common office of the Blessed Virgin; it is associated with the Votive Masses of Our Lady for Saturday composed by Alcuin (d. 804). By the tenth century the office was recited daily, and after it was reorganized by Peter Damian (d. 1072) it grew into common use.

The Little Office became part of the *Book of Hours* in honor of Mary, and in 1952 was revised with psalms, canticles, hymns, responsories, antiphons, and collects for the six periods of the liturgical year. Included were twenty-eight feasts of Our Lady. According to Vatican II, the Little Office is now part of the public prayer of the Church.

The Little Office is meant as a way of living the hours of each day in tandem with Mary and her Son. Thus it contains prayers for each hour of the day.

Little Office of the Immaculate Conception A office purportedly written by Saint Alphonsus Rodriquez (1532–1617), a Spanish Jesuit who was admitted to that order as a lay brother and who, for forty-six years, served as a doorkeeper at the College of Majorca where many students and visitors came to his lodgings for advice and spiritual direction.

Living Rosary, The A public ceremony in which a group of people arrange themselves in the form of a rosary. Each person alternates praying the first part of an Our Father or a Hail Mary, with the group as a whole responding with the remainder of the prayer.

Loreto, House of On the Italian shore of the Adriatic in the small town of Loreto lies a shrine built over a small house. According to tradition, this is the same house in which Mary was born and which was used by the Holy Family during their life in Nazareth. It was transported to Loreto by angels in 1291 after first being set down at Tersato in Dalmatia. A great basilica has been built around this small house, and inside stands a statue of Our Lady of Loreto, commemorating Mary in her role as mother of the Holy Family. Despite objections raised to the authenticity of the means of transporting the house, the shrine is visited by many pilgrims, including Pope John XXIII and Pope Paul VI.

Louis Marie Grignion de Montfort, Saint See Montfort, Louis Marie Grignion de.

Lourdes, Our Lady of Title of Our Lady arising from her eighteen apparitions to Bernadette Soubirous in 1858 in a small village in the foothills of the Pyrenees. In the apparitions, Our Lady called herself the Immaculate Conception, a title unfamiliar to Bernadette since the Immaculate Conception had only been declared dogma in 1854. In the apparitions, Our Lady also asked Bernadette to drink at a spring that came forth as she dug in the mud. This same spring now flows at a rate of 32,000 gallons a day and has been instrumental in physical healings. She also requested that a chapel be built near the spot where people could come to pray, and requested penance for the sins of the world.

Initially, the apparitions were met with disbelief, but in 1862, the Bishop of Tarbes approved devotion to Our Lady of Lourdes. A chapel and a minor basilica were built at Lourdes, until the huge influx of pilgrims necessitated the building of a still larger basilica, the Rosary Basilica with fifteen chapels, one for each decade of the rosary. In addition, the underground

Church of Pope Saint Pius X was consecrated in 1958, the centenary year of Our Lady's apparition.

***Lux Veritatis* (luxs veh-ree'-ta-tis)** In English, "Light of Truth," the encyclical of Pope Pius XI issued in 1931 on the fifteen-hundredth anniversary of the Council of Ephesus, which affirmed Mary as the Mother of God.

M

Madonna, The In English, "my lady," a word from the Italian used to designate Our Lady, usually images of her in pictures, statues, or stained glass, holding the Christ Child in her arms. Many painters titled their works using the word *Madonna*: for example, Raphael's *Madonna of the Chair*; Boticelli's *Madonna of the Magnificat*; Jan van Eyck's *Madonna of Lucca*; and Leonardo Da Vinci's *Madonna of the Rock*.

Magnificat Mary's canticle of praise and thanksgiving found in Luke 1:46–55. The *Magnificat* is striking in its reminders of Old Testament phrases, and is reminiscent of the composition of the song of Hannah in 1 Samuel 1–10. The song is a hymn of thanksgiving for the Lord's gifts to the lowly, and a prophetic work that symbolically reveals the destiny of Israel as the new City of God and announces the whole plan of salvation.

***Marialis Cultus* (mah-ree-aĥl-is cool'-tis)** In English, "For the Right Ordering and Development of Devotion to the Blessed Virgin Mary," an Apostolic Constitution issued by Pope Paul VI in 1974. This document urges the faithful to pray the rosary and the *Angelus* and guides devotion to Mary in light of the spiritual renewal of Vatican II. It includes the criteria for deciding which Marian practices are acceptable, and points out the important link between Marian devotion and the struggle for social justice.

Marian feasts Feasts honoring the Blessed Virgin Mary can be grouped into three levels. The oldest, most significant, and most central feast is the feast of the Virgin Mary, the Mother of God, which celebrates Mary's divine maternity.

The second group is made up of those feasts that celebrate events from Mary's life. These feasts concentrate on Mary's holiness and include the Annunciation, the Visitation, the Presentation, and the Assumption.

The third group is comprised of feasts that celebrate Mary as protector and model. Feasts in this level are the Blessed Virgin of the Holy Rosary, Our Lady of Mercy, Our Lady of Mount Carmel, and so on.

Marian Movement of Priests An international organization of clergy and religious whose aim is spiritual renewal through consecration to the Immaculate Heart of Mary.

Marian Year A twelve-month period proclaimed by the pope in honor of the Mother of God. This year of celebration is marked by special prayers, hymns, indulgences, and other events. Pope Pius XII proclaimed 1954 as a Marian Year to mark the one-hundredth anniversary of the promulgation of the dogma of the Immaculate Conception.

Marianists A commonly used name for a congregation founded by Joseph Chaminade at Bordeaux, France, in 1817, whose mission is marked by total consecration to Mary. The word *Marianist* is applied to the priests of the Society of Mary (S.M.), the Brothers of Mary, and the sisters known as the Congregation of the Daughters of Mary Immaculate (F.M.I). These congregations grew out of the sodality of the Blessed Mother which Chaminade had organized. Chaminade's exhortation to his followers to "multiply Christians" resulted in the establishing of schools of all kind, the conduct of parish work, the leading of retreats, and to special missions such as the founding of the Marian Library at the University of Dayton, Ohio.

Mariapolis Name given to the annual meeting of members of the Focolare movement founded in 1943 by Chiara Lubich. Members of this group can be celibate women and men who observe poverty, chastity, and obedience; married people who identify with the group's goals; and fraternities of priests who wish to further the group's ideals.

Mariological Society of America A group whose headquarters is at the University of Dayton and whose mission is to promote greater appreciation of, and research in, the study of Marian topics.

mariolatry The sin of idolatry committed by giving worship to Mary that belongs to God. An example is the practice of a fourth-century sect that offered little cakes to Mary as a form of sacrifice. Sometimes this word is used to refer to errors and excesses about Our Lady.

mariology The study of the theology of Mary that focuses on her person, her prerogatives, her mission, and her role in salvation history.

Martyrs, Our Lady of A famous church in Rome that was originally built by Marcus Agrippa in 25 B.C. as a temple for the gods. It was consecrated as a church by Pope Boniface IV in honor of the Blessed Virgin and all the martyrs. This church holds the tomb of the painter Rafael.

Mediatrix See coredemptrix.

Medjugorje (med-joo-gore'-ree) Village in Croatia where six young people are purported to have seen a vision of the Blessed Virgin Mary. The apparitions have continued, and even in the absence of official approval, pilgrims have flocked to this village. The seers maintain that they have seen, heard, and touched Mary, and were given ten secrets containing information about world events.

Memorare A prayer of intercession to the Blessed Virgin which begins "Remember, O most gracious Virgin Mary." This prayer was promoted by Claude Bernard, called the "poor priest" (d. 1641), who was so active in spreading devotion to the *Memorare* that he circulated more than 200,000 copies of it during his lifetime. Bernard's work was with prisoners and criminals, and he seems to have used the prayer to Mary as a means of conversion. This prayer is erroneously attributed to Saint Bernard.

Mercedarians Originally founded by Peter Nolasco about 1189 for the purpose of liberating Christian captives of the Moslems. The Order was dedicated to Our Lady of Mercy.

messages and communications, Our Lady's Mary's messages, claimed to be communicated primarily through her apparitions beginning in 1846, are in the nature of private communications and in no way are to be seen as part of the revelation given by God to Israel and the apostles. Mary's messages have emphasized the fundamentals of Christian life: prayer, repentance, personal goodness, and acquiescence to God's will. They disclose nothing new. At Lourdes, Mary spoke of the necessity of healing and holiness, and announced that she was the Immaculate Conception. At Fátima, Mary asked us to imitate her by consecrating ourselves to the Immaculate Heart and urging us to pray the rosary. At Medjugorje, Mary continues to refocus our attention on the sacramental life of the Church.

Militia of the Immaculate Conception A canonically established pious association for evangelization and catechesis beginning with members' own total consecration to the Immaculate Virgin Mary. This association draws its inspiration from the story of Alphonsus Ratisbon's conversion in 1842 through the mediation of Mary Immaculate. Maximilian Kolbe, learning of this spiritual conversion, was inspired to ask for Mary's intercession for the anti-Christians of his day. With six other Franciscan friars, he founded the Militia in Rome in 1917. Membership is open to both men and women. Father Kolbe was killed in a Nazi concentration camp in Poland in 1941.

Miraculous Medal A medal, to which great miracles have been ascribed, that formed part of Our Lady's apparition to Saint Catherine Labouré in 1830 at the Convent of the Daughters of Charity in Paris. In Mary's second vision to Catherine, she stood on a globe, with her feet crushing a serpent. On a circle in the shape of a medal that surrounded the vision, these words were written: "O Mary, conceived without sin, pray for us who have recourse to thee." Then Catherine heard a voice say, "Have a medal struck after this model. All who wear it will receive great graces; they should wear it around the neck. Graces will abound for those who wear it with confidence."

Morning Star   A title of Mary that made its way into the Litany of Loreto because the Blessed Virgin is like the first star of the day that outshines all others and that ushers in the sun. Thus Mary is the forerunner of the dawning day of redemption and the proclaimer of Emmanuel. She is the star that leads us to our eternal destination.

Montfort, Saint Louis Marie Grignion de (1673–1716)   A French priest and missionary who wrote several influential works about Mary: *Treatise on True Devotion to the Blessed Virgin, The Secret of Mary,* and *The Admirable Secret of the Most Holy Rosary.* The manuscript of *Treatise on True Devotion,* which contains the essence of his thoughts on the Blessed Virgin, was not discovered until 1841, more than a century after his death. In it, Montfort says that true devotion to Mary consists of giving oneself entirely to the Blessed Virgin, in order to belong entirely to Jesus Christ though her. The work also focuses on the Holy Spirit whom Montfort sees as communicator of God's many gifts to Mary.

Montfort Fathers   The Monfort Society of Mary or Company of Mary (S.M.M.) was founded by Saint Louis Marie Grignion de Montfort (d. 1716), author of *The True Devotion to Mary,* for the purposes of preaching and missionary work. Throughout its history, the order has fostered devotion to the Blessed Virgin Mary.

month of Mary   Just as Saturday is seen as Mary's day of the week, May is seen as the month of the year devoted to Mary. Blessed Henry Suso (d. 1365) of Germany is credited with weaving a garland of flowers and crowning a statue of Mary during the springtime of the year. By the sixteenth century, Saint Philip Neri (d. 1595) urged young Romans to pay homage to Mary during the month of May. By the eighteenth century, handbooks were published giving suggestions for private devotions to honor Mary during May. At the same time, Marian celebrations moved from family or religious houses into the parish church—fostered by the popularity of Alphonsus Muzzarelli's book *The Month of May.* In modern times, Pope Paul VI wrote a short encyclical on the month of May in which he urged making use of the devotions to Mary during this month to pray for peace.

month of the rosary   October is considered the month of the rosary. The remote beginnings of the dedication of October to Our Lady were the rosary devotions held in commemoration of the victory of Lepanto in October 1572 and the institution of the feast of the Holy Rosary by Pope Gregory XIII in 1573. This devotion became even more widespread when Pope Pius IX granted indulgences to all who attended such October observances.

Pope Leo XIII was considered the pope of the rosary, and in one of his many rosary messages the pope refers to his joy as seeing the month of the rosary approach once again. Pope John XXIII's first Marian encyclical opens with a grateful memory of the series of rosary letters of Pope Leo XIII.

Mother of God The most important truth about the Blessed Virgin Mary is that she is the Mother of God. This title of Mary was applied to her at the Council of Ephesus in 431 and confirmed at the Council of Chalcedon in 451. This divine motherhood is the source of all Mary's privileges and graces. It is the source of all the honor that is given to her. Through the centuries, the Church has constantly avowed, as at the third Council of Constantinople, that Jesus Christ was born "of the Holy Spirit and the Virgin Mary, rightly and truly the Mother of God according to his human-ity...."

Though the title "Mother of God" is not found directly stated in the New Testament, similar terms are used, as when Elizabeth calls Mary the "Mother of my Lord," and as in Luke 1:32 where Mary's future Son in called "Son of the most high."

As well, Mary's position as the Mother of God was enshrined in sacred Tradition as early as the time of Saint Hippolytus (d. 235) who asks of those about to be baptized: "Do you believe in Christ Jesus, the Son of God who was born by the Holy Spirit of the Virgin Mary?" (*CCC* §495)

Mother of the Church A title of Our Lady proclaimed by Pope Paul VI on November 11, 1964, at the close of the third session of Vatican II. He de-clared Mary as "Mother of the Church," that is, mother of the whole people of God, in response to requests from bishops attending the council. This was an explicit affirmation of the idea of Mary as Mother of the Church that had been accepted by popes before him. John Paul II later inserted this title in the Litany of Loreto, stressing the complete motherhood of Mary toward the Church, "as Mother of the Head and Mother of the mem-bers of the mystical body." (*CCC* §963–965)

motherhood of God, Mary's A central truth of Christianity that Mary conceived by the Holy Spirit, the second Person of the Blessed Trinity and that she truly was the mother of Jesus Christ, the Savior, one undivided person in which there are two natures—one human and one divine. This dogma was formally clarified by the Council of Ephesus in 431. (*CCC* §721–725)

Scripture implicitly attests to Mary's divine motherhood and calls her "Mother of Jesus," and "Mother of the Lord" (Lk 7:43).The first mention of the actual title "Mother of God" is made by Saint Hippolytus of Rome (d. 235).

The fact that Mary is the Mother of God explains the total perfection of Mary—here on earth and in heaven. In the *Dogmatic Constitution on the Church*, one of the documents of Vatican II, the Church says that the "wor-thy Mother of God" is redeemed by reason of the merits of her Son" and is "united to Him by a close and indissoluble tie." Mary is "endowed with the high office and dignity of being the Mother of the Son of God and, as a consequence, the beloved daughter of the Father and the temple of the Holy Spirit. Because of this sublime grace she far surpasses all creatures, both in heaven and on earth" (§53).

mysteries of the rosary The mysteries of the rosary represent those fifteen themes which form the contemplative focus of each decade of this prayer. They are organized into the Five Joyful Mysteries: (1) the Annunciation, (2) the Visitation, (3) the Nativity, (4) the Presentation, and (5) the Finding in the Temple; the Five Sorrowful Mysteries: (1) the Agony in the Garden, (2) the Scourging at the Pillar, (3) the Crowning with Thorns, (4) the Carrying of the Cross, and (5) the Crucifixion; and the Five Glorious Mysteries: (1) the Resurrection, (2) the Ascension, (3) the Descent of the Holy Spirit, (4) the Assumption of the Blessed Virgin Mary, and (5) the Crowning of the Blessed Virgin Mary in Heaven.

The mysteries developed in three stages. At first, in the twelfth century, a phrase referring to an important event in the life of Jesus or Mary was announced before the recitation of a psalm. Later, the psalms were no longer recited, and the introductory phrases were expanded into longer reflections, still relating to topics surrounding Jesus and Mary, with each topic followed by Hail Marys.

In the next stage, people would recite fifty joyful meditations followed by Hail Marys, fifty earthly sorrows followed by Hail Marys, and fifty heavenly joys followed by Hail Marys.

Finally, in the fifteenth century, in order to make the prayer available to those who were unable to read, the number of mysteries was reduced to fifteen—five for each set along with one hundred and fifty Hail Marys.

In a 1973 pastoral letter, the American Catholic Bishops recommended extending and/or substituting mysteries in order to foster a better understanding of discipleship.

mystery plays and Mary Medieval religious dramas that were performed outdoors for the uplifting of the masses. Occasionally plays honoring Mary were acted out on days special to her as when the Assumption play was performed on August 15. The Marian plays, for the most part, however, were part of the liturgical cycle and celebrated the Annunciation, the Nativity, the Purification, and the Presentation.

Mystical Rose A title of Our Lady in the Litany of Loreto based on the stature of the rose as the queen of flowers and Mary as the queen of saints. Mary can also be seen as the greatest mystic since she kept all things "hidden in her heart."

N

name of Mary, Most Holy A feast of Our Lady celebrated on September 12 and honoring her most holy name, for as Saint Francis of Assisi says: "When I pray 'Hail Mary,' the heavens smile, the angels rejoice, the earth is happy...." Saint Jerome says that Mary means "enlightening"; others have maintained that it means "beloved of God," "perfect one," or "wished-for child."

The whole of Spain and the Kingdom of Naples were the first to celebrate the feast of the Most Holy Name of Mary; however, in gratitude to Mary for the defeat of the Turks at Vienna (1683), Pope Innocent XI extended this feast to the universal Church.

Nazareth A town in northern Israel near Haifa, the site of the Annunciation, the home of the Holy Family, and the place where Christ was rejected. An imposing modern basilica, the Church of the Annunciation, is built over what is claimed to be part of Mary's home.

new Eve The idea of Mary as the new Eve is one that has been richly considered: Paul portrays Christ as the new Adam and so Saint Irenaeus sees a parallel: "It was right and necessary that Adam be restored in Christ...that Eve be restored in Mary...." Saint John Chrysostom made clear the salvation aspect of the Eve-Mary comparison, contrasting "a virgin had cast us out from paradise, through a virgin we have found eternal life," or as *Lumen Gentium* points out: "death through Eve, life through Mary."

novena A format of prayers and praises, said for some particular occasion, that is repeated nine times. Novenas may be made privately on an individual basis or publicly in church, often accompanied by Benediction. The first novena in honor of Mary was one begun by the Franciscans in preparation for the feast of the Immaculate Conception. Mary is popularly honored in the United States by novenas to the Miraculous Medal, to Our Lady of Perpetual Help, and to Our Lady of Sorrows. Indulgences are usually attached to the completion of a novena.

O

Oblates of Mary Immaculate A congregation of men (O.M.I.) founded in 1816 by Charles Joseph de Mazenod in France, the Oblates' original purpose was parish and mission work, though their focus expanded to include the establishment of seminaries for the education of the clergy. Today the Oblates conduct missions, retreat houses, and parishes and care for Marian shrines including the Shrine of Our Lady of the Cape in Quebec, Canada, and the Shrine of Our Lady of the Snows in Illinois.

Office of Our Lady, Little   See Little Office of the Blessed Virgin Mary.

Our Lady   The usual title for Our Blessed Virgin that is affectionately used most often by English speakers. The English poet Cynewulf, toward the end of the eighth century, used the expression "Our Lady Saint Mary." The French have used the title to signify one of their great churches—*Notre Dame.*

Our Lady of Sorrows   See Sorrows of Our Lady.

Our Lady of the Cape   A shrine in Canada located midway between Quebec and Montreal on a cape that juts out into the St. Lawrence River. This shrine, a place of pilgrimage, grew out of a small chapel which housed a wonder-working statue of Our Lady given by a parishioner to the Confraternity of the Rosary in 1845. Many pilgrims are especially devoted to the rosary, and on August 7 to August 15, a great novena to Our Lady of the Rosary is conducted.

Our Lady of the Rosary   Title of the Blessed Virgin in honor of the most widely said and most highly indulgenced prayer to her. In 1572, Pope Pius V instituted the feast of Our Lady of Victory in thanksgiving for God's deliverance of Christendom from the Turks in the Battle of Lepanto. This victory seemed to be facilitated by the prayers of the rosary confraternities in Rome that took place during the battle. Later, Pope Gregory XIII changed the name to the feast of Our Lady of the Rosary, which was eventually extended to the whole Church and set for observance on October 7, the date of the Battle of Lepanto.

Our Lady of the Snows   An alternate title for the feast of the Dedication of the Basilica of St. Mary Major, arising out of a dream in which Mary appeared to the pope and asked him to build a church on the site of a snowfall which took place in the middle of summer.

Our Lady's Rosary Makers   Organization instituted to supply missionaries with free rosaries for distribution throughout the world.

P

Panagia **(pah-nah-gee'-ah)**   In English, "The All-Holy," a Byzantine title for the Mother of God and also the triangular loaf of bread praised in Orthodox monasteries with the words, "Great is the name of the Holy Trinity. All-Holy God-bearer, help us." This observance is thought to recall the Assumption of the Blessed Virgin and is sometimes used as an intercession for travelers.

Perpetual Help, Our Lady of   An image of Our Lady now located in the Church of St. Alphonsus Liguori in Rome. This image had been stolen from its place of honor in Crete and placed in the Church of St. Matthew in Rome in 1449. This church was plundered, and the image was thought to be lost. More than fifty years later, this image was found again, and the pope ordered the picture transferred to the Redemptorist Church which had been built over the site of the original St. Matthew's.

Devotion to Our Lady of Perpetual Help became so popular that the confraternity was quickly granted status as an archconfraternity. To join the Archconfraternity of Our Lady of Perpetual Help, a person is enrolled in the confraternity listing of a church associated with the Redemptorist Order. Members then make an act of consecration to Our Lady of Perpetual Help and partake of all the indulgences and spiritual benefits that accrue to members of this organization.

Perpetual Rosary The continuous saying of the rosary by the members of a group who arrange themselves so that at each hour of the day or night, the rosary is being said in honor of Jesus and his Mother for the benefit of those who are at the hour of their death.

perpetual virginity, Mary's The doctrine of faith that Mary was a virgin before, during, and after the birth of Jesus Christ. This threefold character of Mary's virginity was stressed by the Lateran council in 649. That Mary conceived as a virgin by the power of the Holy Spirit is attested to by the Gospels of Luke and Matthew and is expressed in the Apostles' Creed. This doctrine of faith asserts the fact of Mary's continued virginity during the physical events of Jesus' birth (however this occurred) and ever after. Saint Basil says: "The friends of Christ do not tolerate hearing that the Mother of God ever ceased to be a virgin."

pietà (pee-ay'-tah) Any artistic image of the Blessed Virgin Mary holding the body of Christ after it has been taken down from the cross. Such images became common at the end of the Middle Ages as popular devotion to the sorrows of Our Lady grew. The most famous *Pietà* is Michelangelo's in St. Peter's Basilica in Rome.

pilgrimages and Mary A pilgrimage is a journey to a holy and sacred place. Pilgrimages were a fixture of medieval society; great pilgrim highways led to Rome, to Jerusalem, to Santiago de Compostela, to Walsingham. After the Reformation in Europe, however, the popularity of pilgrimages declined, only to swing upwards in favor in the nineteenth century when Our Lady began appearing all over Europe—at Rue de Bac in 1830, at La Salette in 1846, at Lourdes in 1858, and at Pontmain in 1871. The early twentieth century saw a continued increase in pilgrimages to the shrines of Our Lady after the Blessed Virgin appeared at Fátima in 1917, at Banneux in 1933, at Beauraing in 1933, and at Medjugorje beginning in 1981.

Pontifical Marian Academy Founded in 1946, this international institute promotes devotion to Mary and studies about her. It holds congresses and coordinates Marian studies worldwide.

Pontmain Village in western France where, in 1871, Our Lady appeared to a group of children in the form of a woman wearing a black veil, a blue robe decorated with golden stars, and a crown of gold. As those who gathered prayed the rosary, Our Lady unfurled a banner which said: "Pray, my children, God will answer you in a short while; my Son will let himself be moved."A year later the Bishop of Laval acknowledged the apparition as authentic; over 100 years later, pilgrims still come to pray to the Blessed Virgin Mary.

Portiuncula (pohr-tee'-uhn-cue-lah) A word meaning "a small portion,"used to describe the small portion of land accepted by Saint Francis of Assisi (from a nearby Benendictine monastery) as a place for his followers to live and worship. On this land was a small chapel which was restored by the friars. This small church is now in the middle of a large basilica known as Our Lady of the Angels.

  The Portiuncula Indulgence was the result of a vision of Our Lady received by Saint Francis. She told him that a special plenary indulgence could be obtained for the dead as often as a person would visit the small chapel on August 2. Pope Honorius III granted this indulgence under the condition that the Our Father, Hail Mary, and Glory to the Father be recited six times per visit for the Holy Father's intentions. Now the Portiuncula Indulgence can be transferred to any parish church provided certain standards are met.

predestination of Mary An act on the part of God which established Mary's role in the Incarnation as the Mother of God and which awarded her total respect for her freedom of person and choice. Vatican II says that the Blessed Virgin was "eternally predestined, in conjunction with the divine Word, to be the Mother of God" (*Lumen Gentium* §46). *(CCC 488–493)*

prefaces of Our Lady Liturgically, a formal proclamation of praise in the Eucharistic Prayer. The number of prefaces was limited severely by the Council of Trent, but at the middle of the twentieth century, the Second Vatican Council's revised Missal for the universal Church increased the number of Prefaces to over eighty. This revision also left the national conferences of bishops free to request more. Thus, the publication of the *Collection of Masses for the Blessed Virgin Mary Approved for Use in the Dioceses of the United States of America* in 1992 adds over forty more prefaces to the Roman rite for English speakers.

Presentation in the Temple, feast of the This feast, celebrated on February 2, has an varied history. It was formerly known as the Purification of the Blessed Virgin, the feast of the Candles (or Candlemas), and the Feast of Saint Simeon the Patriarch. The current title reaffirms Jesus Christ's centrality as the Messiah while unifying the other themes: Mary and Joseph who come to the Temple to present Jesus to his beloved Father and to the people he has come to save; Mary whose active offering indicates her part in the Redemption; Simeon's prophecy which signals the mission of Jesus Christ and Mary's suffering that will take place because of this mission.

privileges of Mary   The special attributes of Mary that distinguish her from all other human beings. These are her freedom from original sin, her freedom from all other sin, and her resulting fullness of grace; her virginity; her lack of ignorance; her spiritual maternity; her secondary mediation role in our salvation; her role in the Church and her right to the devotion of its members.

processions and Mary   Religious processions are solemn and sacred walks where people go from one place to another. The Mass in the Roman rite contains a liturgical procession that occurs when representatives of the people bring the unconsecrated water and wine to the altar. The Eucharist may be formally honored in a liturgical procession on the feast of the Body and Blood of Christ. Devotional processions honoring the Blessed Virgin are also popular, and in some places and at some times occur in honor of her feasts, as do the processions for the Assumption and Candlemas (now known as the feast of the Presentation in the Temple). Other processions occur in the context of public ceremonies at sacred shrines, as at Lourdes, and as part of the celebrations attached to the Marian months of May and October.

Q

Queen of All Saints   A title of Mary included in the Litany of Loreto and a manifestation of her position as the most perfect of all human beings and her power in heaven as the Mother of God.

Queen of Peace   A Marian title inserted into the Litany of Loreto by Pope Benedict XV during World War I as a plea for peace among people and among nations. Mary brought Jesus who is the King of Peace, who spoke the words: "Peace I leave you, my peace I give to you." In consequence, Mary is the Queen of Peace, and she appeared as such at Fátima, where she promised to bring peace to the world if the faithful would do penance and say the rosary. In the Mass commemorating the feast of the Blessed Virgin Mary, Queen of Peace, the faithful ask God that through her intercession he will grant to us the spirit of love, the gifts of unity and peace, and tranquillity in our times.

Queen of the Americas Guild   An organization designed to spread the message of Our Lady of Guadalupe.

Queenship of Mary   Pope Pius XII's encyclical *Ad Caeli Reginam* inaugurated the feast of the Queenship of Mary and ordered it observed on May 31. The queenship of Mary follows from her divine maternity and is further supported by texts from ancient Christian documents, from the prayers of the liturgy, from works of art, and from the pious practices of the faithful. It follows by analogy that if Christ is the King, then Mary is our queen, for as Saint John Damascene states: "She indeed became mistress of all creation when she became mother of the Creator."

Queen of the Apostles   A name of Mary in the Litany of Loreto arising out of her superior position in the community of the early Church and her presence at the events of Pentecost. As the first disciple, Mary spread the message of salvation to the house of Elizabeth, just as the apostles were filled with the Holy Spirit on Pentecost and hastened out to preach the Gospel of Christ to all nations.

R

***Redemptoris Mater* (ray-dem'-tor-is mah'-ter)**   In English, "The Mother of the Redeemer," an encyclical, or formal pastoral letter, issued by Pope John Paul II in March 1987 in preparation for the Marian Year of 1987–1988. This year was seen as a preparation for the celebration of Christianity's third millennium.

***Regina Caeli* (ray-jee'-nah chay'-lee)**   The first words and title of an antiphon of Our Lady whose creator is unknown. The hymn dates back to the twelfth century and is sung or said during the Liturgy of the Hours at Eastertide. Its use as a substitute for the *Angelus* dates from the time of Pope Benedict XIV. The *Regina Caeli* is a hymn of joy at the Resurrection and in it the Blessed Virgin Mary is acclaimed Queen of Heaven.

relics of Our Lady   Strictly speaking, relics are remains of the bodies of saints, including skin, bones, clothing, or objects used for penance. In a wider sense, objects that have come into contact with the body of a saint are also considered to be relics. It is highly unlikely that any authentic relics of Our Blessed Virgin exist, though the Cathedral of Chartres claims a relic of the veil of Mary, presented to it by Charlemagne; the shrine of Our Blessed Virgin at Messina in Sicily maintains that it possesses a letter dictated by the Mother of God, congratulating the people of Messina on their conversion to Christianity; and the city of Aachen claims to possess the cloak of the Blessed Virgin along with a host of other relics.

religious institutes of women and Mary   Of the numerous institutes of religious women, many bearing Mary's name. Here are some: Sisters of the Assumption of the Blessed Virgin, founded in 1853 in Canada; Institute of the Blessed Virgin Mary, founded in the seventeenth century in Belgium; Institute of Our Lady of Mount Carmel, founded in 1854 in Italy; Sisters of Charity of Our Lady of Mercy, founded 1832 in Holland; Sisters of Charity of the Blessed Virgin Mary, founded in 1833 in the U.S. by Mary Frances Clarke; Franciscan Missionaries of Our Lady, founded in France in 1854; Franciscan Sisters of Our Lady of Perpetual Help, founded in 1901 in the United States; Sisters of the Humility of Mary, founded in 1854 in France; Sisters of the Immaculate Heart of Mary, founded in 1848 in Spain; Company of Mary, founded in 1607 in France; and so on.

rosary   A string of beads or the series of prayers said on them. There are several different types of rosaries said in honor of Our Lady, as well as other non-Marian rosaries, such as the Rosary of the Names of God.

Rosary, Dominican   A rosary popularized by the members of the Dominican Order, consisting of fifteen decades of ten Hail Marys with an Our Father preceding each decade. During each decade, one of the fifteen principal mysteries of the Redemption is meditated upon. Because the hundred and fifty Hail Marys correspond to the hundred and fifty psalms, the complete rosary is sometimes called Our Lady's Psalter.

In English, we use the term *rosary* to refer to both a five-decade rosary and to the complete fifteen-decade rosary. For purposes of clarity, some people speak of a third of a rosary, that is, five decades.

Strictly speaking, the fifteen Our Fathers and the hundred and fifty Hail Marys are the only recited prayers that belong to the rosary. But other prayers have come to be added through custom. In the U.S., the rosary is preceded by the Sign of the Cross, the Apostles' Creed, an Our Father, three Hail Marys, and a Glory to the Father, usually said on the hanging part of the rosary separated from the circle of beads. However, in other countries, these prayers come at the end of the rosary. Another widespread practice is that of ending each decade with a Glory to the Father or when the rosary is recited for the dead, "Eternal rest grant unto them, O Lord...."

The development of the rosary has occurred in several stages. Its origins are in the monastic prayer based on the recitation of a hundred and fifty psalms. To give the laity a form of everyday prayer, they were encouraged to recite a hundred and fifty Our Fathers and were given beads to help them count.

Parallel to this, those devoted to the Blessed Virgin said the angelic salutation of Gabriel in groups of fifty, one hundred, or a hundred and fifty. Next psalters of Jesus and Mary evolved by adding a phrase that referred to one or the other in each psalm. Eventually the psalms were omitted, and the phrases—making up an abbreviated life of Jesus and Mary—were retained. By the early 1400s, the Carthusians decided to attach fifty commemorative phrases to fifty Hail Marys.

The next step was to simplify the mysteries, since fifty were too many to remember. Gradually, the arrangement of Our Fathers and Hail Marys joined into the present-day rosary which was approved by Pope Pius V in 1569.

Rosary Confraternity A pious association first organized in the fifteenth century whose members undertake to say the complete fifteen mysteries of the rosary each week. In the document establishing the rules and privileges of the Confraternity, Leo XIII gives the Dominican master general the right to promulgate this confraternity and all of its devotions. To become a member, one must have his or her name inscribed in the membership register wherever the confraternity is accorded canonical status. A succession of popes has granted various indulgences to Confraternity members for praying the rosary, for visiting the sick, for completing the Devotion of the Fifteen Saturdays, for any pious work, and so on. Membership is open to both men and women but, often in the United States, pious associations of women only have arisen.

Rosary Sunday An informal name for the feast of the Most Holy Rosary in Dominican churches. On this day, roses are blessed and distributed in honor of Our Lady.

S

Sabbatine Privilege A belief that those who wear the Carmelite Brown Scapular, who observe chastity according to their station in life, and who daily recite the Little Office of the Blessed Virgin Mary or who abstain from meat on Wednesdays and Saturdays will receive Mary's special protection, especially on Saturday, the day dedicated to the Blessed Virgin. This privilege is purported to have been derived from a bull issued by Pope John XII in 1322. Even though this bull is regarded as inauthentic, the privilege has been accepted in Church practice.

Saint Mary Major, feast of the Dedication of the Basilica of The Basilica of Saint Mary Major is one of the most important churches dedicated to the Mother of God. It was erected by order of Pope Sixtus III (d. 440) on the Esquiline hill in Rome in the early centuries of Christianity. Its construction was undertaken in memory of Mary *Theotokos*. At one point, the church was known as Saint Mary of the Crib from the timbers—supposedly from the crib at Bethlehem—that lie under its high altar. It also was known as Our Lady of the Snow from a story in which the Blessed Virgin Mary appeared to Pope Liberious and asked that a church be built on the spot on the Esquiline hill that was covered in snow. This vision was said to have occurred in August, generally the hottest month of the year in Rome.

The feast of the Dedication of the Basilica of Saint Mary Major spread outward from Rome and was made a feast of the universal Church by Pope Pius V (d. 1572).

***Salve Regina* (sal'-veh ray-gee'-nah)** The first words and title of an antiphon of Our Lady said or sung at various hours of the Divine Office. It is thought to have been composed by Hermann of Reichenau (d. 1054). This hymn to Our Lady has been greatly loved since the Middle Ages. In it, Mary is praised as the Mother of Mercy, an advocate who will help the faithful through the exile of earthly life.

The *Salve Regina* was the first hymn to have been sung in the New World—by the sailors accompanying Christopher Columbus in 1492. Just as sailors in the Middle Ages sang the *Salve* at the end of the day, so too did the laity join monks and friars in an evening *Salve*. Pope Leo XIII asked that the *Salve* be used after all the Low Masses for Russia, but this practice is no longer observed.

Saturday of Our Lady The observance of Saturday as Mary's day seems to have come about during the tenth century as a commemoration of her sorrow at Christ's death and his disciples' abandonment of her during the day after his death. From that time forward, Saturday became associated with the Blessed Virgin in other ways, and the custom arose of celebrating a Mass in her honor on Saturdays. About this time, the Little Office of the Blessed Virgin came to be recited on Saturdays, especially by the Benedictine monks of Monte Cassino and Cluny. From the Benedictines, this practice spread to other religious orders who wished to show their devotion to Mary. Vatican II, in its liturgical reform, maintained the commemoration of Mary on Saturdays. The revised Roman Missal of 1963 gives three common forms of the Mass of the Blessed Virgin, plus one each for the seasons of Advent, Christmas, and Easter.

scapular A garment that hangs down the front and back of the body and has a hole in the middle for the head. This garb was part of the habit of older religious orders. Gradually, lay members of religious orders took to wearing miniature decorated scapulars connected by cords under their clothes to represent the larger scapular. From this practice, wearing of the scapular spread to the laity at large. There are more than fifteen scapulars approved for use by the Church but the most popular and widely worn is the Brown Scapular.

Scapular, Black A scapular originating from the Order of Servites which is worn in honor of the seven sorrows of Mary. Also black is the Scapular of Our Lady, Help of the Sick, the badge of the Confraternity founded by Saint Camillus de Lellis for the aid of the sick, approved in 1860 by Pope Pius IX.

Scapular, Blue   A scapular in honor of the Immaculate Conception. This practice arose out of a vision of the Blessed Virgin to Mother Ursula Benincasa, founder of the Theatine nuns in 1617. It is worn by all those who are members of the Confraternity of the Immaculate Conception.

Scapular, Brown   The most highly developed of the scapular devotions is that of the Brown Scapular of Our Lady of Mount Carmel worn and fostered by the Carmelites. The Brown Scapular is seen as a means of protection insofar as one who faithfully wears this scapular until death while endeavoring to lead a sinless life will be granted the grace of perseverance at the hour of death. This belief in Mary's final intercession arises from an apparition presumably made to Saint Simon Stock.   See **Sabbatine Privilege.**

Scapular, Fivefold   Scapulars of the Passion, the Holy Trinity, the Seven Sorrows, Mount Carmel, and the Immaculate Conception worn as one on a single set of cords.

Scapular, Green   This is not a scapular in the strict sense since it is a single square of green cloth hung around the neck by a cord. On one side is the image of Our Lady and on the other side is the image of her heart, with the words: "Immaculate Heart of Mary, pray for us now and at the hour of our death." This badge was instituted for the conversion of those without faith and it originated in Our Lady's appearances to a Daughter of Charity of Saint Vincent de Paul in the 1840s in France.

Scapular, White   White scapulars include the Scapular of the Immaculate Heart of Mary, approved by Pope Pius IX in 1877; the White Scapular of Our Lady of Good Counsel, approved by Pope Leo XIII for the purpose of invoking Mary's guidance upon its wearer; and the White Scapular of Our Lady of Ransom bearing the cross of Aragon, which originated in the thirteenth century in connection with the Fathers of the Blessed Virgin Mary of the Redemption of Captives.

scapular medal   A medal that may be used in place of the cloth scapular in recognition of the changes in modern life. Anyone invested in any Scapular may substitute a scapular medal which need only be carried on the person. This is not intended as a new form of devotion, but merely as a convenience for the faithful and to encourage its continued practice.

Schrocken Rosary   A form of the rosary named after a village in the Alps, which is made up of sixty-three beads. The Hail Mary said on each of these beads is the biblical salutation, excluding the final part of the prayer. At the end of each Hail Mary, a meditational sentence is read aloud by a reader as the congregation reaches the end of the Hail Mary. The final three additions said after the last Hail Mary on the hanging portion of the beads are significant. They are (1) Grant that we may hear with devotion the word of God; (2) Grant that we may keep the word of God in our hearts; and (3) Grant that we may attain the happiness of heaven through Jesus Christ. There are no Our Fathers in this chaplet.

The Secret of the Rosary An influential book authored by Saint Louis Marie Grignion de Montfort (d. 1716).

Seven Joys, Rosary of See Franciscan Crown.

Seven Sorrows of Mary See Sorrows of Our Lady.

Servites A religious community founded by seven prominent citizens of Florence in 1233. The Order of the Servants of Mary include priests, brothers, contemplative nuns, and tertiaries. One of the original intentions of the Servites was devotion to Our Lady, particularly Our Lady of Sorrows—which they accomplish through promotion of the Black Scapular, the Crown of the Seven Sorrows of Our Lady, and the Way of the Sorrowful Mother.

shrines, Marian See Section Ten, page 241.

Sisters of Mary of the Presentation (S.M.P.) A congregation founded in Broons, France, in 1828 by Mother Saint Louis Le Marchand and Father Joachim Fleury to educate people in the faith after the religious suppressions of the French Revolution. They also care for the poor, the sick, and the needy. During the first part of the nineteenth century, the sisters were exiled to the Isle of Guernsey because their order had been dissolved and they had been evicted from their schools and their motherhouse. Some sisters emigrated to Canada and the United States during this period.

Sisters, Servants of the Immaculate Heart of Mary (I.H.M.) Founded in 1845 in Monroe, Michigan, by Mother Teresa Maxis Duchemin and Louis Florent Gillet, C.Ss.R. They engage in parish and campus ministries, education, health care, and social services.

sodalities of Our Lady The first sodality was founded by Jesuit John Leunis in Rome in 1563. The initial meeting of the sodality was graced by a statue of Our Lady, and it was the intent of the founders to make devotion to her a hallmark of their fledgling group. The movement spread rapidly and soon included groups for schoolchildren, men and women, and various others organized along vocational lines. In the United States during the nineteenth century, sodalities could be found in many parishes, and their monthly meetings emphasized devotions to Our Lady, daily Mass, and good works for the less fortunate. Since the revised norms laid down by Pope Paul VI, sodalities are known as Christian Life Communities.

Solemnity of Mary Four celebrations honoring the Blessed Virgin Mary in the cycle of the liturgical year are designated as a solemnity: the Immaculate Conception (December 8); Mary, Mother of God (January 1); The Annunciation (March 25); and the Assumption of Mary (August 15).

Sorrowful Mother, Sanctuary of Our Servite Father Ambrose Mayer founded the National Sanctuary of Our Sorrowful Mother in 1923 in fulfillment of a childhood pledge. Popularly known as The Grotto, this shrine is a sixty-two-acre retreat near the center of Portland, Oregon, which features a marble replica of Michelangelo's famous *Pietà*.

Sorrows of Our Lady A devotion to Our Lady centering on Mary's compassion as she stood at the foot of the cross and, by extension, on Mary's sorrows suffered in the course of the Passion, and, more broadly still, to Mary's sorrows throughout the whole of her life. Devotion to the Sorrows of Mary began as a popular movement in the fourteenth century and was expressed in prayers, meditations, poems, and hymns.

The number and subject of the Sorrows of Our Lady varied but what we think of as the traditional list is one promoted by the Servite Order to commemorate Mary's participation in the sufferings of Jesus the Savior: (1) Simeon's prophecy; (2) the flight into Egypt; (3) the loss of Jesus; (4) the meeting of Jesus on the road to Calvary; (5) the Crucifixion; (6) the taking down from the cross; and (7) the burial of Jesus.

The Rosary of the Seven Sorrows consists of seven groups each of seven Hail Marys and one Our Father said while meditating on the Sorrows of Our Lady. This chaplet is concluded by three additional Hail Marys in memory of Our Sorrowful Lady's tears and requesting true sorrow for sin.

The image of Our Lady of Sorrows shows her heart pierced by seven swords, recalling the prophecy of Simeon ("a sword shall pierce your heart") and the seven sorrows.

The feast of Our Lady of Sorrows was fixed by Pope Pius X as the day after the Exaltation of the Holy Cross, that is, on September 15.

Stabat Mater (stah'-baht mah'-ter) A well-loved hymn of Mary's sorrows which in English begins "At the cross her station keeping," and is a prayer requesting the same compassion from Mary as she showed to Jesus at the foot of the cross. Thought to be composed by Jacob da Todi (d. 1306), the *Stabat Mater* is often sung at a service of the Stations of the Cross and as an optional Sequence for the Mass of the Seven Sorrows of Mary on September 15.

Stabat Mater Speciosa (stah'-baht mah'-ter spay'-cee-oh-sah) This hymn is often seen as a companion to the *Stabat Mater*. It celebrates Mary's joy at Christmas and was repopularized by Frederick Ozanam, founder of the Society of Saint Vincent de Paul.

Stations of the Seven Sorrows A devotion commemorating Mary's seven sorrows and similar to the Stations of the Cross. These seven stations are

42

found in churches of the Servite Order and are sometimes called the *Via Matris* (vee'-ah mah'-tris), or the Way of the Sorrowful Mother.

Sub Tuum (sub two'-um) Title of one of the oldest intercessory prayers to the Blessed Virgin in existence, discovered in 1917 on an Egyptian papyrus fragment thought to be from the third or fourth century. One translation of this prayer is "Under your mercy, O holy Mother of God, we take refuge. Do not reject our supplications in necessity, but deliver us from danger. You alone are chaste. You alone are blessed."

T

Theotokos (thay'-oh-tow-kus) In English, "Godbearer," or "God's forth-bringer," a title used by Saint Cyril, Archbishop of Alexandria at the Council of Ephesus in 431. This council confirmed that Jesus is one divine person, not two as the Nestorians erroneously claimed, and that Mary therefore was the Mother of God, not just the mother of the human substance of Jesus.

Three Hail Marys Archconfraternity popularized by French Capuchins and associated with the devotion of the Three Hail Marys which is a series of seven prayers to Our Lady, one for each day of the week, written by Saint Alphonsus Liguori (d. 1787). Each prayer is followed by the Hail Mary said three times. There is also a devotion that involves saying three Hail Marys daily in honor of the wisdom, power, and loving mercy of the Blessed Virgin Mary.

titles of Mary The great variety of expressions of honor and dignity, love and reverence, used in litanies, sermons, devotions, and theological writings. Some Marian titles are biblical in origin, such as Handmaid of the Lord or Mother of my Lord. Other Marian titles also designate particular feasts, images, shrines, and places associated with Our Lady. Some of these are Our Lady of the Poor, Our Lady of the Smile, Our Lady of the Blackbirds, and so on. There are compilations of Marian titles derived from various sources and arranged alphabetically.

True Devotion to the Blessed Virgin Mary, A Treatise on The major work of Saint Louis Marie Grignion de Montfort. This work outlines the characteristics of true devotions to the Blessed Virgin which consists, says de Montfort, of "giving oneself entirely to the Blessed Virgin in order to belong entirely to Jesus Christ through her." He characterizes true devotion as having five qualities: being inward in spirit and heart; tender, with a childlike confidence; holy in emulation of Mary's virtues; loving because Mary is worthy of love; and unwavering in perseverance.

V

Visitation of Mary   The meeting of Mary and her cousin Elizabeth as told in Luke's Gospel. Mary's decision to journey to see Elizabeth who also conceived in a miraculous way recalls the Marian types of Judith and Jael, and signifies Mary as the heiress to Abraham. The Visitation is the occasion for the *Magnificat*. Tradition identifies the spot where the two mothers met as a place near Jerusalem called Ain Karim. It has two churches to commemorate the meeting and the birth of John the Baptist.

W

Weeping Madonnas   Statues or pictures of Mary that have been reported to shed tears. Examples that have survived ecclesiastical consideration are those that occurred in Treviglio in 1522, in Rho 1583, and in San Severino in 1519.

Z

***Zia Puebla* (zee'-ah pweh'-blah)**   A mission church near Albuquerque, New Mexico, which is the site of a pilgrimage, *fiesta*, and procession on August 15.

Shrines of
Our Blessed Virgin Mary
Around the World

The word *shrine* is usually given to a particular holy place regarded as sacred and spiritual. This sacredness may arise from many sources: a statue or an image, a tomb or a relic, or a remembrance of some religious event that occurred there. Usually a shrine is a pilgrimage destination, often associated with devotion to Mary. Shrines are also the sites of Marian apparitions, such as Lourdes, Knock, La Salette, or Montserrat.

An apparition is a term used to designate the inexplicable and extraordinary appearance of someone who is usually deceased. Most frequently during the history of the Church, apparitions involve appearances of the Blessed Virgin Mary.

Given an increasing number of claimed apparitions of Mary, it is important to have the authenticity of an apparitions established. A primary aspect of this authenticity is that the message or messages transmitted through an "apparition" should be in harmony with the teachings of the Church. In modern times, each claimed apparition is checked by the local bishop, who may appoint a commission to study the situation and who may also seek the opinion of Rome.

Though some apparitions have been recognized as authentic, such affirmation does not mean that a belief in a particular appearance is required of all Catholics. Recognition merely implies that the Church does not regard belief in the apparition as harmful to the faithful.

1. Africa

ALGERIA

Our Lady of Africa A bronze image of Our Lady brought to Africa from France in 1840 where it was entrusted to the Cistercian monks. Later the founder of the White Fathers enshrined this image in the basilica at Algiers.

SOUTH AFRICA

Mary, Mediatrix of All Graces   Atop a hill at a spot near Durban stands a statue of Mary, Mediatrix of All Graces. It has become a place of pilgrimage, especially on May 31, when the sick are blessed and a torchlight procession occurs.

UGANDA

Mary, Queen of Africa   This statue of Mary, which contains both a cross and the Moslem crescent, was crowned in 1954 and is located at Koboko.

2. Asia

CHINA

Our Lady of Zo-Se   Situated on a hill near Shanghai near the ruins of a former Buddhist monastery, this shrine grew out of a small church built by Jesuit Father Della Corte. Inside this small chapel, Father Corte placed a picture of Our Lady Help of Christians. After being saved from floods and attacks by bandits, Father Corte's congregation began building a larger church dedicated to Mary. On the campanile of the church is a statue of Our Lady, holding the Child Jesus aloft.

INDIA

Our Lady of Bandel   Pilgrims visit a church at Bandel, north of Calcutta, to honor Our Lady of Safe Travel, represented by a statue which was saved from desecration by a Portuguese merchant.

Our Mother of Divine Grace   This shrine lies on the southern bank of the Ganges River at Mokameh, about two hundred miles from Calcutta and fifty miles from Patna. The church, begun in 1943, is Hindu in architectural style and the Madonna is dressed in a sari with Hindu features. The church is the center of great devotion, and pilgrims walk for miles to reach it.

JAPAN

Our Lady of Akita From 1973 to 1975, Agnes Sasagawa Katsuko, a member of a religious order called the Institute of the Servants of the Eucharist, received visions of Our Lady which began with an address by her guardian angel who urged her not to be afraid but to pray for the reparation of the sins of all humankind.

Led to the chapel late that night, Sister Agnes heard a voice coming from the statue of Mary even though the nun had lost her hearing several months previously. And earlier that evening a painful, cross-shaped wound had appeared in the palm of Sister Agnes' right hand. Soon after the announcements of Mary had ceased, the right hand of the statue was also bleeding.

Several weeks later, Sister Agnes' guardian angel again said to her: "Pray for the conversion of all sinners, while adoring the Sacred Heart of Jesus and his Sacred Blood." At the sound of the angel's voice, her wound was healed.

During the next eight years, the statue of Mary in the sisters' chapel would shed tears intermittently, an occurrence witnessed by many thousands of people. The actual messages lasted about a year and a half, always emphasizing reparation for the sins of humanity through prayer, penance, and sacrifice.

The statue wept for the one hundred and first (and last) time on the feast of Our Lady of Sorrows, September 15, 1981. The following year, Sister Agnes recovered her hearing. On April 22, 1984, the Bishop of Nigata, Japan, declared the apparition to be authentic and authorized veneration of Our Lady of Akita.

Our Lady of Oura One of the first priests to arrive after Japan was reopened to the outside world in 1854 was the chaplain of the French consulate, Father Petit-jean who erected a modest church called Oura on a hill near the city of Nagasaki. One day he noticed a group of Japanese onlookers outside the church. He invited them inside and as he proceeded with his prayers, they whispered into his ear, "The hearts of all here are the same as yours." Here was a group of Japanese Christians who had maintained their faith for more than two hundred years—without benefit of clergy. The church of Our Lady of Oura was partially destroyed by the atom bomb dropped on Nagasaki.

PHILIPPINES

Our Lady of Antipolo This major sanctuary is dedicated to Mary and houses a statue of Our Lady which was installed in 1653. It was carved of wood which has discolored over the years and it stands atop a shrine of solid silver. Thousands of pilgrims crowd the shrine during the month of May when Our Lady is crowned with precious jewels following a colorful and elaborate procession.

Our Lady of the Turumba So called after the hymn of praise sung to Mary by pilgrims to the shrine. The image of Our Lady of the Turumba represents Our Lady of the Seven Swords; its face and hands are of ivory, it is clothed in a silken robe, and gold bracelets adorn its arm. This image is said to have been discovered submerged in a lake where men were fishing.

RUSSIA

Our Lady of Vladimir A Russian icon brought from Constantinople to Kiev and subsequently taken to the city of Vladimir, and finally to Moscow where it was taken in order to protect the city against a Tartar invasion in 1395. A monastery was erected on the spot where the population of Moscow met the holy image on August 26, and that day has commemorated ever since the salvation of Moscow.

VIETNAM

Our Lady of La-Vang Established in 1800 as a result of a reported vision of Our Lady, this shrine is located in the garden city and old capital of Hué. It receives thousands of pilgrims each year.

3. Holy Land

Basilica of the Annunciation An imposing church funded by Catholic communities from throughout the world and completed in 1969, this church is erected over what is claimed to be part of the home of the Blessed Virgin Mary in Nazareth. It commemorates the mystery of the Incarnation and the Annunciation of the angel Gabriel to Mary with the news of Our Lord's impending birth. Four other houses of worship have preceded the present basilica on this site.

Church of the Visitation The church in Ain Karim, a few miles west of Jerusalem, that marks the place where Mary hastened to meet her cousin Elizabeth. This church, completed in 1955, was built over the remains of earlier Byzantine and Crusader buildings. In the lower chapel of this church is an old well where ancient tradition holds that waters sprang joyfully out of the rock when the Virgin Mary greeted her cousin. Outside in the courtyard are displayed the Blessed Virgin's *Magnificat* in forty-five different languages.

In the upper church are paintings depicting the Virgin throughout the centuries, as well as holy women of the Old and New Testaments.

Dormition Abbey The cone-shaped gray roof and its nearby bell tower are distinctive identifiers of the Dormition Abbey in Jerusalem, a church dedicated to the "falling asleep," or peaceful passing of Mary from this life to the next. Tradition asserts that the Virgin Mary spent the latter years of her life on Mount Zion.

This church was consecrated in 1910 and is in the care of a community of Benedictine monks. Inside this spacious church is a fine mosaic of the Virgin and Child Jesus along with the eight Old Testament prophets who foretold the coming of the Messiah.

4. Europe

AUSTRIA

Our Lady of Mariazell A mecca for pilgrims from all of Central Europe, this shrine is located in the mountains some fifty miles southwest of Vienna. The shrine originated through the efforts of a Benedictine monk named Magnus, who in 1157 set up a statue of

Our Lady and the Infant Child on the spot that today is marked by a splendid three-towered basilica.

BELGIUM

Our Lady of Banneux The title of the Blessed Virgin Mary under which she appeared eight times to eleven-year-old Mariette Beco in Banneux in 1933. During these apparitions, she asked Mariette to build a little chapel by the side of the stream she had said was "reserved for all nations, for the sick." She also identified herself as the mother of the Savior, the mother of God, and admonished her to "Pray hard." Between the time of the last apparition and its approval by the Church in 1949, many miracles were accomplished. Thousands of pilgrims make their way here each year to receive the healing blessing of Our Lady.

Our Lady of Beauraing Between November 1932 and January 1933, Our Lady appeared to five children of the Deggeimbree and Voisin families in the small town of Beauraing, in the south of Belgium. In her thirty-three visions, Our Lady asked the following: that a chapel be built in her honor, that sacrifices be made for sin, that people pray always. She also identified herself as the Immaculate Virgin and gave the children a miraculous vision of her radiant Immaculate Heart. In 1949 the appearances were given ecclesiastical approval; since then, millions of pilgrims have made their way to this small Belgian village.

Our Lady of Oostacker A Belgian shrine to Our Lady of Lourdes which began as an aquarium used to display the Marquise de Courtbourne's collection of rare fishes. The aquarium was housed in a small house that had been the home of the Marquise's brother who had lived his last years there in prayerful solitude. When the parish priest came to inspect the new aquarium he suggested that it might be possible to incorporate a figure of Our Lady as she had appeared at Lourdes in the cleft of the rocks of this artificial cave. This was done in 1872, and almost immediately people came to visit the shrine in ever increasingly numbers. When Peter de Rudder's shattered leg was healed and made whole through intercession to Our Lady of Lourdes, the popularity of the shrine was sealed. Today a large church exists there and many testimonies as to cures and other favors granted are on display there.

CROATIA

Our Lady of Bistrica   A statue of the Blessed Virgin brought to Bistrica by refugees from the Turks, it was almost forgotten until 1684 when the church in which it stood became a place of pilgrimage and, later on, the Croatian national sanctuary.

CZECHOSLOVAKIA

Our Lady of Hostyn   Most significant shrine of the district of Moravia and the home of the pilgrimage church of the Assumption of the Blessed Virgin Mary. This shrine dates from the Mongol invasion of 1241, when Moravians took refuge in the forests on the mountain of Hostyn and were soon encircled by the Tartars. Those Christians were soon suffering from lack of water and were in imminent danger of being overrun by their attackers. They implored the help of the Mother of God and suddenly an enormous storm broke out, bringing relief to the Christians and causing thunder and lightning to destroy the Mongol tents, ensuring their retreat.

The memory of Our Lady's intercession was the occasion of the commissioning of a portrait of the Blessed Virgin Mary, painted on lindenwood, with the Infant Jesus in her hands, and directing bolts of lightening into the Tatar camps. Pilgrimages in honor of Our Lady of Hostyn have been recorded as far back as the year 1625. The number of chapels needed to accommodate as the pilgrims grew, and in 1748 a Baroque church was completed with six altars.

ENGLAND

Our Lady of Evesham   According to tradition, Our Lady appeared to a herdsman and gave him the task of asking the Bishop of Worcestershire to build a shrine in her honor in the forest in which she had appeared. No record exists of the building of this church, but it is maintained that Lady Godiva rebuilt this shrine in 960. It was a great pilgrimage place until the Reformation. In modern times, the Catholic Church has erected a new shrine to Our Lady of Evesham.

Our Lady of Mt. Carmel   Located in Aylesford in Kent, this place of pilgrimage commemorates the apparition of Our Lady to Saint Simon Stock, the prior general of the Carmelite Order. In this vision, the Blessed Virgin handed Simon Stock the Brown Scapular—the sign of her protection for all of her children. The Carmelite monastery was pulled down during the dissolution, but the Carmelites regained possession in 1949. The chapel still holds the relics of Saint Simon Stock.

Our Lady of Walsingham   According to an account written in 1465, the shrine of the Annunciation at Walsingham in the county of Norfolk was founded by a widow named Richeldis de Faverches around the year 1061 in response to a vision of Our Lady. The chapel was intended to be built to the dimensions of the Holy House at Nazareth and, according to legend, angels were instrumental in selecting the final site. Throughout the later Middle Ages, Walsingham was the most visited shrine of Our Lady in England.

The shrine was destroyed in 1538, and the statue of Our Lady was burned along with others in London. In 1897 Catholic devotion to Our Lady of Walsingham was rekindled at Saint Mary's Catholic Church at King's Lynn twenty-five miles away from the shrine at Walsingham. In 1934, the restored Slipper Chapel, one mile from Walsingham, was opened for Catholic worship. In this chapel was set up a statue of Our Lady of Walsingham, carefully recreated from the medieval design on the priory seal. Once again, this shrine to Our Lady is the focus of renewed devotion and pilgrimage.

FRANCE

Our Lady of Chartres   In Chartres, a city southeast of Paris, is found a Gothic-style cathedral, known for its architecture and its stained-glass windows. Tradition asserts that this cathedral stands on the spot of the oldest grotto to Mary in the Western world. Early Christian missionaries are said to have found a statue of a woman holding a child, known since the founding of the cathedral as Our Lady of the Underground or Our Lady of Chartres. Other objects of pilgrimage at the Cathedral of Chartres are the statue of Our Lady of the Pillar in the upper church and a reliquary said to contain the veil of the Virgin that once belonged to Charlemagne.

Our Lady of La Salette The tearful Mother of God appeared to two children on September 19, 1846, just outside a small village near Grenoble in southeastern France. She complained of people's irreligious ways and their working on Sunday, threatening famine if they did not revise their ways and be reconciled to God. In 1851, the Bishop of Grenoble declared that belief in the apparition was justified. Even before that, a Christian renewal began which influenced people like Don Bosco, Madeleine Sophie Barat, Léon Bloy, Blessed Julian Eymard, and Saint John Vianney. The basilica of Our Lady of La Salette was consecrated in 1879. The Missionaries of La Salette were approved in 1890 to care for the sanctuary and the needs of the pilgrims.

Our Lady of Le Puy Le Puy, just south of Lyon, is home to one of the most ancient shrines dedicated to the Blessed Virgin. A fifty-five-foot tall statue of Our Lady of France greets each person entering the city. This crowned figure is standing on a globe, her foot crushing the head of the serpent, and in her arms is the Child Jesus. In the city is the Cathedral of Le Puy which holds the image of the Black Madonna, a replica of the ancient one that had been dragged in a tumbrel during a mock trial at the time of the French Revolution, and then beheaded, and burned. The present statue is made of black marble and shows Our Lady seated holding her Son on her knees. According to tradition, the original statue was brought to Le Puy by Saint Louis, who had received it during his imprisonment by the Sultan of Egypt.

Seventeen kings of France, seven popes, and saints such as Dominic, Vincent Ferrer, Antony of Padua, and Francis Regis have made pilgrimages to Le Puy. Unable to make the pilgrimage herself, Joan of Arc sent her mother to represent her.

Our Lady of Lourdes   Lourdes, a town in the southwest of France and the site, in 1858, of eighteen apparitions of Our Lady to young Bernadette Soubirous, is today a pilgrimage-shrine of worldwide significance. In her appearances Our Lady called herself the Immaculate Conception, requested that a chapel be built on the spot where people might come in procession, and requested prayerful penance.

The Bishop of Tarbes proclaimed the legitimacy of the apparitions in 1862, and by 1871 the Basilica of the Immaculate Conception was dedicated. By 1889 the Basilica of the Rosary was completed along with several hospitals and a medical bureau to assist in the validation of the many cures which had occurred.

Our Lady of the Miraculous Medal   In the heart of Paris is the Convent of the Daughters of Charity where Our Lady appeared to Saint Catherine Labouré in 1830 and asked her to have a medal made with the inscription "O Mary conceived without sin, pray for us who have recourse to thee." So many miracles were attributed to this medal that it became known as the Miraculous Medal.

The gift of the Green Scapular was revealed to the novice Justine Bisqueyburu in 1840 at the same convent where the Miraculous Medal was presented. Our Lady appeared to Justine in a vision and asked that the Daughters of Charity distribute the Green Scapular which bears a picture of the Blessed Virgin Mary on one side and on the other side the image of her Immaculate Heart.

Pilgrims to the shrine will also see the incorrupt body of Saint Catherine Labouré, a reliquary holding the body of Saint Louise de Marillac; a reliquary holding the incorrupt heart of Saint Vincent de Paul, and a large statue of the Blessed Virgin marking the place where Mary appeared.

Our Lady of Pellevoisin   Pellevoisin is a small town about one hundred miles southwest of Paris. Here in 1876 Our Lady appeared fifteen times to Estelle Faguette who was suffering from the ravages of tuberculosis. Through these visions Estelle obtained a cure for her illness and was introduced by Mary to the Scapular of the Sacred Heart. In her final vision, Mary invited Estelle to kiss the Scapular of the Sacred Heart that she was wearing and said, "Nothing would be more pleasing to me than to see this livery on each of my children; see the graces I will pour on those who will wear it with confidence." This shrine is in the care of a community of contemplative Dominican nuns whose chapel is the room were Estelle experienced the apparitions.

Our Lady of Rocamadour   According to legend, this shrine began as a hermitage which was founding in the first century by a man named Zaccheus of Jericho. It was maintained that Zaccheus, who died in 70 A.D., knew Jesus and conversed with him. After Zaccheus died, his hermitage became a place of pilgrimage. Several centuries later, Rocamadour became one of the most famous shrines in Christendom when a miracle-working statue of the Blessed Virgin was brought to the site which is near the present-day Toulouse. The figure is of cedar blackened with age. Our Lady is seated and appears to be resting her weight on her hands which are supported on the arms of her chair. The Child Jesus is balanced on her knee, dressed in a simple robe like hers. In his left hand he holds a book of the Gospels; his right hand is extended in blessing. Today more than 1.5 million pilgrims visit Rocamadour every year and many place testimonies of favors in the *Book of Miracles*. The complex includes the Holy Redeemer Basilica, Our Lady's Chapel, Saint Michael's chapel, a museum, and a crypt of Zaccheus who had taken the name of Amadour.

GERMANY

Our Lady of Altötting   An miraculous image of Our Lady dating from the 1200s which stands in a silver-plated alcove of the Holy Chapel of Altötting, east of Munich. The chapel, octagon-shaped and build of volcanic rock, date from around A.D. 680 when Saint Rupert was supposed to have baptized Otto the Bavarian. This richly endowed shrine has escaped many threats, including epidemics, barbarian invasions, and wars.

Our Lady of Kevelaer   This shrine owes its origin to a peddler, Hendrik Busmann, who heard a command to build a shrine at a certain spot near the town of Kleve. Encouraged by his wife who had also had a vision, he built a little holy place, and in it he put a reproduction print of the Luxembourg statue of Our Lady, Consoler of the Afflicted. So many people flocked to the shrine known as Our Lady of Kevelaer that it became necessary to build beside it a church which was finished in 1645. This first church is now called the Candle Chapel where pilgrims now bring giant candles, some ten feet long. In addition, an impressive Gothic-style cathedral was built in 1858. Much of the shrine was saved from destruction by a German Catholic soldier who, ordered to blow up the spire of the church, refused and was court martialed.

Our Lady of Dettelbach   Our Lady of Dettelbach, near the city of Würzburg, is a shrine of Our Lady housing a small *pietà*. It was established by the owner of a vineyard toward the end of the fifteenth century. After the miraculous cure of a man who had been seriously injured in a quarrel, the shrine received increasing attention from pilgrims. The original wooden chapel built next to the small shrine has given way to a large church in which the *pietà* is enthroned under a massive marble canopy.

HOLLAND

Our Lady of 's Hertogenbosch   The cathedral in Brabant named after Our Lady was built in the fifteenth century. The image of Our Lady of 's Hertogenbosch is housed in the chapel of that cathedral. Damaged and dirty, it was first discovered in 1380 in a junkyard, but it soon attained renown for the wonders associated with it and was installed in the cathedral in a place of honor.

HUNGARY

Our Lady of Györ   This image of Our Lady shows her kneeling beside the Infant Jesus, asleep in bed, with a crown on his head. This picture is often called the "Irish Madonna" because it was brought to Hungary in 1655 by the exiled bishop of Confert in Galway, Ireland. Bishop Walter Lynch spent ten years in the city of Györ and, as he was preparing to return to Ireland, he fell ill and died. On his deathbed, he bequeathed the picture of the Irish Madonna to the people of Györ. The arrival of this treasured relic from Ireland marked a series of victories over the Turks and the averting of many national disasters; thus Hungarians attach great important to this picture of the Madonna who is a symbol of religious and national significance.

IRELAND

Our Lady of Knock In August 1879, on a rainy evening, Our Lady revealed herself to a group of villagers in the town of Knock, in County Mayo, Ireland. These people saw the crowned figure of Our Lady, accompanied by Saint John the Evangelist and Saint Joseph, on the face of a church wall in the parish courtyard. A shrine built on this spot is the destination of many thousands of pilgrims.

Our Lady of Limerick A statue of Mary and her Child presented by Patrick Sarsfield to the Rosary Confraternity of Limerick in 1622. It was given in reparation for his father's part in the murder of Sir John Burke. After 1698 it lay buried until 1733, when it was set up in Fish Lane chapel. The statue of Our Lady of Limerick was transported to a new Dominican church in 1816. At the base of this statue is a chalice which was hidden during the time of the "general exile."

ITALY

Our Lady of the Catacombs The fresco of the Blessed Virgin seated with the Child Jesus on her knee is painted on the wall in the Catacomb of St. Priscilla and dates from about A.D. 170. It is a very early precursor of the icons, paintings, and other representations of Our Lady that have inspired devotion to the Virgin Mary and Mother of God.

Our Lady of Good Counsel In Genazzano, a town about thirty miles southeast of Rome, stands the pilgrim-shrine that is home to the image of Our Lady of Good Counsel which miraculously descended from a cloud and was left on the walls of the uncompleted church named after her. The appearance of the "Madonna of Paradise," as she was also called, occurred in 1467, and investigations by two bishops confirmed that more than one hundred miracles had occurred in Genazzano between April when the picture appeared and August.

A basilica was built by the end of the fifteenth century, and veneration of Our Lady of Good Counsel spread all over the world. The people of Genazzano celebrate the appearance of this image of Our Lady with a procession of great verve and beauty.

Our Lady of Loreto   The little town of Loreto is the scene of a monumental shrine to Our Lady—a domed basilica built completely around the Holy House of Nazareth in which the Virgin Mary was born. According to tradition, this is the original house of Nazareth which was transported by angels, first to Tersato in Dalmatia, and then to Italy to rest on the Recanati road at Loreto.

Though the story of the translation of the Holy House is open to question, these objections do not change the fact Loreto has long been a site of religious devotion.

Our Lady of Pompeii   Our Lady is honored under this title at a sanctuary near the ruins of Pompeii. The complex includes a pilgrim hospice, a school, and a splendid church erected in 1939.

The origins of this shrine are found in the efforts of a lawyer of Pompeii named Bartolo Longo who had established the local Rosary Confraternity. In search of an image of Our Lady for the confraternity, he went to Naples where he purchased a dilapidated old painting of Our Lady of the Rosary, with Saint Dominic and Saint Catherine of Siena. Soon miracles were reported in connection with the picture, pilgrims started to come, and out of this small beginning grew a large establishment in honor of Mary.

Our Lady of the Sacred Letter   The title of the celebration in honor of Our Lady held at Messina in Sicily. This title refers to a letter that was claimed to have been dictated by Mary to followers of Saint Paul at Messina. No authenticated reference to any such letter has been found.

Our Lady of the Snows The original name of the Basilica of Saint Mary Major in Rome arose out of a legend in which a wealthy and pious Roman was told in a dream to build a church in honor of Our Lady on the spot on the Esquiline hill that was covered in snow in the middle of summer. In the Borghese chapel of this basilica rests the most venerated image of Our Lady in Rome, an ancient Byzantine painting know as Saint Mary, Protectress of Rome.

Santa Maria Delle Grazie One of the best-known shrines to Our Lady of Grace in Italy, the refectory of this monastery in Milan houses Leonardo da Vinci's painting of the Last Supper. It also is the center of the veneration of Our Lady of Grace as a result of an image ordered painted by Lodovico Sforza at the end of the fifteenth century. According to tradition, the virulent epidemics of the plague seemed to stop before reading Milan once the image of Our Lady of Grace had been installed.

POLAND

Our Lady of Czestochowa The most famous of Poland's shrines, the icon known by this title was brought to Poland from the Ukraine in 1382 by Duke Ladislas of Opole who built a chapel and founded a monastery to care for the image. After an attack of anti-papal Swedes was repulsed through the leadership of the abbot of the monastery in 1655, Our Lady of Czestochowa was proclaimed "Queen of the Crown of Poland." It is a national shrine and is visited by millions of pilgrims each year.

PORTUGAL

Our Lady of Fátima The title referring to the apparitions of Our Lady to three young Portuguese children in the village of Fátima, seventy-five miles north of Lisbon. The visions of Our Lady were preceded by three apparitions of an angel who taught the children prayers and who urged them to say the rosary and make sacrifices for the reparation of sins.

In the apparitions of Our Lady she appealed for prayer and penance, urged the consecration of Russia to her Immaculate Heart, and asked for the observance of First Saturdays in reparation for sins. The first vision occurred on May 13, 1917, and the final vision took place on October 13, 1917, along with the dramatic episode of the dance of the sun. The bishop of the diocese in which the apparitions occurred formally gave his approval of devotion to Our Lady of Fátima in 1930.

From a tiny chapel built over the spot of the apparitions, today's Fátima has grown to a huge complex including the Basilica of Our Lady of the Rosary, with fifteen altars in honor of the fifteen mysteries of the rosary, a hospital, a Medical Bureau, a Perpetual Adoration Chapel, and a monument to the Sacred Heart.

Since the visions, millions of pilgrims have visited to honor Our Lady and seek her intercession.

SCOTLAND

Our Lady of Carfin   Just after World War I, the parish priest of a church in the Lanarkshire coal fields organized unemployed workers to build a Lourdes grotto to Our Lady. Finished in 1922, the shrine soon was receiving thousands of pilgrims. The original one-acre site was enlarged and among other Marian shrines replicated there is the Holy House of Loreto.

SPAIN

Our Lady of Montserrat   Situated near Barcelona, Montserrat is the name of a four-thousand-foot mountain where, in the ninth century, legend has it that a black, wooden statue of Our Lady with an orb in her hand and with the Holy Child on her lap was discovered in a cave. Though attempts were made to move the statue, it never reached its destination because the small wooden figure became too heavy to move. A church and then a basilica were built on the site of the discovery of the Black Madonna of Montserrat, and pilgrims and many saints have visited to ask Our Lady's intercession. During the Spanish Civil War of 1936–1939, the Benedictine monastery there was closed and more than twenty of its monks were murdered, including the Prefect of the Vatican Library.

258

Our Lady of the Pillar A pilgrim-shrine at Saragossa in Spain where rests a small statue on a pillar of jasper that is said to have been given to James the Apostle in a vision. Our Lady asked that a church be built on the spot of her apparition and named after the image and column on which it stood. Though the original chapel has long since been destroyed, in its place is a magnificent basilica wherein the fifteen-inch statue now resides.

SWITZERLAND

Our Lady of Einsiedeln Twenty miles southeast of Zurich, Einsiedeln is home to Benedictines where a monastic hermit named Meinrad set himself off from the rest of the monks and built a solitary sanctuary deep in the forest. In this sanctuary he kept a statue of the Black Madonna, a symbol of his deep devotion to Our Lady. In 861, this holy man was murdered by two men who had hoped to find riches and other jewels in Meinrad's hermitage. They were apprehended after two ravens noisily and insistently followed them into town. Almost from the time of Saint Meinrad's death, pilgrims made their way to this sacred site.

According to legend, in 948, Christ himself consecrated Meinrad's Lady Chapel, and the local bishop was notified of this occurrence through a vision. This miraculous event was confirmed by Pope Leo VIII sixteen years later in a papal bull.

Our Lady of the Rock This shrine, dedicated to Our Lady, is located near the city of Locarno, on the border between Switzerland and Italy. The origin of this shrine dates to 1480 when Brother Bartolommeo d'Ivrea set up a sanctuary on the mountain above Locarno. According to tradition, the Virgin Mary appeared to him on the feast of the Assumption and confirmed his desire to consecrate the mountain in her honor.

Brother Bartolommeo started work on several chapels in honor of Our Lady and, after his death, a string of chapels were completed, connecting the monk's cave at the top of the mountain with the valley below.

5. North America

CANADA

Our Lady of the Cape On a little cape jutting out into the St. Lawrence River, Jesuit priests erected a small chapel dedicated to Saint Mary Magdalene. Inside the church was a statue of Our Lady donated to the parish in 1845 in honor of the Confraternity of the Rosary. Parishioners decided to build a new church to supplant the old chapel, but were stymied because the river had not frozen solidly enough to permit transport of the building stones across the ice. However, during a novena to Mary, the weather turned bitingly cold, and teams of horses made one hundred and fifty trips across the ice to bring sufficient building stones to land. The new church was dedicated in 1888 and soon became a shrine of national importance.

Saint Mary Among the Hurons Established by Jesuit Jerome Lalemant in 1639 at what is now Midland, Ontario, as a place of pilgrimage for the Hurons. In Indian burial sites uncovered close to this shrine, rosaries were found around the necks of each person buried there. At the same time that Saint John de Brébeuf and Saint Gabriel Lalemant were martyred by the Iroquois in 1649, this shrine was also destroyed. In modern times the shrine has been restored and a chapel of Our Lady erected.

MEXICO

Our Lady of Guadalupe In December 1531, Our Lady appeared on three occasions to a poor Indian convert, Juan Diego, on Tepeyac Hill, not far from what is now Mexico City. She asked Juan Diego to convey to Bishop Juan de Zumárraga her wish that a church be built on the spot where she stood. She promised: "None who seek me here in true need or affliction shall go away unconsoled." The Bishop was not inclined to believe the Indian and asked that he return with a sign. When he saw Our Lady next, she instructed him to return to the original spot where she had appeared, pick the flowers that were blooming there, and bring them to the bishop.

Though this was not the season for flowers, Juan did as Our Lady instructed, putting the flowers he found on Tepeyac Hill inside his large cloak. When he brought these to the bishop, petals dropped from his cloak and, on the inside, was the miraculous picture of Our Lady which may still be seen above the main altar of the Basilica of Our Lady of Guadalupe.

A small chapel was erected at the site of the apparitions, probably around 1531, and three others at later dates. The largest church was begun in 1695, completed in 1709, and raised to the rank of a basilica in 1904.

In 1946, Pope Pius XII declared Our Lady of Guadalupe the patroness of all the Americas. In 1988, the liturgical celebration of Our Lady of Guadalupe on December 12 was raised to the status of a feast in all dioceses in the United States.

UNITED STATES

National Shrine of the Immaculate Conception   Conceived by Bishop Thomas J. Shahan in response to the naming of Mary, under her title of the Immaculate Conception, as patroness of the Unites States, this basilica, located in Washington, D.C., is a huge hymn to Mary.

In the center of the Crypt Church is a carved altar dedicated to Our Lady of the Catacombs. It has been used for the celebration of Mass since 1927 and was a gift from more than thirty thousand women named Mary. The shrine's great upper church was added in 1954, followed by many chapels, each reflecting the religious heritage brought to America by waves of immigrant Catholics.

Our Lady of La Leche   Located on the grounds of the Mission of *Nombre de Dios* (the name of God) in St. Augustine, Florida, this shrine was originally established by Spanish settlers around 1615. Once ruined in battle, rebuilt, and then destroyed by a hurricane, the present chapel and shrine was built in 1915. Enshrined there is a replica of the original statue of *Nuestra Señora de la Leche y buen parto*—Our Lady of the Mild and Happy Delivery. The shrine is visited by all those with special intentions but most especially by mothers-to-be and families.

Our Lady of Sorrows   Popularly known as "The Grotto," this shrine located on sixty-two acres near the center of Portland, Oregon, was founded by Servite Father Ambrose M. Mayer, O.S.M., in fulfillment of a childhood pledge. The shrine features a marble replica of Michelangelo's *Pietà* set into a rock cave carved into the base of a cliff, a Meditation Chapel, a Peace Garden, and a life-size statue of Saint Francis of Assisi.

Our Lady of Victory   This shrine was the culmination of the work of the Reverend Nelson H. Baker. Built near Buffalo, New York, in honor of his personal patron to whom he credited his success in aiding thousands of infants, young people, and adults who had fallen on hard times. The copper-domed basilica is crowned with four copper angels, raising their trumpets in four directions around the dome. Inside, the focal point of the main church is the statue of Our Lady of Victory underneath a marble canopy supported by a large gold cross. Overhead, a bright blue dome depicts the Holy Spirit. Also inside are magnificent sculptures, the fourteen Stations of the Cross, and numerous smaller altars.

Our Lady of Zhyrovytsi   Located at Olyphant, Pennsylvania, this shrine memorializes the miraculous icon of Our Lady of Zhyrovytsi found in the Church of Saints Sergius and Bacchus in Rome where it had been transported from the Ukraine. This outdoor shrine shows Our Lady in a red gown covered by a deep blue tunic. In her right arm she holds the Infant Jesus. Inscribed on an oval around the figures are the words of the "Hymn to the Blessed Virgin" taken from the liturgy of Saint John Chrysostom.

6. Central America

DOMINICAN REPUBLIC

Our Lady of Altagracia   The painting honoring Our Lady under this title was brought to the New World a short fourteen years after the discovery of America. It was enshrined in a parish church in Higuey, and later a large basilica was built to accommodate the large number of pilgrims who visit the site.

COSTA RICA

Our Lady, Queen of the Angels   This shrine honors a miracle which took place on the feast of Our Lady Queen of the Angels (August 2) 1635, when a statue of the Madonna and Child was discovered in a forest. The young girl who discovered the statue took it home twice, and twice the statue mysteriously returned to the place were it was originally located. A shrine was built on this forest site, and Our Lady Queen of the Angels was declared patroness of Costa Rica in 1824.

7. South America

ARGENTINA

Our Lady of Cuyo   A statue of Our Lady resting in a sanctuary at Mendoza. Its history goes back to the earliest Spanish days when it was in the possession of the Jesuits. When they were driven out of Argentina in 1767, the statue came into the possession of the Franciscans. Our Lady of Cuyo was the object of special devotion to General José San Martin, leader of the war for independence against the Spaniards. In 1812 he sent him military baton to the shrine as a thanksgiving for graces granted.

Our Lady of Luján   The small statue representing Our Lady of Luján is housed in one of the most significant cathedrals in the world located near the Luján River in Argentina. This statue was in a caravan headed toward the town of Córdoba when the horses refused to go any further. Despite every effort, the horses could not be budged. But they started off again as soon as the small terra cotta statue they were carrying was removed from the wagon and carried into a nearby ranch house.

The ranch owner gave the statue into the care of a slave who insisted that a chapel be built for it. Soon miraculous events set in, and pilgrims visited from all over. Today the area is a great religious center, and Our Lady of Luján has been declared the protectress of Argentina, Uruguay, and Paraguay.

BOLIVIA

Our Lady of Copacabana   Indian fishermen were caught in a terrifying storm on Lake Titicaca near the ancient town of Copacabana. Thinking they would perish immediately, they prayed and, while doing so, the Blessed Virgin appeared to them, and led them safely to shore. They decided to build a shrine and to place a statue in it that reproduced the vision they had seen. The statue was completed in 1576, and the first chapel was built in 1583. The church here was elevated to the rank of a basilica in 1940, and is the focal point of celebrations on Our Lady of Copacabana's feast day which occurs in August. Our Lady of Copacabana is the patroness of Bolivia.

BRAZIL

Our Lady of Aparecida   In 1717, a group of Brazilian fishermen were fishing on the river Parahybam with little success. They were about to return home when the last throw of their net brought up a small wooden statue of Our Lady. The statue was considered a sign of grace and, with the consent of the ecclesiastical authorities, a shrine and chapel were erected. In the course of almost three hundred years, this little shrine grew into Brazil's major sanctuary.

COLOMBIA

Our Lady of Chiquinquirá   In 1586, in the Andean town of Chiquinquirá, near the city of Medellin, a cousin of a Spaniard named Don Santana was praying before a tattered painting of the Madonna. As she prayed the rosary, Our Lady appeared and left behind her beautiful image on the canvas. This miracle soon became renowned, and a stone church was built to house the pilgrims who visited Our Lady of Chiquinquirá. A basilica was built over the ruins of the early church by the Capuchins in 1824.

ECUADOR

Our Lady of Quinche   In 1586, the Indians of Lumbici asked a Spanish sculptor to create an image of Our Lady out of native cedar. This image was finally installed near Quinche, Ecuador, where a chapel was soon built and later, a larger church. This statue is carried in processions on important occasions throughout the land of Ecuador. She is affectionately referred to as "The Little Beloved One."

VENEZUELA

Our Lady of Betania   In March 1976, on the feast of the Annunciation, a wife and mother of seven, Maria Esperanza, received her first apparition of the Blessed Virgin at a grotto on her farm in Betania, Venezuela. Mary said to Maria: "My daughter, I have given you my heart. I give it to you and will always give it to you." Mary awarded Maria Esperanza a mission of kindness, fidelity, service, and sacrifice, while assuring her that she would always be her refuge. The Madonna concluded this apparition by saying "I am the Reconciler of all Peoples," the title by which she is now known in Betania.

Further apparitions occurred, especially on March 25, but the most spectacular appearance occurred on March 25, 1984, where a crowd of over one thousand people witnessed the Blessed Mother bathed in a brilliant light and accompanied by the sweet fragrance of roses.

These apparitions have enkindled a search for God and the spiritual life and a renewed love of the Church. Consequently, Bishop Pio Ricardo welcomed the Virgin's request to build a church to "Our Lady, Reconciler of Peoples" and, in 1987, after consultation with the Vatican, declared the apparitions authentic.

Our Lady of Coromoto   In 1651, the chief of the Cospe Indians living near the village of Guarare in Venezuela, were on their way to get water when Our Lady appeared to them. In later apparitions she asked them to receive baptism, and gave them a painting of herself with the Infant King Jesus in her arms. This image was venerated for over two hundred years in the parish church of Guarare and today is housed in a Baroque basilica, the destination of thousands of reverent pilgrims.

SECTION ELEVEN

Calendar of Our Lady

JANUARY

1. Solemnity of Mary, the Mother of God (Celebrated on December 26 in Syrian Churches, and January 16 in the Coptic Rite)
2. Our Lady of the Pillar (Spain)
3. Madonna of Sichem (Palestine)
4. Our Lady of the Flowers (Beauvais, France)
5. Our Lady of Prosperity (Italy)
8. Synaxis of the Miracle of the Wedding Feast at Cana Performed at Mary's Request (Constantinople)
9. Feast of the Translation of the House of the Annunciation to Varani (Italy)
11. Our Lady of Egypt
12. Memorial of the Icon of the Blessed Virgin Mary of the Akathistos Hymn (Mount Athos)
13. Our Lady of Virtues
14. Our Lady of Consolation (Naples)
15. Our Lady of Prompt Succor (New Orleans, Louisiana)
    Mother of God, Mother of Seeds (Oriental churches)
    Our Lady of Banneaux (Belgium)
16. Immaculate Heart of Mary, Refuge of Sinners (France)
17. Our Lady of Lights (Cistercians)
18. Our Lady of Dijon (France)
19. Our Lady of Grace (Carmelites of Avila, Spain)
20. Manifestation of the Blessed Virgin Mary to Alphonse de Ratisbonne Judeo
21. Feast of Our Lady of Alta Gratia (Santo Domingo)
23. Feast of the Betrothal of Our Lady (Palestine)
24. Feast of Our Lady of Fontana (Italy)
25. Feast of the Blessed Virgin Mary, Our Lady of Sorrows (Marburg, Germany)
26. Our Lady of the Long-Fields (Spain)
30. Feast of the Translation of the Relics of Saint Anne, Mother of the Blessed Virgin Mary (France)
31. Feast of the Hidden Life of Mary

FEBRUARY

2. Feast of the Presentation of the Lord and the Purification of the Blessed Virgin Mary
4. Feast of the Ten Virtues of the Blessed Virgin Mary (purity, prudence, humility, faith, compassion, devotion, obedience, poverty, patience, love)
5. Commemoration of Our Lady of the Sacred Letter
6. Our Lady of Louvain (Belgium)
7. Feast of the Sacred Heart of Mary (Calabria, Italy)
8. Madonna of Miracles (Rennet, France)
9. Our Lady of the Lily
10. Our Lady of the Dove (Italy)
11. Our Lady of Lourdes
12. Commemoration of the Most Pure Heart of the Blessed Virgin Mary
13. Feast of Our Lady, Queen of Orphans (Montpelier)
    Our Lady of Pellevoisin (France)
14. Coronation of the Blessed Virgin Mary, Mother of Hope
15. Notre Dame de Paris
16. Madonna of the Thorn (France)
17. Our Lady of Constantinople
19. Our Lady of Good Tidings (France)
21. Our Lady of Good Haven (France)
23. Madonna of the Rocks (Spain)
26. Madonna of the Fields (Paris)
27. Our Lady of Lights (Lisbon, Portugal)
28. Our Lady of Tears (Lombardy)

MARCH

1. Feast of Our Lady, Mother of the Divine Shepherd (Gubbio)
2. Feast of Our Lady, Mirror of Justice
5. Our Lady of Good Aid (France)
6. Our Lady of Nazareth (Portugal)
7. Madonna of the Stars (Portugal)
11. Our Lady of Suffering
12. Our Lady of Miracles

14. Our Lady of Kostrama (Russia)

16. Our Lady of the Fountain (Constantinople)

17. Institution of Our Lady's Office

18. Commemoration of the Appearance of Our Lady of Mercy to Saint Bernard: 1536

19. Feast of Saint Joseph, Spouse of Our Lady

20. Our Lady of Calevourt (Belgium)

21. Our Lady of Bruges (Flanders)

24. Our Lady of Saidnaia (Syria)

25. Solemnity of the Annunciation of the Lord to the Blessed Virgin Mary

26. Our Lady of Soissons (France)

27. Feast of the Apparition of Our Lord to Our Lady After His Resurrection

28. Feast of the Blessed Virgin Mary of the Martyrs

29. Apparition of Our Lady to Saint Bonet (7th c.)

31. Our Lady of the Holy Cross (Jerusalem)

APRIL

1. Feast of the Blessed Virgin Mary, Queen of Poland

2. Visitation of Our Lady at York (1263–1389)

5. Apparition of Our Lady to Pope Honorius IV to Confirm the Order of Our Lady of Mount Carmel

7. Our Lady of the Forsaken (Valencia, Spain)

8. Feast of the Miracles of Our Lady (Belgium)

10. Our Lady of Laval (France)

11. Madonna of Montserrat

12. Our Lady of Charity (Toulouse, France)

13. Our Lady's Apparition to Blessed Jane of Mantua

14. Feast of Our Lady of Vilna

15. Feast of Our Lady of Deliverance (Sicily)

18. Our Lady of Fourviers

19. Our Lady of Good Counsel (Limoge, France)

20. Our Lady of Schier (Bavaria)

21. Confraternity of the Immaculate Conception: 1506

22. Feast of the Blessed Virgin Mary of the Way (Pamplona)

26. Our Lady of Lujan (Argentina)
28. Our Lady of Quito (Ecuador)
29. Our Lady, Queen of the Angels
30. Our Lady of Africa (Algiers)

MAY

1. Nativity of the Blessed Virgin Mary (Abyssinian Rite)
2. Our Lady of Reparation (Rome)
3. Our Lady of Jasna Gora, Queen of the Crown of Poland
4. Our Lady, Altar of Heaven (Spain)
6. Our Lady, Queen of the Prophets
7. Seven Joys of Our Lady
8. Our Lady, Mediatrix of All Graces
   Our Lady of Pompeii
11. Our Lady of Aparecida (Brazil)
12. Humility of Our Lady (Louis de Montfort)
13. Our Lady of Fátima
15. Our Lady of the Sheaves (Syrian Rite)
16. Vision of Our Lady to Catherine of Alexandria
18. Notre Dame de Bonport (France)
20. Feast of Our Lady, Consolation of the Afflicted
21. Feast of Our Lady of Vladimir (Russia)
    Feast of Our Lady of the Cenacle
24. Mary, Help of Christians
    Our Lady of the Highway
25. Our Lady of the New Jerusalem
26. Our Lady of Caravaggio (Milan)
28. Feast of the Relics of Our Lady (Venice, Italy)
30. Our Lady of Hanswijk (Belgium)
    Our Lady of Fair Love
31. Feast of the Visitation

JUNE

1. Our Lady of Kevelaer (Germany)
   Our Lady, Cause of Our Joy (Canada)

2. Our Lady of Edessa (Asia Minor)

4. Our Lady, Queen of Peace (Calabria, Italy)

6. Founding of the Nuns of the Visitation of Our Lady by Saint Francis de Sales

7. Immaculate Heart of Mary
Our Lady of the Valley

8. Our Lady of Wisdom

9. Mother of Divine Grace (United States)

10. Madonna of Granganor (East Indies)

12. Vision of Our Lady to Saint Herman

15. Dedication of First Church to Mary (Syria)

16. Our Lady of Aix-la-Chapelle

17. Our Lady in Porticu (Wales)

18. Vision of Our Lady to Saint Agnes of Mount Politan

19. Veneration of Our Lady Comb at the Church of Saint John the Evangelist (Treves, Germany)

20. Our Lady of Consolation (Turin)

21. Our Lady of Mararieh (Egypt)

25. Mary Declared to Be the Mother of God by the Council of Ephesus

26. Our Lady of Meliapour (East Indies)

27. Our Lady of Perpetual Help

28. Dedication of Notre Dame de Paris: 1325

30. Our Lady of Calais

JULY

2. Feast of Our Lady of Montallegro (Italy)
Feast of the Deposition of the Mantle of Our Lady, Mother of God, at Blachernae: 458

3. Our Lady of La Carolle (Paris)

5. Our Lady of Cambrai (France)

6. Our Lady of Iron (Blois, France)

7. Our Lady of 's Hertogendoseh (Netherlands)

8. Madonna of Kazan (Russia)

9. Our Lady of Chevremont (Belgium)

Our Lady of Chiquinquiré (Ecuador)
10. Our Lady of Good Health (Canada)
Prodigies of Our Lady
12. Our Lady of All Graces
13. Our Lady of Providence (Naples)
14. Our Lady of the Bush (Portugal)
16. Our Lady of Mount Carmel
Our Lady of Avioth (France)
Our Lady of Einsiedeln (Switzerland)
17. Humility of Our Lady
18. Our Lady of Good Deliverance (France)
21. Our Lady of Verdun (Lorraine)
22. Our Lady of Safety (Holland)
23. Order of Prémontré Instituted Through Revelation of Our Lady
25. Feast of the Dormition of Anne, Mother of the Blessed
Virgin Mary (Byzantine Rite)
26. Our Lady of Faith
Our Lady, Help of Those in Their Last Agony
28. Our Lady of Providence
30. Our Lady of Gray (Besancon, France)
31. Our Lady of the Slain (Portugal)

AUGUST

1. Our Lady of All the Earth (Naples)
2. Our Lady of the Angels of Portiuncula (Assisi, Italy)
3. Our Lady of Bows (London, England)
4. Madonna of Dordrecht (Holland)
5. Dedication of Saint Mary Major
6. Our Lady of Copacabana (Bolivia)
7. Our Lady of Schiedem (Holland)
10. Our Lady of Ransom (Spain)
11. Translation of Two of Our Lady's Robes to Aix-la-Chapelle:
A.D. 180.
13. Our Lady, Refuge of Sinners
15. Solemnity of the Assumption and the Feast of the Dormition
of Our Lady, Most Holy Mother of God (Byzantine Rite)

17. Madonna of Grace (Italy)
18. Coronation of Mary (Central America)
19. Our Lady of the Don (Russia)
    Holy Heart of Mary
21. Institution of the Order of the Thirty Knights of Our Lady
    Our Lady of Knock (Ireland)
22. Queenship of Mary
24. Our Lady of Czestochowa (Poland)
27. Seven Joys of Our Lady (Traditional)
28. Our Lady of Kiev (Poland)
30. Notre-Dame de Délivrande (Martinique)
31. Feast of the Girdle of Our Lady (Byzantine Rite)

SEPTEMBER

1. Our Lady of Hal (Belgium)
   Our Lady, Consoler of the Afflicted
2. Our Lady of Ebron (Germany)
3. Our Lady of Penha (Brazil)
5. Our Lady of the Woods (France)
6. Our Lady of the Fountain (France)
8. Feast of the Birth of Mary
   Our Lady of Bandra (India)
   Feast of Hagia Sophia or Divine Wisdom (Russia)
9. Our Lady of Aranzazu (Spain)
   Our Lady of Le Puy (France)
10. Our Lady of Zion
11. Our Lady, Help of the Infirm
12. Holy Name of Mary
13. Our Lady of Guadalupe
    Our Lady of Mariazell (Austria)
15. Our Lady of Sorrows
    Our Lady, the Amiable Mother of Starkenburg (Missouri)
16. Our Lady of Good News
17. Grandeurs of Our Lady (Paris)
18. Our Lady of Life (Syria)
19. Our Lady of La Salette

20. Our Lady of Silver Feet

22. Our Lady of Epakuses or She Who Listens Well and Grants Requests (Mount Athos)

25. Our Lady of the Oak (Viterbo)

27. Our Lady of Happy Assembly

29. Our Lady of Good Memory (Genoa, Italy)

30. Our Lady of Beaumont

OCTOBER

2. Feast of the Protection and Intercession of the Blessed Virgin Mary (Russia, Serbia, Bulgaria, Romania)

3. Our Lady, Mother of the Divine Redemption (Spain)

4. Our Lady of the Cape (Cap de la Madeleine, Canada)

6. Our Lady of La Plebe (Venice)

7. Our Lady of the Most Holy Rosary

8. Our Lady of Gifts
Our Lady, Queen of Hungary

9. Our Lady of Ephesus (Moscow)

10. Madonna of the Cloister (Besancon, France)

11. Mary, Mother of the Church

12. Our Lady of the Pillar (Saragossa, Spain)

13. Our Lady of Iviron (Russia)

14. Our Lady of Larochette (Near Geneva, Switzerland)

15. Our Lady of the Schools

16. Our Lady of Purity (Portugal)

17. Feast of the Vesting of Our Lady of the Underground

18. Our Lady of Rheims

19. Feast of the Inner Life of Mary (Sulpicians)

20. Feast of Our Lady, Mother Most Admirable

22. Our Lady of Boulogne-sur-Mer (France)

23. Our Lady of Comfort (France)

26. Our Lady of Victories (St. Louis, Missouri)

27. Our Lady of Charity (Cuba)

28. Our Lady of the Trellis (France)

31. Consecration of the World to the Immaculate Heart of Mary by Pope Pius XII in 1942

NOVEMBER

3. Our Lady of Mokameh (India)
4. Our Lady of Paradise (Sicily)
5. Establishment of the First Sodality of Our Lady at the Jesuit College at Rome
7. Our Lady of Suffrage
8. Our Lady of Hope
12. Our Lady of the Tower (Eriburg, Germany)
13. Dedication of the Abbey of Bec in Honor of Our Lady
14. Our Lady of the Grotto (Lamego, Spain)
16. Mother of Divine Providence
17. Founding of the Confraternity of Our Lady of Sion: 1393
18. Our Lady of Chiquinquirà (Venezuela)
19. Our Lady of Good News
20. Our Lady On Guard (Italy)
21. Presentation of Mary in the Temple
22. Founding of the Confraternity of the Presentation of Our Lady of the Teutonic House of Jerusalem by Saint Omer: 1841
25. Our Lady of the Rock (Fiezoli, Tuscany)
27. Our Lady of the Miraculous Medal
28. Our Lady of Walsingham (England)
29. Our Lady of the Crown (Palermo, Italy)
30. Saint Mary of Zion (Ethiopic Rite)

DECEMBER

1. Our Lady of Ratisbon (Bavaria)
2. Our Lady of Didnia (Cappadocia)
3. Our Lady of Filermo (Malta)
4. Madonna of Holy Purity
   Feast of the Virgin Mary Most Powerful
8. Solemnity of the Immaculate Conception and
   Feast of the Maternity of Saint Anne, Mother of Mary
12. Our Lady of Guadalupe
13. Our Lady of the Holy Chapel (Paris)
14. Our Lady of Albe la Royale (Hungary)

16. Confraternity of Our Lady of Deliverance in France: 1583
18. Expectation of the Blessed Virgin Mary
19. Our Lady of Etalem (Bavaria)
22. Notre Dame de Chartres
25. Nativity of Our Lord
27. Founding of the Order of the Knights of Our Lady: 1376
28. Feast of the Holy Family
29. Our Lady of the Spire (Germany)
31. Our Lady of the Closing Year

Appendix

APPENDIX

Outline of Major Texts About Mary
in the *Catechism of the Catholic Church*

The Apostolic Constitution written by Pope John Paul on the publication of the *Catechism of the Catholic Church* ends with the following prayer to Mary:

I beseech the Blessed Virgin Mary, Mother of the Incarnate Word and the Mother of the Church, to support with her powerful intercession the catechetical work of the entire Church on every level, at this time when she is called to a new effort of evangelization. May the light of the true faith free humanity from the ignorance and slavery of sin in order to lead it to the only freedom worthy of the name: that of life in Jesus Christ under the guidance of the Holy Spirit, here below and in the Kingdom of heaven, in the fullness of the blessed vision of God fact to face!

A. I believe in Jesus Christ, the only Son of God.

1) Born of a woman (Gal 4:4) [422]
2) Jewishness of Jesus: born a Jew of a Maid of Israel [423]
3) True God, true Man (Christological debate)

- Ephesus: 431 (no juxtaposition—Nestorious): truly Mother of God
- Chalcedon: 451 (no monophysitism): Virgin Mary, Mother of God
- V Constantinople: 553 (One of the Trinity): Mother of God, ever Virgin

4) Conceived by the Holy Spirit, born of the Virgin Mary [484–512]

Event—Agent—Fruit: Christ

1) Predestination
2) Immaculate Conception
3) Annunciation (Fiat)
4) Divine Motherhood
5) Virginity of Mary
6) Mary—ever Virgin
7) Virginal Maternity of Mary in God's plan of salvation

B. I believe in the Holy Spirit [721–726]

Spirit of Christ (=Holy Spirit) in the fullness of time (NT, as opposed to OT = time of promise)

1) Mary = masterpiece of joint mission of Spirit and Son
2) Mary = dwelling place, temple of Son and Spirit offered to Father
3) Thus Mary understood as Seat of Wisdom
4) Beginning manifestation of God's marvelous deeds in Mary through Spirit:

   • Spirit prepares Mary by his grace
   • Spirit accomplishes in Mary the plan of God
   • Spirit manifests Son of Father who became Son of the Virgin
   • In Mary, Spirit establishes relation/communion between Jesus Christ and representatives of humanity in need of redemption
   • In the Spirit, Mary becomes Woman, New Eve ("mother of the living"), Mother of the "total Christ"

C. I believe in the holy Catholic Church [963–975]

Church in the Plan of God, major images, attributes, organization, communion of saints....

Mary, Mother of Christ, Mother of the Church (VI)

- True Mother of God, redeemer
- Mother of members of Christ
- Mother of the Church

1) Mary's maternity of/for the Church

- Totally united to her Son in her life
- Totally united to her Son in her Assumption
- Mary is our mother in the order of grace
- Model of faith and charity for Church
- Through cooperation in Christ's salvific work, she becomes, in the order of grace, our Mother
- Mary's maternity in economy of salvation until consummation

2) Cult (devotion to) of the Holy Spirit

- Integral part of Christian worship—legitimate special devotion
- Virgin honored as mother of God; protection, refuge
- Essentially different from cult of adoration (Trinity); Marian devotion in service of divine worship
- Expressed in liturgical celebration and Marian prayer (rosary)

3) Mary—eschatological icon; we contemplate Mary in the mystery of the Church

(a) now and

(b) at the end of her pilgrimage

- Mother of the Lord, Mother of the Church inaugurates ultimate achievement of heavenly Church
- Sign of Hope and Consolation

D. The Prayer of Mary [2617–2619]

In the fullness of time,

Jesus prays

Jesus teaches how to pray

Jesus listens and acts on behalf of our prayer

The prayer of Mary

1) Mary's prayer revealed at the Annunciation and Pentecost as unique cooperation in God's plan; fiat in the Christian prayer: to be completely God's, since he is completely ours

2) Mary's prayer of intercession in faith expressed in Cana and Calvary

3) Mary's *Magnificat* is both canticle of the Mother of God and of the Church, whose hope has been fulfilled

E. Prayer in communion with the Holy Mother of God [2673–2679]

In "Ways of prayer" (prayer to the Father, to Jesus, with [as the Holy Spirit], we are told how to pray in communion with the Holy Mother of God

1) Mary the *Hodegetria*: She points the way to Jesus, who is the way of our prayer
Spiritual maternity

2) Mary is the sign, transparence unto Jesus, the way of our prayer

3) Prayer to Mary is centered on Christ's person as manifested in his mysteries

   Double movement:

   (a) Praise for great things the Lord accomplishes in/for his humble servant (= Hail Mary)

   (b) Entrusting to Mary all praise/supplication of God's children (= Holy Mary)

4) Mary is the perfect *Orans*, figure of the Church:

   (a) assent to God's plan

   (b) inviting Mary into "our being"

   - We pray with Mary, and we pray to Mary
   - Mary's prayer sustains, supports the prayer of the Church

Reprinted from Betrand Buby, SM, *Mary of Galilee: Woman of Israel—Daughter of Zion*, vol. II; Staten Island, New York: Alba House, 1995. Reprinted by permission.